BETWEEN SISTERS

BETWEEN SISTERS
SECRET RIVALS, INTIMATE FRIENDS

▽

Barbara Mathias

Delacorte Press

Published by
Delacorte Press
Bantam Doubleday Dell Publishing Group, Inc.
666 Fifth Avenue
New York, New York 10103

Library of Congress Cataloging in Publication Data

Mathias, Barbara.
Between sisters : secret rivals, intimate friends / by Barbara Mathias.
p. cm.
Includes bibliographical references (p.   ).
ISBN 0-385-30450-1 (hc)
1. Sisters.   2. Women—Psychology.   I. Title.
BF723.S43M38   1992
155.44′4—dc20   92-9836
CIP

Manufactured in the United States of America
Published simultaneously in Canada

November 1992
10 9 8 7 6 5 4 3 2 1

To my sisters,
Mary, Ruth, and Janet.
And in loving memory
of our mother,
Frances Elizabeth.

Contents

Preface

THIS IS A BOOK about how a woman relates to her biological sister. It is both a study of and a reflection on the joy and complexity of being sisters. My aim is to encourage women to discover and examine what impact their sisters had in their development and how their sisters have served as prototypes for relations with others both inside and outside the family. If you and your sister are estranged or you are ambivalent about your relationship, this book may enable you to accept each other as you are in order to reach a feeling of accord. But there are no tidy answers here, no promises for bonding in ten easy steps. A thorough examination of your sisterhood, however, will begin the process of reconsideration. The rest will be up to you.

I am also writing this book with the intention of interesting therapists, analysts, and counselors to further research and recognize the value of the biological sister relationship in the development of women. For while sisters are paramount in women's lives, their presence and impact are, to date, rarely and fully considered in psychological theory and training. The significance of how differently two or more women may be raised by the same parents is ignored, thus implicitly denied. Even with the growing number of books on mothers and daughters there is little acknowledgment of the powerful, lasting influence on how sisters share and relate to their mothers. It is as if we are all only daughters, the dream of every little girl. But with this fantasy played out in popular psychology books, we get only half the story, and are cheated out of a full understanding of our feminine psychology.

There have been several studies on siblings as early as the 1920s, as well as the influence of birth-order research in the 1960s; but even with the influx of family system theorists in the 1970s, and Stephen Bank and Michael Kahn's work in the early 1980s on sibling bonding, there is still no honed focus on the biological sister-to-sister relationship. This is mainly due to the plodding growth of women's psychology, but ironically, it is also a product of the feminist movement, which typically glorified the sisterhood of women, thus discouraging a more realistic look at the ambivalent, sometimes wretched condition between biological sisters.

The Complexity of the Meaning of "Sisters"

Your sister is your other self. She is your alter ego, your reflection, your foil, your shadow. She can represent both sides of you at the same time, thus throwing you into an emotional tailspin. You are different in detail of how you live your lives, but not in substance. Interchangeably, you go in and out of each other's shadows. She is your hero, or she disappoints you beyond words. You are afraid that there are parts of her that remain unexpressed in you. No matter how many years apart, the fact remains that you were raised in the same family, you shared the same parents, and *you share in the experience of your gender.* As one therapist who was helping her sister through a crisis told me: "If we think of our sisters as extensions of ourselves, it is little wonder that we are drawn to them for additional strength, especially in times of need."

The very word "sisters" has come to mean a bond of soulmates who naturally provide love and support. But for many women, the definition can be far more complex and unpredictable. Indeed, there are sisters who are so close in love and mannerisms that they seem one and the same. And there are sisters who are "complete opposites" yet comfortable with each other ("No one believes we are sisters," these women enjoy saying). But there are also sisters who despise each other so passionately, they can't stand to be in the same room with each other. And there are sisters who say they feel "nothing" for each other and are cold in their affection. Perhaps most common of all, there are the sisters who feel ambivalent about their relationship at different stages in their lives. These women typically can waver between deep affection to anger, then back to an empty or neutral state, depending on their stage of crisis and life's changes.

One of the most incongruous features of biological sisterhood is the ability to go in and out of the relationship *without losing the connection.* A few never lose their momentum or the intensity of the relationship, but most of us bring our sisters in and out of the shadows without ever considering that this is unacceptable or unusual.

The foremost theme in this book is that no matter how difficult or satisfying the relationship is, *biological sisters have a complex and inextricable bond based on their feminine psychology: this is the sister connection.* The relationship can appear to be latent, but it invariably rises at different stages in a woman's life; and whether the relationship is healthy or destructive, it is usually impossible for the woman to ignore its presence *because she has been trained since infancy to be sensitive and aware of relationships.*

The second theme is that the *biological sister relationship affects a woman's psychological development.*

Many women told me that they had "forgotten" or "didn't communicate" with their sisters during certain times of their life. It may have been their early childhood lost to memory, or in grade school when they didn't want each other around, or in their twenties when they were wrapped up in separate careers and goals. But there were times in even the strongest of adult relationships when the sister has been an absent figure, then suddenly comes on the scene like a savior or a flaming demon. She matters, she cares, she makes you mad, she is in the way, or she is essential to your survival. Over and over again, I heard of how a sister "suddenly" gave support during a divorce, or death of a spouse or child, or a severe illness. Ronnie hadn't spoken to her two sisters in twenty years, but when their mother's alcoholism had to be faced, her sisters returned with a support that never skipped the beat of time.

Milestones in Caring

Christine Downing wrote in *Psyche's Sisters,* "The rediscovery of the sister is also a new and necessary discovery of self."[1] I agree, and add that that discovery most often occurs during a woman's middle years, when she not only comes to understand herself but is willing to "move on" and change her relationships with family. A more pragmatic and contemporary reason for women to be concerned about their differences with their sisters is the likelihood that they will be combining their efforts to care for their elderly parents.

Deemed the "sandwich generation," middle-aged children are caught between responsibility for their own children and for their parents. The majority of those caretakers, an estimated 80 percent, are daughters. Recent studies tell us that the average woman spends seventeen years[2] caring for her children and eighteen years caring for her aged parents. Given this circumstance, it is little wonder that women become acutely aware of their biological sisterhood as they and their parents age. The inevitable question for the sisters is, How are we going to *share* this responsibility? A few of the sisters I interviewed were bitter about the imbalance of the responsibility. But most women, like Frances and Dorothy (see Chapter 10), were grateful that they could share equally and yet be flexible in their exhausting care of their ailing parent.

Sisters don't have to take a lifetime to come together, or wait for change and crisis to bring them face-to-face. They can learn to understand their family differences or to lower their expectations of each other. If the goal is to change from a destructive bond to a loving bond, it takes concentrated reexamination. Quarreling or estranged sisters have to relinquish expectations of each other and to do that they have to understand the source of the expectations.

The Survey

In the course of a year, I interviewed more than seventy-five women about how they feel about their sisters, how they manage the relationship, and how it affects their lives. There was no questionnaire provided, nor was there a standard format to the interviews. This was intended not to be a sociological or scientific model, but rather, a collection of observations presented by myself, a journalist who for fifteen years has written articles on family, women's issues, and psychology. I imagine I am very much like the reader, a woman who enjoys using her intuition and listening to others in order to help understand herself and those around her.

The ages of these women range from fifteen to eighty-seven, and they came from all over the United States, as well as Mexico, Israel, Germany, and England. Half sisters and stepsisters are not included because I feel that their circumstances are special and are a separate topic. Nearly 15 percent of the sample represents minorities. The sample is also diverse in its economic representation: I talked to women who make six-figure salaries and women who are struggling on a minimum wage. Many of the women came from economic backgrounds far different from what they are in now, so there is a generational contrast as well. The education levels represented ranged from three years of high school to six years of postgraduate work.

In some instances I interviewed both sisters or several sisters in one family, as well as their mothers and their sisters. I met with numerous sets of twins (including a deaf woman whose deaf twin had died), as well as sisters of twins and triplets. Birth order, family spacing, and the number of sisters are important considerations in this discussion: 40 percent were the oldest sister; 30 percent were middle sisters; and 30 percent were the youngest. Half of the women had more than one sister; and slightly more than half had brothers. Sisters closest in age were twelve months apart to the exact day; sisters farthest apart were twenty-two years.

In this survey there are numerous examples of sisters whose childhood and adolescence were affected by such family dysfunctions as alcoholism, depression, manic-depression, schizophrenia, and sexual abuse. I do not focus on these dysfunctions as the singular source of roles and identities, as they would be considered, for example, in a book on adult children of alcoholics. Instead, the particular dysfunction is described and included within the whole description of the family. For instance, if two estranged sisters grew up with a depressed mother, the impact of the depression is recognized and examined, but so too are other contributing factors, such as the economic state of the family, the spacing of the children, and the presence of grandparents.

One cannot look at the dynamic of sisters without looking at the whole family, and that means listening to and absorbing stories of joy and tragedy. I feel honored to have met these women and remain grateful for their willingness to talk to me. To keep their anonymity, I have not used last names and have changed first names, and in some instances identifying characteristics.

A Family History of Sisters

My most precious credential for writing this book is that I am the oldest of four sisters, and the third child of seven. I love all three of my sisters, but my different relationship with each one aptly illustrates how complex sisterhood can be. I'm the most emotional and ambivalent about Mary, whom I have covertly envied since she usurped my throne when I was four and she was born. Ruth is seven years younger than I am, but we are comfortably close, aided by her humor and generosity. We have had our rough spots, mostly a result of my different life-style on the East Coast (she lives in the Midwest in the same neighborhood where we were raised), but fortunately the contrast doesn't seriously threaten our bond. Janet was born when I was twelve and more than ready to be her surrogate mother. Now as adults we sometimes circle each other as if we are strangers who want to get to know each other, but aren't quite sure what our needs are. It's an awkwardness that I trust will dissolve with age and more opportunities to be together. My experience also extends to my mother, who was the youngest of eight sisters (in a family of twelve) and was deemed "the listener" because as a child she was allowed into her sisters' bedrooms as they prepared for a date or for school, and in time she silently knew all their secrets. My own childhood was filled with comfortable evenings and Sunday afternoons with my many aunts from both my mother's and my father's side. My favorite was my father's youngest of three sisters, Elsie—I secretly pretended that she was the older and accepting sister I always wanted.

Though their stories are not told in this book, without the example of my three daughters (and their interaction with their two brothers), I would not be as fully educated in the complexity of sisters. Brothers cannot be ignored in all this; indeed, they are often the silent players in the games of love and envy between sisters. My two older brothers, Dick and Bob, were "my team" before Mary came. And our "baby" brother Paul was born when Mary and I were young teenagers, creating a considerable imbalance in our scheme of surrogate motherhood. In the early 1970s, Bob suddenly died of a massive heart attack at age thirty-three, six months after my father's death at age fifty-eight, also from a massive heart attack. Their deaths marked a drastic change in our family dynamics. With the original (Dick, Bob, and Barbara) "team" broken, I was fortunate to *rediscover* my family of sisters. Now, after many years of joy, error, and ambivalence, I recognize how crucial my relationship with my sisters is in the definition of my self.

Martha Gallahue is a lay analyst in New York who conducts "Sister-to-Sister" workshops with her two sisters from Ohio: Mary Beth Koechlin, a sociologist, and Rosemary Mullen, a learning disability teacher. During the course of writing this book, I spoke often to Gallahue and also had the pleasure of attending one of the workshops at the YWCA in New York. One day when we were commiserating on how little is written on sisters, she encouraged me by saying that anecdotes could be just as valuable as theory at this early stage in recognizing the dynamics between sisters. "I wish I had as many stories to tell as you've collected," said Gallahue. Clearly, this collection of stories is not an in-depth psychological study, yet it presents in-depth feelings as the impetus for further study. I emphasize, however, that there is an implicit value in the stories themselves, even when they are told to me second and third time around, or when they don't "fit" with the stories told by a sister from the same family. We each behold our lives differently, and our stories should be received individually. As Robert Coles points out from a timeless lesson he learned from his psychoanalytic supervisor, Dr. Ludwig: It is the *stories* that count, not just the theory,[3] and whenever possible the therapist should listen to those stories with "a minimum of conceptual static" in his or her head.[4]

Foremost, my aim in this storytelling is to expose women to the light-and-dark world of biological sisterhood and to enable them to reexamine their own experience. It is both a dare and an invitation, long overdue for most of us.

BARBARA MATHIAS

1

▽

The Feminine Incentive to Bond

WHEN I CALLED Tess to set up her interview, she told me she had been recently reunited with her two sisters from whom she had been estranged for nearly twenty years. "My middle sister, Lynn, has returned to Europe where she lives with her family, but my oldest sister, Peg, will be in town tomorrow," she said. "Would it be all right if she came with me and we could talk to you together?" I was amazed that she had to ask, but I soon learned that that was part of Tess's unassuming manner.

The next day, Tess and Peg arrived at my home five minutes early and openly apprehensive. I had never met either of them before, so I was particularly struck by how dissimilar they were in appearance. Peg at fifty-eight was a large, handsome woman with olive complexion and short dark hair; and Tess, forty-six, was petite in build and height, with very soft, pale features and light brown wispy hair. Wearing spectacles that gave her a suburban schoolgirl look, Tess was dressed forgettably in muted preppy colors, and with no jewelry, while Peg wore a bright, deep pink blouse, casual black pants, and sandals, and boasted several rings on each hand.

1

As soon as Peg saw the tape recorder placed on the coffee table, she cheerfully took charge and directed Tess to "sit close" to her so the conversation could be clearly recorded. "I'm a filmmaker," she told me, "I know about these things. And don't worry"—she laughed, pushing gently next to Tess, who dutifully sat dead center on the long couch—"we like each other now."

"We all blamed each other for our unhappiness," Peg went on somberly, alluding to the history to come. It seems that their estrangement was ambivalent, but easy to maintain with the women living in separate cities. No one did anything until six years ago, when Peg got "fed up" with the void in her life without her sisters. Gradually she began to make calls and write letters, chipping away at the walls between them. "We are talking like humans," said Peg, "and that is satisfactory to me. For the first time we have had the opportunity to become friends as adults with all that baggage we carried from the past cut away. Each one of us, of course, is a separate, different person, with some familiarity, energy or feelings, but it is really as if we are meeting for the first time with a familiarity."

With this rush of feeling, Tess took her sister's openness in stride, sitting with her hands neatly folded in her lap, saying very little but all the while watching Peg closely. When I asked them to tell me about their family history so I could understand what caused this estrangement, their story unfolded as separate eras divided by their age span and the state of their parents' marriage. The first era took place in the fertile valleys of Chile, where they lived in luxury with their Italian-born mother and their American-born father, a business executive who had inherited his comfortable job through the marriage. The three girls were cared for by a full staff of servants while their parents busied themselves with friends, parties, and tennis matches. It sounded bliss-

2

ful, but it wasn't, especially from a child's point of view. According to Peg, who has the strongest and most passionate memories of that time, both parents were "bored and spoiled" and would quarrel incessantly in front of their children. Their father, especially, wanted attention and would "throw tantrums" when anyone favored his daughters or wife. Their mother, a timid woman who longed for the family she had left in Italy, shrank under her husband's hysterics. Things were "so horrible," said Peg, "that I left home at seventeen, and Lynn was close behind."

The family's second era was just as explosive, but more fragmented. It began when their parents divorced, which was not long after Peg and Lynn had gone and Tess was just seven years old. A lonely child, Tess never questioned why she and her mother later moved to the States and her father remained behind. "My mother never talked about anything real, she never told me they were divorced," explained Tess quietly. "I think she was trying to protect me." Eventually, the father also moved to the States, the money had dwindled away, and "ugly secrets" were divulged to the sisters in a vicious postdivorce period that went on endlessly and created further alienation and confusion within the broken family.

As adults, the sisters' differences centered on their acceptance or rejection of their mother. Peg believed her to be a controlling, unfeeling woman who refused to claim any intimacy with her daughters or to admit to "the family's bad past." Tess firmly argued that her mother "tried her best" to reach out to her children, especially in her later years when she was dying of cancer and only Tess was by her side. Lynn was depicted as someone with a "strong chip on her shoulder," who even today was shaky in her reconciliation because she lived so far away and felt that Tess and Peg had more access, thus more sympathy, to each other.

At one point in the interview, Tess opened up and started recounting how she felt "abandoned" by her sisters when they, as young adults, had left the country, leaving her alone with their depressed mother. Without looking at Peg, she spoke evenly but sadly about how when she was fourteen her mother returned to her family in Italy in order "to find herself." Tess unhappily had no choice but to live with her father and his new wife—no one had even told her that her father had remarried, further indication of the family's lack of communication and denial. I was so taken in by her story that I was as startled as she was when we suddenly heard Peg sob.

"What?" asked Tess, turning to her sister and lightly touching her arm with her hand. "What's wrong?"

"I'm just *feeling* so much for you," cried Peg. Seeing the confused look on Tess's face, she said unconvincingly, "Don't worry about it. I cry a lot. It's a kind of sympathy, not because I'm sad."

Throughout the interview Peg would occasionally cry, or her voice would catch with emotion, but Tess remained without tears and yet her facial expression and responses clearly showed that she was touched by her sister's compassion. "I rarely cry," she told me. Their stories weren't all tragic. Peg and Tess comfortably shared the good times with me: the silly quarrels and tricks between the young sisters, how they played with their animals under the shade trees, and the birthday ritual of parading to the bedroom of the birthday child before breakfast, carrying gifts and singing at the top of their lungs.

These two sisters who were studies in contrast were linked by their concern for one another. One is openly emotional, the other is cautiously stoic, and more importantly, each still holds her separate opinion of their mother. They can also maintain their separate approach to life. Peg, a self-educated woman who never married, travels around the world in her job as a television documentary filmmaker; Tess, who has her master's in education, prefers to stay at home with her two children. When Peg was emoting about how wonderful it was when the three sisters shared breakfast and talked last month, Tess dryly interjected that she was more uptight because breakfast was at her house and she worried if the eggs were cooked right, and if her husband was going to get impatient with three days of houseguests.

After so many years of being apart, Tess and Peg told me they were "realistically facing" the task of accepting each other's ways. I had no doubt they knew how dramatically different they were, in personality, in life-style, and in perspective of their pasts, and yet their incentive and willingness to connect with each other were deeper and stronger than their differences.

One of their stories in particular demonstrated to me how conflicted they were about their past, but how much they desired the strengthening of the bond between them. When Peg was twenty-seven and Tess was fifteen, Peg accused Tess of stealing a favorite bracelet during a visit in the father's home. The bracelet was never stolen, just "borrowed," said Peg, who reassures us that she has it in her possession. But Tess, unsure of what really happened, sees the event symbolically, as a crime of the heart.

"I have to tell you about the bracelet," insisted Tess to Peg. "I've been thinking and thinking about it. And I wonder, why would I have taken it? I think I wanted to be close to you somehow, and yet you got angry at me and it was not the right response. I wanted you to say, 'all right, keep it, it is a part of me.' But I would have had to be forty-five to start thinking like that. I didn't know what I was doing at the time."

As Tess spoke this insightful analysis of the "stolen" brace-let, Peg listened with no argument. She didn't dismiss Tess's feelings. The very fact that Tess has "been thinking and thinking" about the bracelet incident, and that she can see it as a need to be part of her sister's life, was enough to tell Peg how much she cares. As they were leaving I walked the two women out onto the front porch, and they told me about their outing the day before on the waterfront. They had been worn out from talking, so they sat on a park bench and were silently looking at the river when two ducklings swam by and circled each other as if they were lost. "We both turned to each other and said at the very same time, 'Where's their mother?' " said Peg dramatically, "and sure enough, within seconds they took off and headed straight downstream, where we could see the mother duck was wait-ing with her other ducklings." We all laughed, no further explanation had to be made. I felt drawn and attached to these two and wished them well.

The Key to the Sister Bond: Our Feminine Qualities

There is no greater incentive behind sister bonding than the fact that we share the same feminine psychology, that is, as women, we define ourselves in relation to others. Little girls, unlike little boys, emerge from their early development with less autonomy and a stronger basis for experiencing an-other's needs or feelings as one's own. Recent studies now show that such feminine "traits" as nurturing, sensitivity, and need for intimacy may be biologically as well as cultur-ally based. (These traits are not exclusively female; they can certainly be part of a man's identity, just as aggression and objectivity is the masculine quality in a woman's identity.) Traditionally, the psychological literature presented women's focus on relationships and involvement as a fault, a failure, a weakness in the development of the self. Because women don't learn autonomy as men do, women were depicted as "lesser than" a whole person. In the early 1980s, Carol Gilligan's work on the "female style" of moral development demonstrated that such a judgment stems from a male-based psychology and that when we recognize women's different development from men, their so-called weakness in being sensitive to others is actually a strength.[1] I would add that it is also a tremendous advantage, and a cherished gift. Like most women I know, I work hard for my independence, but I would never give up my need to relate to others. Gilligan revealed a truth most women intuitively know but have been unable to express until now.

Sisters rarely totally abandon each other. Their love may be ambivalent for periods of time, but it is not in their feminine character to turn their backs and never return. I consistently heard and saw sisters cry or embrace each other in the midst of the most painful situations and judgments. And when I heard women speak angrily or in tears about some discord with their sisters they thought would never be resolved, I felt their frustration was really over the fact that they cared so much, or too much, not that they didn't care at all. When twenty-nine-year-old Angela moodily described her younger sister, Denise, as "living day by day, always busy, out on the streets, and partying," she kept interjecting in disbelief, "This is my *sister* I'm talkin' about! My *sister!*" Angela and Denise grew up without a father and with an overworked mother. Now the two young sisters are single parents themselves, each struggling to manage her affairs without child support. Angela works full-time and goes to night school so that she can eventually get a better job. Denise drifts between low-paying jobs and relies on her grandmother for childcare and lodging. In an angry voice, Angela tells me, "I can't bear to watch Denise stay in jobs where she can't improve and just do as she pleases with her life. She has no consideration for anybody, she's not mature, but she thinks she is."

Given all her financial pressures, it is little wonder that Angela is unhappy with her life and critical of Denise. And yet Angela displays a deep family allegiance as she worries about her younger sister and keeps trying to help her find an apartment and a job. "She doesn't get on my nerves, that's just her, the way she is," relinquishes Angela. "I love her."

Sisters, like Angela and Denise, can be dramatically different in their approach to life and still achieve a close and loving relationship. Like Tess and Peg, they can energize and enrich each other by accepting each other for who they are—two separate people, not reflections but separate souls with separate spirits who are bonded in gender and family. There are countless sisters who have responded to and used their feminine intuition to grow beyond their differences. In their renewed connection, they represent the ultimate promise of all sisters—acceptance and love.

2

Tracing Our Sources of
Separate Identities

FEW OF US WOMEN live the fairy-tale existence of "Snow White and Rose Red," the compatible, nearly alike sisters whose only distinction was that Rose Red loved to chase butterflies in the forest, while Snow White kept close to her mother in the cottage. And yet so many of us want the fantasy quality of *sameness* with our sisters, especially those closest in age. We want them to be as we are, not in looks necessarily, but in spirit and temperament. We blindly believe that if we are sisters, we should naturally think, act, and live the same. Or is the concern deeper and more complex? If we believe the long-held myth that our sisters are the reflection or the extension of ourselves, and if we feel so connected with our sisters, it may be that their differences are so upsetting or threatening that we are asking, Is that how I am? or, Is that how I would like to be?

Rebecca learned that she has a sister she has never seen. As her father lay dying from cancer, an aunt told her that a year before her father and mother were married they had a baby girl who was placed for adoption because they couldn't afford to keep her. A year after they were married, they had

9

Rebecca, and several years later another daughter, Terry. Laden with guilt, mainly inflicted by the maternal grand-parents, the parents never revealed to their two daughters that they had another sister.

"I'm confused," said Rebecca. "I can't ask my father about this because I don't want to upset him when he is so ill. I don't know if it is true, and I don't know if I should try to find my sister or not."

"Why wouldn't you?" I was amazed that she would even hesitate.

"I'm afraid she will be different from me. She'll have different values, talk differently, or just be completely oppo-site from the way I am. And she may not like me."

I assured her she wouldn't be in a situation much different from most women. Sisters *are* different from each other and there are certainly no guarantees that our sisters are ever as we want them to be, or that they will like us.

We know that daughters (and sons) born from the same parents and raised under the same roof, who shared every-thing from their bedroom to their school friendships, can be similar, or complete opposites to each other, but they are rarely identical. Despite this common knowledge, over and over again most of the women I interviewed pointed out to me, or complained, or labored over the fact that their sisters were "different" from them. As one woman put it, "Every time I'm talking to my sister I'm wondering how she can be this way. I know I'm not like that." Other similar frustrations that I heard:

"I don't understand my sister."

"Why doesn't she give up her crazy life-style?"

"Can't she see what she is doing to herself?"

"I wish I could be more like her."

"I love her, but we will never be close, we are so different."

"If she weren't my sister, she would never be my friend."

*   *   *

We—myself included—apparently have a low tolerance for our sisters' differences and idiosyncrasies. The underlying reason is in our gender, which is both a blessing and a curse. As we have discussed, girls grow up to define themselves in relation to others; but we also learn not to differentiate fully from others, not to claim autonomy without risk, and not to raise our voices loudly or aggressively for fear of losing love. And yet, when our sisters don't fit the mold of our expectations and conventions, we are critical and judgmental. Young schoolgirls can be heartlessly cruel to girls who don't fit their clique or their ideal, just as they can be with their sisters who embarrass or disappoint them.

The process of accepting our sisters doesn't come easily, or automatically. Sisters need first to understand why it is that one is different from the other. The question is not so much *how* you differ, but *why* you differ. Gaining an understanding of how those differences were initially and subsequently formed should enable you to look beyond the criticism. By examining your family history you learn how you and your sister acquired or developed your roles and identities in the family, and how you learned to respond to each other. This focus on the past won't preclude your dilemma with the present. But if you are in the middle of a difficult divorce or job change, and your sister is giving you all the wrong and unwanted advice, knowing the origins of your differences may help you have a different or less dramatic reaction to her methods of sistering.

The External Factors Beyond Our Control

As data gathers on families and human development, particularly from the work on siblings by psychologists Stephen

11

Bank and Michael Kahn, it is generally agreed that not one but a combination of factors determines our familial identities and differences. Among the more significant factors, we can name: birth order, access to siblings, gender impact, temperament, family size and spacing of children, parental influence, status of parents' marriage, parents' emotional health, physical health of family, economics of family, geographic location and mobility, and cultural and religious influences.

It is also important how all these factors were presented *generationally*, with the grandparents and their children. When trying to understand your relationship with your sister, consider such factors as the spacing between your mother and her sisters, or your grandmother's health during your mother's childhood, or how your grandfather affected the family dynamics.

No one factor, such as family economics or the parents' health, is the sole impact on the sisters' relationship. Rather, sisters, like all siblings, are products of continually developing and interacting factors and events that are often out of their control. When we study our past, we have to train our eyes and ears not to linger on one scene of rejection, or hear one time when our cries went unanswered, because all these influences are fluid and ever changing. When a woman told me over and over how her older sister "never" showed any interest in her or her family's life, all the while she was focusing on their early childhood when her sister was "cold and aloof," and didn't want to include her younger sister in her play with her best friend. I asked how old her sister was when their baby brother was born. "Sixteen," she said. "I was twelve."

Who took care of the baby if your mother was working full-time? I asked (she had told me earlier that the family couldn't afford any hired help).

much of it documented by German sociologist Walter Toman in a long-term study begun in 1951, involving 3,000
families: the oldest child being the most responsible, the
middle child rebelling and seeking attention, the youngest
child following her siblings' example carefully but willing to
take risks.[1] But because of all the multiple factors that affect
the family, I found notable exceptions to the rule.

Adele, who is five years younger than her only sister,
Evelyn, explains in good humor how she and her sister
switched the usual birth-order roles:

"I was the goody-two-shoes, Evelyn was the rebel. I went to
Sunday school, Evelyn wouldn't go because the minister
thought she was 'too fast,' either she chewed gum or wore
makeup too soon. I was always so sweet, reciting the Twenty-
fourth Psalm to Aunt Mary. I was in Brownies and Girl
Scouts, and Evelyn wasn't. I was in the choir, Evelyn was and
still is tone deaf. She had fast friends, and at fourteen I
remember she was very developed and she dated a sailor
and rode out of town on a motorcycle. Wow! She even *smoked*
a cigarette in the bedroom. That's just not like a firstborn
is it?"

Birth-order myths are legitimate for *each individual* family,
not necessarily for your family. A good example of the excep-
tion to birth order was told by Leah, the third child and the
second oldest daughter in a family of six children. Leah,
twenty-eight, considered herself the peacemaker between
her sisters, a role we normally attribute to firstborns. How did
she gain that role and why did her thirty-five-year-old sister
Trudy, the oldest, avoid it like the plague? (The only brother,
who is the second oldest, was first depicted by Leah as an
invisible sibling with little consequence in this family of
women. Later, she said in strong language, which she rarely
used, "He's selfish and inconsiderate, a spoiled brat.")

Leah's mother, Helen, always ha[t]
dren. Orphaned in childhood and [r]
homes, Helen had no strong role m[o]
only wanted her six children to b
direction from Leah's father, he, t[o]
but he worked long hours and weel[
when he was home the long silenc[
wife Leah grimly remembers as "d[
house."

Trudy had no desire to play surr[o]
of siblings that came along so late i[n
twelve, she wasn't included in her t[
borhood friendship with a family o[
exactly the same ages as they. The si[
bikes, play in the log cabin in their [
divide up their "sleepovers" so that [
the other's house on weekends. "In [
movies, our three friends are in a
"Our mothers were also good frie[
think back, Trudy was there, just n[

Despite or because of the age ga[
now confidantes, especially about th[
their parents' recent divorce. With
jostling between the parents' two [
referee, diplomatically letting her si[
they are hurting each other's feelin[
the two youngest sisters are "free sp[
what is happening in the world aroun[
a "hot temper and no patience" for l[
lighthearted self-centeredness. "Tru[
always talk about themselves and thei[
peace between them," says Leah con[
hide my criticism."

With
maker [
family:
ments,
the fam[

Clini
roles to
But the
and of[
years. [
tensity,
themse[
psycho[
and un[
her fat[
indepe[
mother[
didn't [

Leah[
friends
until w[
friends
older t[
think [
that L[
help h[
her in [
people
which [

Access:

In birt[
far apa[

There was a long pause, until another memory changed the picture considerably. In a softer voice, she said, "My sister took care of him. She didn't finish school. And she let me take care of him when I got home from school. We both adored him."

We can't possibly examine all these external and internal influences in one chapter; that process will continue throughout the book. But here, let us discuss a few of the more essential influences that contribute to sisterly differences.

Birth Order

The concept that your birth order determines your personality and your destiny has been with us since people began telling myths and stories to their families and about their families. So often when a woman asked me about my book, she would immediately cite her birth order in order to explain her relationship with her sister. Birth orders give us a universally accepted framework for who we are. Sisters who were the oldest were especially eager to proclaim that their position endowed them with an "innate" tendency to care about and understand their sisters. They were, it seemed to many of them, the ever responsible ones. (Was this why more firstborns responded to my request for interviews?) When one woman, who was the oldest of three sisters, asked me if I, too, was the oldest in my family, I answered, "Yes, but why do you ask?" "Only an oldest sister would care enough to write a book like this; you want to sort everything out," she said proudly. That may be a nice compliment, but I don't buy it for the whole population of oldest sisters.

Birth-order formulas are fun, but their accuracy and dependability are questionable. Certainly, many of the sisters described in this book fit the classic birth-order mythology, much of it documented by German sociologist Walter To-man in a long-term study begun in 1951, involving 3,000 families: the oldest child being the most responsible, the middle child rebelling and seeking attention, the youngest child following her siblings' example carefully but willing to take risks.[1] But because of all the multiple factors that affect the family, I found notable exceptions to the rule.

Adele, who is five years younger than her only sister, Evelyn, explains in good humor how she and her sister switched the usual birth-order roles:

"I was the goody-two-shoes, Evelyn was the rebel. I went to Sunday school, Evelyn wouldn't go because the minister thought she was 'too fast,' either she chewed gum or wore makeup too soon. I was always so sweet, reciting the Twenty-fourth Psalm to Aunt Mary. I was in Brownies and Girl Scouts, and Evelyn wasn't. I was in the choir, Evelyn was and still is tone deaf. She had fast friends, and at fourteen I remember she was very developed and she dated a sailor and rode out of town on a motorcycle. Wow! She even *smoked* a cigarette in the bedroom. That's just not like a firstborn is it?"

Birth-order myths are legitimate for *each individual* family, not necessarily for your family. A good example of the excep-tion to birth order was told by Leah, the third child and the second oldest daughter in a family of six children. Leah, twenty-eight, considered herself the peacemaker between her sisters, a role we normally attribute to firstborns. How did she gain that role and why did her thirty-five-year-old sister Trudy, the oldest, avoid it like the plague? (The only brother, who is the second oldest, was first depicted by Leah as an invisible sibling with little consequence in this family of women. Later, she said in strong language, which she rarely used, "He's selfish and inconsiderate, a spoiled brat.")

Leah's mother, Helen, always hated to discipline her children. Orphaned in childhood and raised in numerous foster homes, Helen had no strong role model for motherhood and only wanted her six children to be her friends. As far as direction from Leah's father, he, too, was a loving parent, but he worked long hours and weekends as a salesman, and when he was home the long silences between him and his wife Leah grimly remembers as "deadly for everyone in the house."

Trudy had no desire to play surrogate mother to this clan of siblings that came along so late in her life. When she was twelve, she wasn't included in her three sisters' close neighborhood friendship with a family of three sisters who were exactly the same ages as they. The six young girls would ride bikes, play in the log cabin in their adjacent backyards, and divide up their "sleepovers" so that one or two were always at the other's house on weekends. "In all our photos and home movies, our three friends are in all of them," says Leah. "Our mothers were also good friends. Sometimes when I think back, Trudy was there, just not *with* us."

Despite or because of the age gap, Trudy and Leah are now confidantes, especially about the family dynamics since their parents' recent divorce. With all four of the sisters jostling between the parents' two households, Leah plays referee, diplomatically letting her sisters know if and when they are hurting each other's feelings. According to Leah, the two youngest sisters are "free spirits" with little care for what is happening in the world around them; and Trudy has a "hot temper and no patience" for her two younger sisters' lighthearted self-centeredness. "Trudy complains that they always talk about themselves and their friends. I manage the peace between them," says Leah confidently, "because I can hide my criticism."

15

With Leah's story, we see that her family role as peace-maker comes from a combination of factors particular to her family: the spacing of siblings, the siblings' innate tempera-ments, the parents' broken marriage, and, most important, the family history of the mother.

Clinicians tell us that parents necessarily assign different roles to their children in order to keep order in the family. But there is another incentive, far more subtle in its delivery and often rarely expressed or recognized until our adult years. Each one of us contains, to varying degrees and in-tensity, our parents' undesirable traits and dreams of themselves. Alice Miller describes the process in more psychoanalytic terms as the child's receiving the "split-off and unintegrated parts" from the parents.[2] Trudy, who was her father's favorite for many years, probably absorbed his independent, serious side; while Leah is probably the mother figure her own mother always wanted to be, but didn't know how.

Leah continues in her pattern of maturity, by choosing friends older than herself—something she hadn't noticed until we talked about it during the interview. "A couple of my friends are exactly Trudy's age, and my best friend is a year older than Trudy. There is no explanation for this, except I think I am older for my age." One further explanation is that Leah developed her early maturity out of a need to help her mother and as a response to her siblings who like her in that role; in time, the ability to manage and anticipate people's feelings became a valuable part of her identity, which thrives with friends considerably older.

Access: More than Meets the Eye

In birth-order mythology, we are told that siblings who are far apart in age are less likely to be as close as siblings close in age,[3] and many of the stories in this book certainly support that. But when sisters told their stories, I often wondered how often spacing was used as a crutch or an excuse for lack of intimacy. There were several instances of sisters, such as Trudy, who in their preteens felt "displaced" by the arrival of one or more baby sisters. Age wasn't the *reason* they had low access, it evolved into a convenient cover for the unresolved jealousy. The age difference merely *served* to keep them nonintimate. On two separate occasions, I met two women who were ten years older than their sisters, with no other siblings. In both cases, the women were steely cold and couldn't understand why the subject of sisters "was so interesting." On further discussion, I learned that these women both felt their parents had made much too much fuss over their baby sisters. The jealousy was heightened when the older sisters left their homes to pursue their education and careers, and their young sisters were alone with the parents. Neither one of these women wanted to be in the survey (and they weren't), but their attitude left an impression on me.

One woman unwittingly debunked the low-access myth when she cheerfully said, "I finally figured out why my sister and I are so close; it's because we are so far apart in age." Eight years, to be exact. Another woman, ten years younger than her sister, testified how she at first had to live with the myth perpetuated by her parents that her sister, who was away at college, was the "smartest, prettiest, and most accomplished." After she learned to "demystify" her sister's reputation, they became close friends, and their age span didn't matter. And the sisters Ramona and Tina (see Chapter 9) who win the prize for being the farthest apart—twenty-two years—were unquestionably one of the closest and most loving pair of sisters I had met.

Subgroups of Sisters Within the Family

I did find support for Toman's birth-order theories on how subgroups of siblings necessarily form within larger families (four or more children).[4] When there were several sisters, or sisters in a large family with both genders, identities and roles were repeated by sisters well down the line. In families of four or more, the siblings divided into subgroups and the roles were conveniently and economically repeated so that the family would run efficiently. This was especially the rule for sisters who were expected to help with the care of the younger siblings. It was interesting when two sisters from a family of six children, proudly, but *separately*, told me that they were "*the* solution solver," that is, each thought she was the only sister the other siblings turned to for advice. When the oldest sister heard that the second oldest said the family always leans on her, she was incensed. "My sister doesn't know what she is talking about, she's fooling herself. *I'm* the one they lean on." Neither sister was wrong. Both were legitimately serving as pillars of support, but for different groups of siblings. The oldest sister advised the second and fourth siblings, and her sister (the third in line) advised the last two siblings.

Parental Influence: The Many Faces of Mom and Dad

A common source of angst between sisters is that they perceive or recall their involvement with their parents differently. To one sister, Mommy was charming and attentive in their childhood, while another sister remembers that same mommy as cold and unavailable. In Woody Allen's 1991 film *Alice,* the two sisters in a "dream scene" argue over the memory of their parents. "Dad was a naval hero . . . Mom was wonderful . . . a starlet," says Alice breathlessly. "Dad was a bore," cracks her older sister, Dorothy, "and Mom was a drunk."

Discrepancies over how we view our parents can be due to actual different experiences because of the sisters' birth order and the family history, and/or the sisters' individual development. We know that no two siblings experience or remember family history identically. As one thirty-five-year-old woman said in exasperation: "I know in recent years when I talked to my sister about our father, I was amazed that her reactions to him were completely opposite from mine. She doesn't realize that he was a liar, or remember that he would go through our family money when we were growing up. She idealizes him more . . . she doesn't remember that he never did anything with us, he was really the absent father."

In my survey, problems surrounding the different memories and perceptions of the alcoholic or drug-addicted parent(s) were frequently mentioned. Typically, the parent's addiction in the early stages had a totally different impact for the oldest daughter than it did for the middle or younger daughter. In one case, the oldest sister recalls that her mother had mood swings and an unpredictable temper in her early years of drinking. By the time the youngest sister was in grade school and the older sister was out of the house in college, their mother was "always in a drunken sleep and unable to get off the couch."

Unquestionably, their mother's alcoholism left lasting effects on both sisters, but it was complicated for several years when the painful memories were denied by the youngest sister, who wanted to believe she had a perfectly attentive mother.

Alcoholism, a progressive disease that affects the entire family, is an ideal example of how a dysfunction within the family can produce contrary and diverse perspectives between and among sisters. According to Dr. Timmen L. Cermak, the founding member and first president of the National Association for Children of Alcoholics, the role-playing within an alcoholic family is usually "rigid," with little room for being allowed "other feelings."[5]

But even with that rigidity, the effect of the parent's alcoholism on the child still greatly depends on the age the child is when the family life is disrupted by the alcoholism. "Infants will, thus, be affected differently—and probably more profoundly—than teenagers," says Cermak.

As one woman lamely tried to explain to her older sister, "Mom was just depressed when you were living in the house. By the time I was ten, you had gone, and Mom was having hallucinations."

Parental Favoritism Seen from All Sides and Always Wanting a Boy

Addiction isn't the only dramatic source of discrepancies. There are also the uncanny and varied memories of parental favoritism. I especially heard sisters disagree on who was Daddy's favorite. Many were honestly confused because their fathers sent such mixed messages about who was loved the most. Whether the sisters agree on which parent favored whom, parental favoritism is the seeding ground for competition between sisters, which serves as a prototype for how we compete with our daughters, women friends, and colleagues. The next two chapters focus solely on the dynamics of that competition, but here let us examine how and why we have differing memories of our parents' attentions.

One reason for preference is knowing or *feeling* the parents, particularly the father, were disappointed in the birth of a girl. When both daughters, or more, are a disappointment to the parents, they can at least gain strength from each other and possibly defy such insensitive bias, but when one sister is revered and the other is treated as a misfortune, the issues between them may become dramatically complex. Note, throughout the book there is considerable testimony to gender bias.

"My father desperately wanted a boy."

"I always knew my being a girl was a problem for my parents."

"They gave me a boy's name."

"They were thrilled with my sister, but they wanted me to be a boy."

Women often told me that they thought they or their sisters were favorites with their parents because of some physical similarity, such as: "I have my father's eyes." "My sister is thin like my mother." "My father and I are both fair." "My sister takes after my mother's Irish side." Whether based on fact or not, in the eyes of a little girl the most apparent and non-threatening reason for a father's favoring her or her sister would be the color of their hair or the sound of their laughter. I also heard more guilt-ridden or emotional explanations; again, they reflected the young age of the perceiver, but these perceptions were carried through adulthood. "My sister was a nicer baby so she was the favorite; I was the crabby one." "My sister is funny, my father always wanted my mother to be funny." The most often mentioned explanation: "I was my mother's favorite because I am most like her, and my sister was my father's favorite because they are most alike" (or vice versa).

Parents are only human, so they can change their favoritism, depending on what stage of life they are going through or what needs they may have when one child comes along and fulfills or appeals to those needs. Unfortunately, sisters who are sensitive to their parents' waning attentions feel the

21

change very deeply. Leah, whom we discussed earlier, is proud that her father had "different times of favoritism for all of us." But when he chose Trudy, the oldest sister, she admits, "I was unquestionably the most jealous I have ever been in my life."

Unwittingly, Leah has worked out her jealousy and need for security by becoming romantically involved with David, an old friend and peer of Trudy's. "I've always known David as Trudy's friend . . . but when we first started dating it was strange. I was thinking, 'this is not right, I'm in Trudy's territory.' The first couple times it didn't work and I felt that I came second, and their friendship dominated. I'm not sure how it was resolved, it just happened as we became more comfortable with each other. He's safe, very safe, and he's so connected to the past. He's very quiet, and his family lives just a town away from mine, so when I go home he stays with his parents; this is very comforting to me."

Different Memories May Mean Different Histories

Details from our family histories help define the reasons for our sisterly differences. A parent's change in job, access to grandparents, economic hardship or success, the changing nature of the neighborhood, a father going off to war—all these external events, well out of the control of the child, create different realities and different perceptions that, good and bad, stay with us throughout our adulthood and interfere with or assist in our bonding.

Claire, the oldest of three sisters, grew up in a closely knit family, first and second generations, all living in a South Philadelphia neighborhood. "We are all Daddy's girls," beams Claire. "Daddy always said to us, 'There is the best, the favorite, and number one.'" Despite his conscious efforts to keep things fair, the sisters still dub Claire as "Daddy's girl" and say that she is "spoiled." Now that they are all in their thirties they still have a "friendly bickering" over who had the best times and the most attention from their parents.

"Things *were* different for me," reasons Claire. "But not because my father favored me. I did a lot of special simple things with my great-grandparents and my grandparents and they weren't around for that. Going to the supermarket or the open-air market with my cousin and my grandparents on Friday night, those are the times in my childhood I really cherish. In the supermarket Grandpa would always take us down the candy aisle and get a few things, then after dinner in Grandma's kitchen my cousin and I would take down the cereal bowls, fill them with the candy, and pretend it was a party. When my sisters came along, the family was doing things on a larger, grander scale like taking the trips to New York with our parents, shopping and attending the theater, but things weren't the same."

Claire also had more of her father's attention in the early years of his profession. "His law office was just around the corner and across the street from my grandparents, so I could spend time there while my mother was helping in the office. My younger sister really got shortchanged from that when he became more successful and moved his office downtown."

The Flowering of Separate Selves

Adult sisters are more likely to achieve a healthy bonding and appreciation of each other if their parents gave them their separate space and value during their developmental years. It is absolutely crucial for a healthy adult-life that the siblings within the family maintain their sense of self as they each take on separate and, ideally, flexible roles. In Leah's family, the father and mother were both loving, but they took little notice of their daughters' different goals and accomplishments, especially later in their teen and young-adult years. The same wasn't true for the only son, who went into business with his father. After several job changes, Leah has a busy and interesting job as a physician's assistant, but her father has never discussed with her either her profession or her plans for the future. "I don't think my father even knows what kind of work I do now," said Leah. "He never asks."

When Susan was just eleven years old, she and her older sister Lauren had already gleaned and dedicated them-selves to two opposing passions of interest—chemistry and psychology. "We used to fight like cats and dogs over which was more important in looking at life," says Susan, who as a child spent hours sighting birds and animals in the woods near her home outside London.

Raised by parents who encouraged all of their children to pursue their separate interests from the time they were tod-dlers, their three daughters went on to elect diverse careers and have remained close in their biological sisterhood: Susan, fifty-five, edits scientific journals; Lauren, sixty, is a child psychologist; and Sara, forty-eight, is an artist. More important to our discussion is how the sisters also differ in temperament, yet are comfortable with and even proud of each other. "I am the most aggressive; Lauren used to com-plain that I boss people," says Susan lightly, "but Lauren is very outgoing and self-confident. I admire her a lot, she rose to the highest position one can as a British civil servant. And Sara, she is the more reticent, very helpful, she cares about people."

I heard numerous family stories where such contrasts in

temperaments were a major cause for dissension. Why is Susan's story a happier one? Certainly, her family life wasn't perfect. Susan recounts her father's long working hours, her parents' "stormy marriage at times," and her stubborn, troublesome stance during her adolescence with her mother. What remained intact, however, was her parents' position that she—and her sisters—could experiment and grow in whatever path they chose. No sister had to act or "shape up" into the example of the other sister. Susan would ride her horse by herself, while Lauren preferred her work in the garden. When Susan despised the traditional restraints on life expected in school or while visiting her aunt, or when her mother had guests, she would "run away," sometimes to the kitchen roof, more often to the woods, where she brought a picnic lunch. When she returned, there was no major reprimand from her parents and there was always that subtle understanding that "independence was encouraged."

Taking Your Family's Pulse

One of the most powerful influences in our childhood and our sister-to-sister relationship, which sisters often neglect to consider in understanding their differences and identities, is *health*. (Traditional psychology and psychoanalysis does recognize the significance of a parent's or sibling's chronic illness in a person's development. Unfortunately, it is one of only a few instances in which the sibling relationship holds weight in therapy or analysis.)

When parents are focused on the care of their poor health or with a chronically ill, or "weaker," child, it is bound to affect the other siblings, as well as the parents' marriage. When a sister or brother is sick, it is likely that the healthier, less envious sister will become her nurse and protector. After all, she has been trained to be sensitive and to nurture, so she is not only drawn to her ailing sibling, but she is acutely aware of how the illness has affected her parents. With whatever resources she has, she tries to share the burden in order to keep whatever equanimity and happiness there is left in the family. But not all sisters can be caretakers. There are combinations of siblings who feel "left out" from all the attention the sick sister receives. A woman in her late seventies complained that her ninety-year-old-sister was "always a baby, always sick." Indeed, she had been a chronically ill child who received extra attention from her mother. The younger sister, however, had never relinquished her anger and jealousy even though her older sister had many adult years of good health.

Linda, Karen, and Holly: Love and Frustration

At first, Linda, twenty-four, would talk only about one major concern. She and her twenty-one-year-old sister, Karen, are both getting married soon, and their parents, who are in their late forties, have just separated. A family that was once so proud of its loving, tight unit, is suddenly dividing and dissolving before Linda's eyes just as she is about to enter marriage. Her mother isn't coping as well as Linda would like her to, and her father is "acting like a child, doing whatever he pleases." It wasn't until our interview was almost half over that Linda told me that her fifteen-year-old sister, Holly, has cystic fibrosis, a fact she would like to keep pushing aside.

"She has been spoiled since day one," says Linda kindly when showing me a picture of her sister. "She's not a good case study for your book because she is different, she's beautiful, active, no one can tell by looking at her that she is sick."

Despite her healthy appearance and her energy, Holly is

expected to live no longer than her mid-twenties. Right now she is being bandied back and forth between her parents for weekends and nights, creating more havoc than in her early infancy when the whole family was threatened by her debilitating illness. "Holly is like my child," explains Linda. "Mom had to work, so I would be watching her, we are very very close, she is very special to me. That's why it hurts so much when I see my parents fighting over Holly, and Holly getting whatever she wants, and there's Karen angry with the world, especially with my father, who now gives all his attention and time to Holly."

When there were just two girls, Karen was his favorite because she was a "little rebel" just like him, said Linda. "That's why it hurts Karen; she's been replaced and she has such a chip on her shoulder." Where does Linda come in with all this attention on her sisters? "I think I always had a special place with my father . . . I always feel exempt from being compared to the other girls. My parents respect me in a certain way, they are pleased with how I came out . . . I'm not saying this to be conceited or anything. Maybe because I'm the oldest I think I'm different and it's not on the same comparison level . . . maybe I'm more of a mother to my sisters. Because of Holly I grew up so fast and became more of a caring and less a selfish person. Holly puts everything in perspective . . . she is very special and we are not going to have her for very long and so you have to look at it like that."

Death in the Family

The impact of a parent's or sibling's death on family members greatly depends on each one's age and developmental strengths at the time, but its effect lasts for a lifetime, again, particularly with the surviving daughters who are often

27

immediately called upon to keep the grieving family intact emotionally and physically whether they are equipped to do so or not.

Flo was only six, and the youngest of five children, when her mother died in 1930, but she can remember vividly the casket in the living room, the soft pink dress her mother wore, and all the flowers and candles. "I remember how everybody was very sad," says Flo, who still recalls the scene in the simple, succinct language of a child. Flo is perhaps the most outspoken of three sisters, and even that is barely an issue. The two oldest, Ceil and Edna, are practically identical in their courteous stoicism. It's as if they have seen it all and will stand by their family at whatever cost.

Immediately after their mother's death, the three sisters and their baby brother were taken in by their mother's sister, a spinster who lived just six blocks away in a small town in Indiana. The oldest brother remained with the father, who soon remarried a young woman only six years his daughter Edna's senior. The father and his new bride went on to have a large family of their own, a fact of life that the three sisters accepted with the understanding that they were still part of their father's life even if it was at times only for Sunday dinner or when helping him out in his grocery store.

When I first met with these three sisters, they presented their childhood as problem free living with an aunt who was dedicated to caring for her dead sister's children. It was only after we talked for almost an hour that they mentioned the aunt's formidable control, her total inability to embrace and kiss the children or to praise them as their mother so often did. They had earlier described their mother as "saintly," a life-loving woman whose main interest was in her family and church, but who also enjoyed music and evening games with the children around the dining room table.

I asked if they had any explanation for the difference between their mother and the aunt. With insight, they cited the fact that their grandfather had died when their mother and aunt were also young, leaving their aunt in charge of her younger siblings, one of whom was a retarded brother. "In retrospect, I now realize that our aunt was very insecure. She later lost both of her two sisters when they were relatively young women, so she was afraid to let us out of her sight or allow us any freedom like other children had," said Edna.

My intention was to interview Edna, Ceil, and Flo, now in or near their seventies, but I was fascinated with how their mother's similar experience of losing her parent early in life had differently affected her and her sister, and then went on to affect them. Unlike the women in the generation before, Edna, Ceil, and Flo have barely discernible differences. Apparently they cherish their mother's love of life and acceptance of each other, and they lived with their mother long enough to be able to withstand their aunt's icy upbringing. I'm sure the fact that they were living all together under the aunt's roof helped immensely in maintaining their brave camaraderie and their joint concern for their baby brother, who was only two when their mother died. Edna particularly kept a watchful eye on her younger sisters and brother. During the interview she refused to acknowledge her role as surrogate mother, but Flo and Ceil told me that they leaned on her routinely.

When we parted, I teased them that their story was amazing because there was no conflict or noticeable differences among the three of them. Several weeks later I received a letter from Edna. After "much thinking" she remembered that she and her sisters differ over the way they do their housework. One was either neater or sloppier than the other, she offered. The letter was written lightly and closed warmly. I imagine it was how her mother would have written it.

29

*   *   *

I first met Charlene when we shared a ride offered by our car service center, which took us back to our respective offices. She intrigued me because she was so good at talking to the driver, a young man who was anxious to get home after he had worked the night shift. Charlene sat in front, I in the back, and we all chatted lightly, but somehow she drew out of him the fact that he was married, had two small children, and kept two jobs, which provided for his family in a way he had not known as a child because his father had abandoned him when he was two. "The most important thing in my life," he told Charlene, "is to be available to my children." Nodding, Charlene told him she understood: "I am the youngest of eleven children, and my mother died when I was just one." I was quiet and in awe of these two people. Before we parted, Charlene and I exchanged names and numbers, and I met with her the following week to discuss her relationship with her sisters.

During our chance encounter, Charlene, who is in her mid-forties, had told me that she was divorced with one adult child, and that she worked full-time as an office assistant and studied nights to be a social worker. I made the assumption that her mother's early death had affected her caring personality and career choice; that is, she became a healer, sensitive to others' needs and problems. But when we met the second time, Charlene presented a totally different perspective.

"I'm a spoiled baby," said Charlene directly, not waiting for any argument. "I didn't know it until I was an adult. And I still have some spoiled behavior now. My oldest sister, Josie, spoiled me a lot, all my sisters did really. They spoiled me because they looked at me and said, 'She never had no mama.' Oh, my, the tantrums I used to put on, and create havoc."

30

When Charlene recently took a friend to her sister Josie's house for dinner, her friend couldn't believe how Josie got up from the table and waited on Charlene. Charlene had never before considered how unusual Josie's attentions and generosity were: "That's the way it's always been. I asked Josie for some dishes that night and she just gave them to me. Anything I see, I can have."

Her role as the baby who always receives and gets her way, often makes Charlene feel uncomfortably separate from her sisters, whom she loves and keeps in daily touch with. "They still look at me as being that little girl. Because I'm spoiled, I say how I feel. I'll tell them when things go wrong, 'I'm just mad and I don't want to talk to nobody.' Emotionally, it's like that little girl internally kicking and having that tantrum. I want my way, and always they give it to me. 'Oh God, please don't let her get mad!'

"I don't like how people tiptoe around me. When I'm angry, I can't say a word, I shut down. When I'm angry I don't call my sisters, I don't talk to them. I'll tell them I'm angry, but not what I feel inside, 'I hate them, I hate them.' I don't verbalize that."

Her pent-up anger may stem from her childhood, when she and her siblings would always try to "keep the peace" in their household. Charlene's father, a religious and strict man, was a sharecropper in North Carolina. When his wife died of a stroke and left him with eleven children, he fought her sisters' wishes to take the younger children into their homes. He insisted that his children remain with him, and besides, he knew that his oldest girl, Josie, like most eldest girls in the large families in the area, was fully prepared to mind children and do chores, so she could easily slip into the role of mother—which she did.

"All of us are very close. We didn't associate much with the outside." Charlene smiled. "Because we lived in a rural

31

section, we were each other's family and friend. Of course, there was some discord, but when that happened you could move from one sister or brother to another. Primarily, there was a lot of love and religion taught in our home so you didn't carry grudges and anger very long. It's still that way today."

Was that where she got the inspiration to be a social worker and help others?

"I'm a people person," laughs Charlene. "I could have done carpentry work, which is not feminine and my sisters wouldn't have liked that (all of my decisions are made with my sisters), so I asked myself, I love being with people, why not social work? I contemplated being a nurse, but I couldn't stand it if people died."

Unfortunately, Charlene's early loss of her mother and the strength of the family, particularly the bond with her sisters, has prevented her from making close friendships outside the family. Enmeshed in her sisters' judgments, love, and support, she insists she doesn't have the time or inclination to meet or get involved with other women. Charlene has several platonic friendships with men, but no close woman friend. "Sometimes when I get mad with my sisters, I think, 'I'll show them, I'll have a friend,'" says Charlene, "but it never happens." Her sentiment is like that of a sulking child who wants more attention from the mother she cannot have. Any "older" sister who takes a parent's place cannot possibly give what the younger sister fully needs and wants; it is little wonder, then, that the frustration lasts a lifetime.

Our roles and identity in a family are shaped by myriad external factors, such as birth order, the changing status of parents' marriage, economics, and health. We also bring our own temperament and style to the scene. Charlene lost her mother when she was only one, a fate over which she had no control; her short temper and strong will, however, help to maintain her place as "the baby" in the family. Another contributing factor to differences is how we perceive our parents in their favoritism and influence; and when the parents are dysfunctional, one sister typically glorifies the parent, while the other sees the tarnish behind the glow. Because women are such *reactors* to others, their roles within the family are often divided into the giver and the receiver; that is, one sister *needs* so much emotionally, so the other *responds* to her. Linda knows she has "grown up quickly" because of the care and concern for her younger sister Holly, who has cystic fibrosis. Leah is balancing her parents' divorce as if it is her own, and has been appointed family peacemaker by her younger sibling and the older sister, who wants to remain uninvolved. When there is less need to react, and more space for the child to create and live in autonomy, there is less distinction between the giving and receiving sisters, such as in Susan's family, where the daughters all grew up in a relatively secure family life knowing that they could pursue their separate interests without comparison.

The inherent problem with this pattern of giving and receiving among sisters is that it provides an atmosphere of inequality and unrest. The sister who gives invariably becomes tired of her role and feels that her sister should be doing her part. The sister who receives soon feels her sister is not giving enough, or she is struggling with her guilt that she, too, should be the all-nurturing woman that society expects her to be. It is a heavy load to put on both sides and it invites disappointment. In the following chapter we will look at dramatic contrasts between sisters that further illustrate how we shape and maintain our sisterly differences in reaction to one another.

3

▽

The Light and Dark Sides
of Sisterhood

EVER SINCE SOPHOCLES created the aggressive Antigone and her complacent sister, Ismende (sisters of Oedipus), we have been plagued, amused, and blessed with the dark and light sides of sisters. While it is true that few of our female protagonists or heroines in literature even *have* a sister, when they do, they are typically and conveniently their moral or psychological antithesis, each struggling against the other's separate identity, and yet drawing from each other's strength. In George Eliot's *Middlemarch* there is the uncanny balance between Celia, the rational sister who still blushes at a gentleman's solicitous remarks, and Dorothea, the idealistic, almost masculine, sister who rarely blushes, and then "only from . . . anger."[1]

In Jane Austen's novels we always find in minute detail the contrast of sisters, not necessarily in a moral sense but rather in personalities and manner—as in *Pride and Prejudice*, when the playful, handsome Elizabeth points out to her beautiful, more pliant eldest sister, Jane: "But that is one great difference between us. Compliments always take *you* by surprise, and *me* never."[2] With Austen we see that dualism within the family isn't limited to choices of what is right and what is wrong. It is also used to depict the dramatic contrasts or subtle discrepancies of how sisters perceive life and live out their lives: in piety or in freedom, in silence or in retort, in giving or in getting, in expectations or in demand. We seem to be fascinated with such contrasts because it is such an anomaly of the feminine. We *expect* women to be universally good and caring, so when a woman is "bad" or a rebel or *just different,* she gains our attention and curiosity. And if she has a sister who is her opposite, or her foil, all the better, the sisters now grab our full attention.

Sexy Versus Dependable

One particular dichotomy that fascinates us in fact and fiction is the so-called sexy sister versus the proper sister, implying that one is bad and the other is good. In Barbara Raskin's 1990 novel, *Current Affairs,* Natalie is a feet-on-the-ground social worker who glibly carries on an "overwrought relationship"[3] with her sister, Shay, a chronic heartbreaker who at forty acts like a teenager at her first party with drugs. "I help, my sister hypes,"[4] complains Natalie to anyone who will listen, including her husband, who was Shay's lover before he met and married good old solid Natalie. The beautiful and famous Shay is an international journalist who flauntingly borrows and discards men the way she does her sister's wardrobe. During one of Shay's whirlwind visits, Natalie second-guesses a conversation with one of her shrinks about her jealousy and frustration: "So how do I live with this sister of mine, who flits in and out of my life, using and abusing me, hogging the limelight, taking liberties and always just a bounce away from actually flirting with my husband?

"Poorly."[5]

If a woman is repressing her sexual needs, or is miserable in her marriage, she may find her sister's more promiscuous, or freer life-style, threatening and annoying. "Why can't I do what she does?" she asks herself. Or, she may be judgmental and wonder why her sister has the license to have sex with whomever she pleases. Marilyn, who has struggled for years with a difficult marriage, tells me that her youngest sister's life of divorce, lovers, and extramarital affairs is "sometimes amusing" but more often a painful frustration.

"I envy her freedom to pick up and take off, her flirtations, her whole damn bravado about all her lovers," says Marilyn. "It infuriates me, though, when she thinks that I want a play-by-play account of all her affairs. She is so self-centered and I feel so stuck and uninteresting. She never asks how I'm doing with my relationship with my husband . . . probably because she knows nothing has changed."

Conflicted with her bad marriage and fear of divorce ("At forty-six, I don't want to do to my children what my parents did to me. They split just when I went off to college"), Marilyn can do nothing but criticize her sister, without ever considering how needy or unfulfilled she may be.

Jo and Kimberly's Story

A totally different reaction to the sexy sister came from twenty-eight-year-old Kimberly, who neither covets nor rejects her sister Jo's style of rebellion but wants to enjoy it and remain her trusting friend. "In high school I was class president and homecoming queen with a boyfriend in medical school," says Kimberly, not in a bragging sense but to show how she was "the predictable sister who did everything straight."

"My youngest sister thought of me as 'the Blessed Virgin

Mary,' " she says with a groan. But her middle sister, Jo, just a year behind Kimberly in school, decidedly went her own way. "Jo always felt she was living in my shadow," explains Kimberly. "She was dyslexic; a cheerleader who didn't hang out with the crowd but smoked in the school bathroom." When Jo got mixed up with a drug crowd, she tried to kill herself, a dark scene her sister will never be able to erase from her memory. "My parents were away on vacation, I walked in the house and I saw this horrible person, some guy with long hair, carrying my sister, who had slit her wrists. It was horrible. Jo and I tried to keep it from my parents, but she committed herself to a drug rehab center when they got back." Once Jo was in rehabilitation, the family went into therapy, a task in Kimberly's eyes that was especially painful for her parents. "I don't know how they survived it. I didn't have to deal with it as much as my parents, but I can remember how the therapist blamed me for my sister's problems; I was really turned off by it. My sister has blocked the whole thing from her mind. She's out of rehab and has gotten a wonderful job, which she loves. I'm very proud of her.

"Jo will always be her own person. One time I was working on Capitol Hill in the office of a conservative senator and Jo came to visit me and she was wearing tight black pants, spike heels, and an angora sweater with big red roses on it. Everyone was speechless," laughs Kimberly. "It was like a scene out of the movie *sex, lies, and videotape* with me as the character Ann, the not-so-extreme sister. I loved it."

It was interesting to me that though Kimberly is so different from Jo, they are confidantes. Several years ago while they were living in separate cities, both sisters "coincidentally" got pregnant. After deliberating with each other, both decided on an abortion—a particularly difficult decision for Kimberly, who is a practicing Catholic like her parents. "Through the whole thing, Jo was a total support to me. My parents don't know about this [the abortions]. Jo is very close to my father, I'm closer to my mother. Dad could never comprehend this happening to me, but he could accept it of Jo. My mother asked about it, but I lied to her. She could accept it from Jo also." Kimberly pauses. "Maybe I'm not giving my parents enough benefit of the doubt."

Kimberly's concerns about Jo's relationships with men show how deeply she cares, despite and because of their differences. "Jo is not attracted to the same kind of men that I am. She's not as picky as I am. This week I'm not speaking to her because of this loser guy she's going with, he's married. I tell her that she is heading for disaster. I told her, 'You are always going to be number two with this guy.' And she told me, 'Well, I was born number two.' I don't like it when she talks that way. She gets real insecure and clings to these people. I think I don't trust men, because of what has happened to me in the past [the abortion]. Whereas my sister will just dive right in and get so absorbed that it consumes her life and she forgets her family."

Gay Versus Straight

When a sister reveals that she is a lesbian, the effect ripples through the family, touching on each and every member, but with a varying and progressive impact. In time, the siblings' and parents' reactions may progress from shock, through denial, through sadness, to acceptance—or to rejection. I learned from the women in my survey, and from the private testimony of my friends, that often the key person in the dynamic between the gay and straight sister is the mother. If she rejects her gay daughter, the straight daughter, depending on her age and emotional development, may "take sides" with her sister, rebelling against the mother; or the straight daughter may follow the role of the mother and turn against her sister. Neither way is rewarding to either sister, or fair to the gay sister. However, if the mother accepts her gay daughter with love and encourages her to pursue her life-style, or at the very least to keep an open dialogue on the struggle within the family, the straight daughter is more likely to follow or attempt to follow her mother's example of acceptance.

"I realized I was gay in 1985, when I was in college," says Caitlin, an attractive, intelligent young woman who has her degree in philosophy and is working in a bookstore until she can find academic work in her field. "My mother is very religious, as I was at the time, so I went to her and said, 'Mom, I might like women and I know this is wrong with God, I want to kill myself.' She said, 'No problem. God loves you for who you are.' I know that she didn't really think at the time that I would stay this way. But if she hadn't been as supportive all this time, I would have been extremely depressed with my struggle with gayness."

Caitlin's family has always taken great pride in their academic achievements. Caitlin has two younger sisters: Penny, twenty-one, is married and has degrees in law and social work; Nan, nineteen, is a student at a leading women's college. There is also an older brother, Phil, who is "mildly autistic" and is described by Caitlin as "not a major player in our family . . . he lived with us, but doesn't talk, though he did manage to get a college degree." Despite their focus on learning, Caitlin's family harbors a painful, destructive secret. In the university town where they grew up, Caitlin's father was a noted university faculty member, a "pillar of the community." He was also physically abusive to his wife and son, and sexually abusive to Caitlin and Nan.

"I equate him with Adolf Hitler," says Caitlin calmly. "He can convince all his friends that he is right and that his family is making it up. But everyone at the university knows that my father is a crazy, dangerous man. People don't like him, despite his intelligence, he is a terrible teacher, not in touch with people. Mom also works at the university, but his friends and mom's friends are separate."

Caitlin hasn't seen her father since her last year in high school, the year of her parents' divorce. Her plan is to take her father to court sometime within the next two years, according to the statute of limitations. Meanwhile, Caitlin has had to face up to two major and related emotional hurdles: her gayness and the sexual abuse.

"When I told my sisters I was gay, at first my sister Penny didn't say anything. Then one night at the dinner table she made it plain that she was very open-minded. I was shocked. Before, it seemed like she didn't want to hear about it. She accepts it, but it's not something we talked about.

"My youngest sister, Nan, has always looked up to me. I took care of her a lot when we were growing up. She thought my being gay was neat, cool. She would tell all her friends that she had a lesbian sister and then see how they reacted. Then she would decide on whether they were her friends. She was always proud of me."

Three years ago Caitlin entered therapy specifically to work on her problems with sexual abuse and her fear of men. Recently, because of her work in therapy, she has experimented with dating men and discovered that she is bisexual. "I talk about the gayness and bisexuality with Nan. She has the same feelings I do, and tells me that now that she's in college she is bisexual. The funny thing is she hates men, but as far as her feelings she is more naturally attracted to men than women, and is more frightened to date women. I'm more naturally attracted to women, but I want to deal with the fear of being hurt by men, so I have decided to date men. I'll be honest with you, it's nicer to date men because

41

you can hold hands in public, and tell people you are dating. In my family of abuse, we had to hide everything. When I'm dating a woman, it's just one more thing I had to hide and it's very uncomfortable."

Other things have changed since the therapy. Just a few months ago Penny came to visit Caitlin, and they had a wonderful time talking and sharing their feelings; it was "a first" for Caitlin. "Penny had always been on the outside of my life. When she was sixteen and I was twelve, she was dating and going on road trips with her boyfriend's band. I traveled two months in Europe with her after I graduated from high school; it turned out that I didn't even know her. She had a terrible time on the trip, she just hated me. Now our relationship has changed drastically for the better. I guess we have grown up. I can appreciate her now, even though I'm very jealous of her success at such a young age."

Caitlin and Penny also realize that they share a common bond in their love and admiration for their mother, while Nan remains angry and separate from her mother, whom she blames for staying in an abusive marriage. Caitlin also has some of those angry feelings toward her mother, but she tells me they are part of her therapy's healing process. She is also patient with her changing relationship with Nan. "I have always spoiled her rotten. I gave her a black leather jacket for her birthday, it cost me a hundred dollars. But she has become demanding. Penny told me that Nan is very spoiled. She will take what she wants and then will treat you badly. I started thinking how I give, but Nan doesn't give, she only takes. She owes me seventy-five dollars. That's been frustrating. I'm going to wait for Nan to grow up and me to grow up. Let Nan go her own way. Penny and I grew up and we are all right," says Caitlin. Then she adds wistfully, "Although Nan and I share a bond being bisexual, and abused."

Unfortunately, Caitlin and her sisters are all reacting to

the years of sexual and physical abuse by the father. Their confusion about their sexuality is not unusual, given the history of their childhood. But in the confusion and the pain, they have managed to sustain their feminine connection with one another. Caitlin's therapy has helped her immensely, but she is also gaining because she brings to her therapy and to her relationship with her sisters her ability to reflect and be patient. Women enjoy reflection and they do it so well. Caitlin's sensitivity to her sisters is actually enabling her to inch toward her self-identity and maturity.

Fertile Versus Infertile

With motherhood as the badge of femininity, an infertile woman invariably feels lesser, and certainly unluckier, than her fertile sister. How can this be? she asks herself. Why can she have children and I cannot? What makes her so special? What is wrong with me?

One divorced woman in her late fifties, whose two sisters are nine and eleven years younger, still feels that her life would not have been filled with so many slights from her mother if she had been able to have children. "In my mother's book, success was having one husband, a home, and children, and being part of the community. My sisters were just that. I felt the black sheep because I didn't have children, though my mother never said that."

Often, much is left unsaid between fertile and infertile sisters and their mothers. A friend of mine told me that she "aches" for her sister and her battle with infertility. She is so careful not to make her feel bad by talking too much about her children, that they have to work hard on not avoiding each other. I also heard considerable testimony that the infertility brought the sisters closer together. Today, with the medical progression of fertility workups and the growing acceptance and availability of adoption, there is more of an arena for sisters to support each other. There is also specialized counseling and literature available to enable women to work out their feelings with someone like a fertile sister. But even with the most sophisticated understanding of the problem, the tension is ever present.

Chris and Carey's Story

Chris could never keep up with her older sister Carey's record of straight A's, so she didn't try. When teachers started calling her "Carey," her parents decided to send her to a public school junior high. Chris's grades improved somewhat, but she always felt in her sister Carey's shadow. Chris gained an edge when she got engaged one year after college graduation and Carey, who is three years older, felt like a spinster with "no serious relationship." On Chris's special day, Carey was a brooding maid of honor. Exactly one year to the day of Chris's engagement party, Carey "evened the score" with her own engagement party. "I know it was no accident," says Carey, who describes herself as one who analyzes everything psychologically. "I was desperate to keep up with my sister." Carey's husband-to-be was ten years older than she; Chris's husband was one year younger than Chris. Carey's was a long engagement, so by the time she married, Chris had been married three years. The first thing Carey wanted to do was have a family. "It was a dream since I was a little girl. I did a lot of baby-sitting when I was a teenager," says Carey. "We grew up in New Jersey in a Catholic neighborhood with families with six, eight, ten kids. My sister and I thought our family was small. My sister used to say she wanted eight children. I always wanted three children, not just one or two; I wanted to diffuse the relationship my sister and I once had, and I always thought it would be fun to have a boy, unlike the matriarch-dominated family we grew up in."

One year after her marriage, Carey was operated on for endometriosis and was diagnosed as infertile. It was a devastating blow. Because Chris and her husband were struggling with graduate school costs, they had waited to start a family; by the time Chris got pregnant with her first child, Carey and her husband had been married three years and were "heavy" into the search for their fertility, through the emotionally strenuous routine of fertility workups—hormonal therapy and inseminations.

"Chris lived in California at the time, so we didn't see each other much and I didn't call too often because I didn't want her to feel bad for me," says Carey. Because of her husband's age, they were professionally advised to stop the fertility workups and start the adoption process as soon as possible. By the time Chris's baby was six months old, Carey learned that she and her husband had a baby boy available to adopt. At this time, Chris moved back to the East Coast and the sisters saw more of each other. Today, Chris has three children, and Carey has two adopted children. At the time of the interview, Carey had just unsuccessfully ended another six-month fertility workup to have a "biological child." Now forty-one, she has reluctantly agreed with her husband to end the fertility workups. "I keep hoping that some miracle will happen, but we've been married fourteen years without it happening."

Because they are busy with their two families, the tension between the sisters has somewhat eased, but not totally. Carey says, "Her children outshine mine, which is hard for me. My kids are wonderful, but neither one of them is going to have great E's for education; the same holds for athletics; both my sister and I are very athletic. I look at her children and they look like us and have the same capacities as I have. My kids are different, wonderful little people. My older boy is kind and amazingly gentle, not like me, but as my sister's children are."

Carey still uses telling phrases, such as, "for my sister, babies just *pop* out." And she begrudges the fact that Chris's first child was planned but the last two were "accidents." The biggest hurdle, however, was when Chris called her six months ago, when Carey had just started on her last fertility workup. "She was actually very upset, crying hard. She and her husband were about to leave on a sabbatical overseas and she learned she was pregnant. She consulted me about having an abortion. It was very difficult for me to handle that. But I acted empathetically, I didn't impose my own feelings." Chris subsequently had the abortion, and Carey never told her how much her not wanting the pregnancy hurt her. "I talked to my friends and my husband, but I couldn't tell her and I don't think she ever thought of it. My sister is very smart, but she doesn't delve into feelings like I do.

"I feel I have a good relationship with my sister, I love her very much. I know we would do anything in the world for each other. We don't have a certain amount of intimacy because of our early competition in school and then later our competing during the infertility. . . . It's possible that it could be a deeper relationship later. I've finished with the idea of biological pregnancy, I think I can get on with life. I *do* have a close extended family with my sister's three children, my plate is full enough."

Carey was giving me a mixed message. On one hand she is aware of the value of having adopted children and the company of the extended family of Chris and her children. But she is still burdened with envy over her sister having a

46

biological family. However, her words, "it is possible it could be a deeper relationship later," are promising, and typical of sisters who have made that leap from ambivalence to caring.

Responsibility Versus Freedom

Most women described the light and dark sides of their biological sisterhood in terms of priorities and responsibilities. I heard numerous testimonies of women who felt locked into a life of hard work and responsibility for their families while they perceived their sisters as doing whatever they pleased with little or no money problems, or few responsibilities. And as for the women who were supposedly "well-off," many of them talked about their *guilt* in leading a better life than their sisters'. One woman, for example, has never told her sister that someone comes in and cleans her house two days a week so that she can manage her full-time job and her family. "I talk to my sister every weekend, she lives on the West Coast and only visits me once a year. She works and has kids, but she can't afford any household help, so my having help two days a week would seem extravagant to her. I feel guilty, so I just keep it to myself."

Much of our guilt and complaints over responsibilities and privilege are leftovers from childhood days when we had to work hard to prove our worth, or gain our parents' favor. There are also families who put value on pain and suffering, a philosophy adopted particularly by the women in the family, who feel that they have to "do it all" in order to prove their worth. These women feel that should success and privileges come their way, they either don't deserve them or having them isn't as valuable as a life of hard work and struggle can be.

When I met Clarissa, she was fresh from a "bad phone

47

call" with her sister Janey. It seems that as Clarissa was telling her sister about her day, Janey offhandedly referred to Clarissa's job as "cushy." Both women are married and have children, and both work diligently, Clarissa as a freelance photographer and Janey as a full-time public relations assistant. "Janey has to report in every day and I don't report to anyone but my clients," said Clarissa. "To her, that probably means I'm eating bonbons and taking hot baths while she's slaving away from nine to five. When I got angry and told her how hard it is to get clients, do decent shoots, sell my pictures, all those things, she just humored me. 'You've got to admit it's cushy,' she said it again! I wanted to strangle her, but I was afraid if I said anything more, I would insult her about her job."

Responsibility for Our Parents

The tension between sisters like Clarissa and Janey is relatively harmless until they have to work together on a common responsibility—the care of their elderly parents. In my survey, the most common concerns about the differences in responsibility were either *"Will my sister, who is out doing her own thing, help with the care of our parents when the time comes?"* or *"Why doesn't my sister do more for my parents . . . why is the load all on me?"*

Lois voiced the first concern with no hesitation. She is harsh and direct about her "strained relationship" with her younger sister, Patsy, but she wants to find a way to reconcile their differences because she is afraid if they don't do it soon, she will be the one left with the sole responsibility for the care of her parents who are now in their seventies.

"I am the first child, the one in control. My sister is the free spirit, very, very different. She moved out West, I stayed here with my parents, so the responsibility is still

48

mine and she is doing her own thing. Yes, it is a bone of contention. I wonder what will happen if something happens to my parents. My sister doesn't come here often. Her husband is a lawyer, but he's a free spirit too and he doesn't have the kind of East Coast–type law job with a lot of pressure. They have a trade-off, they don't have much money but they can go hiking or camping whenever they want.

"When it boils down to it, we have different values. While I have a lucrative career in law and real estate, Patsy's jobs have been social work jobs, consumer advocacy, all those things that people do in the West. Her children go to public schools, my daughter goes to a private school, for the exact opposite reasons, integrated versus nurturing. While my values are a carbon copy of my parents', a throwback to my grandparents'."

Whether one agrees with her sense of values or not, Lois has a workable concern. Her parents are still healthy, and she keeps a polite distance from her sister. If she can learn to accept Patsy's life-style, she may find that in the future they can collaborate on their parents' care. The risk is delaying the reconciliation and hoping the parents live a long and healthy life. Long-established differences between sisters can mushroom beyond proportion when parents suddenly need expensive, time-consuming medical care. At such highly emotional, wrenching times, the burden on sisters touches on the value of their roles within the family. When one is considered the nurturing, responsible sister, and the other the needier or receiving sister, the stage is already set for hurt feelings and guilt. Lois is wise to worry about their differences. If she is as controlled and nurturing as she says she is, however, she will undoubtedly work out some understanding with her sister so things will go more smoothly for everyone involved.

A High Price for Responsibility: Pamela's Story

Pamela is an attractive, intelligent thirty-five-year-old who adamantly claims she will never have children because she had to take care of her four sisters and brother when her mother was chronically depressed. "I got sick of babies. It seemed like you just got rid of one and then another would come," she says unabashedly. When her mother was pregnant with her last child, her father had an affair that precipitated years of quarrels and distrust, until finally they divorced when Pamela was twenty-two and her baby sister was twelve. Easily, the children split into two camps: the three teenage girls living at home chose their mother (the son, rejected by both parents, chose no one); Pamela, the father's constant favorite, was the only child who chose to be on her father's side. Eventually, her father remarried and Pamela and her stepmother became "best friends," while her sisters had little to do with the new marriage. The differences between the sisters simmered while they went through adolescence and young adulthood, though while in college they at least remained in touch with each other for birthdays and holidays. Then, six years ago when Pamela was working in London for an investment company, she received a call from her stepmother saying that her father had prostate cancer that had spread to his bones. "I came back right away and started taking care of him," recalls Pamela. "It was very important to me to be with him as much as I could. This is what tore us [siblings] all apart. I was the closest to him, so I really took care of him. I had never asked my sisters for anything, never, but it got so exhausting (my stepmother had to keep working and she had a long commute on weekends). So one time I asked my sisters to stay for a week or weekend to relieve me. I was getting up every four hours at least to help him urinate, and give him morphine. They wouldn't do it. They said they were too busy. Given a crisis situation, I was expecting them to help out with my father. I went back to London and packed my things to return to him. I took care of him about two months before he died." After his death, Pamela was able to express her anger to her sisters, telling them that through the years she had made such an effort to care for them, and that the one time she really needed them they weren't there. It fell on deaf ears. Or perhaps the guilt-laden message was too much for the three young sisters who as young children had always relied on Pamela. I wondered, though, why they viewed their father with so little compassion.

"Other things came out subsequently," continued Pamela. "I took care of the estate as his executrix. I didn't take very much in fees because there wasn't much money, only a car, a boat, and an annuity. One of my sisters took care of the annuity. I took care of the bills, the assets, all the stupid things you have to do when someone dies. I had to wait for months for my sisters and brother to sign the release. I didn't realize why, I just thought they were being lazy or something. I found out later from my youngest sister that they didn't sign the release because they thought I was stealing money. Would you believe it?"

To this day, Pamela believes that the third oldest sister, Sally, remained loyal to her over the issue of the estate. "In some ways, she and I have the least in common. Sally is gay. When she told me she was a lesbian, we were both living in the same place in the early 1980s. At first I was horrified, then I learned to accept it. The little girl that was born to her bisexual mate is really wonderful; I think of her as a niece. Actually, Sally is my closest sister because we have the same kinds of interests and personality."

The issue of the estate money, however, is still unresolved. And yet it pales in the light of worse accusations following

51

the father's death. At what was to be the close of the interview, Pamela finally revealed the heart of the matter: "There is something else, which I don't feel I have to hide. My two youngest sisters say that my father had an incestuous relationship with them. I couldn't believe it when they told me. I asked myself, 'Pamela, is there anything you don't remember?' But what I do remember was that my father went out of his way not to touch us, or me, in any kind of sexual way whatsoever. He was very definite about that. I have really searched my memory of my father and I know that as I grew and my breasts grew he was very careful not to touch. He had other problems, but nothing like that.

"I don't want to figure it out anymore. It just makes me tired. All I know is that my father didn't abuse me and we had a very good relationship. If something happened with my sisters, wild or wacko, the person is dead and can't defend himself. On one level I can't really handle [the accusation] because my father kept me together. He was the stable one emotionally, he was always there, so supportive. To rip his memory apart, I can't do that."

Shaken with the accusations toward her father, the man she faithfully loved and admired, Pamela has not spoken to her two youngest sisters in two years, and unhappily but stubbornly remains outside her family—the family she once cared for because it was her "sole responsibility." There is no way to determine who is right or wrong. The father is dead, the memories are unclear, the history for each sister, as in any family, is different. But time has its way of inspiration. Just two weeks before we met, Pamela's best friend's parents were killed in an accident in England. Pamela had known them well and was deeply grieved by the news. "I talked to my friend on the phone and she told me that she felt good about their deaths because they were all getting on very well. Her last memory of them was kissing them good-bye and saying, 'I'll see you in a few weeks.' She knows they died with nothing between her and them.

"I started thinking if something happened to my sisters and brother, would I feel bad? You just look at life and you think you don't want somebody to die and not have these issues taken care of. I have to do something about my sisters."

As a child with a depressed mother, Pamela had to take over and be the mother to her siblings, and as a young woman she had to take care of her father. There has been little or no time for Pamela to be a child herself or even to enjoy her young adulthood. Her sisters apparently have their own grievances and needs with their father's abuse and their parents' divorce. Pamela's story is complex and wrenching, but again there is the promise of an understanding and a healthier involvement because she is aware of how important the reconciliation with her sisters is. She too is reflective about her family, like most of the women I spoke with. She can't turn her back on them and feel that she has gained.

The Subtle Differences Over Parental Favoritism

Most sisters' differences are not dramatically defined to outsiders, such as one being infertile, or gay, or promiscuous, or scorned like Pamela. Sisters may appear to others to be totally compatible in their life-style; they both may be married, raising children, working, or they both may be single, working, and leading productive, full lives. What goes on privately between them, however, can be a silent storm of subtle, tenacious visceral differences, built on their opposing experiences and perceptions from childhood. We have seen how sisters view their parents' favoritism differently and how

53

the perception of the favoritism, and the favoritism itself, affect their roles in the family. In time, the issue of favoritism may appear to be lost, as the sisters get older and other issues of contention, such as children or success, become the focal point. But way down deep the sisters are still the two little girls judging themselves in their parents' eyes. They are the good and the bad, the responsible and the irresponsible, the fun-loving and the sad children twirling around their parents looking for love and attention.

Margaret and Phoebe's Story

Margaret tells me that her relationship with her younger sister, Phoebe, is "right now, treacherous and tricky." Ominous words to describe the affairs of two women in their mid-forties who claim they have only each other. Both parents died when the sisters were in their early twenties, leaving them alone with no other family and a discomforting balance of differences and favoritism that didn't disappear with their parents' absence.

According to Margaret, the favoritism was an inevitable product of World War II, when her father fought overseas and she was just two months old. "I am fascinated by what war does to families," says Margaret. "My husband went to Vietnam, so I can relate to what my mother must have felt while my father was gone. During wartime women have to make a special bond with their children, as my mother did with me. It must have been hard for the fathers to get back into that tight circle of women and children." One of the ways was to have another child. Phoebe was born a year after the father's return, when Margaret was five. To this day the sisters' differences revolve around the fact that Margaret was her mother's child and Phoebe was the father's.

54

"I must have had a different bond with my father originally, sort of an anxiety-ridden link to him away, not knowing what was happening. Then he comes back and can't
relate to the first child," says Margaret, switching to the
impersonal third person. "But the next child is born, so he
can relate to her. I've heard this from other families and it
makes me feel better."

But the differences between Margaret and Phoebe go
beyond the war. "We two represent a fairly typical stereotype
of the opposite sisters and all of it was promoted by our
parents, separating us along the way. I was the older responsible one, doing everything right. Phoebe was scary with her
temper, our house was controlled by her anger. One time she
made a terrible scene in a department store because she
wanted a pair of women's pink stockings with sequins on
them. My mother gave in and bought them for her . . . they
were terribly expensive and totally inappropriate for a child.
It must have been terrible for Phoebe to have so much
control; every time she had a tantrum my parents gave her
whatever she wanted."

Margaret and her sister also differed in looks, a bone of
contention only recently and "slightly" resolved. By Margaret's harsh recollection, in grade school she "looked like a
waif" with stringy blond hair and glasses, while little Phoebe
"looked like Elizabeth Taylor."

"When we were out with our parents people would say
how beautiful she was and I must be the smart one," laughs
Margaret. "We've never been able to work this out completely, we fall back into the same traps. Objectively, yes, I
did very well in school. But intuitively she is much brighter
than I am. Phoebe is just realizing this, she has a tremendous lack of confidence." Margaret also knows she is far
more attractive than in her early years and she is just as

beautiful as Phoebe. "But these are patterns that are hard to break. We needed to work this out with my parents as adults, but we weren't able to . . . they died so young."

When talking on the phone or visiting, both sisters often "tense up" over issues surrounding their memories or their different styles of responding. Margaret's early times with her mother were happy, while Phoebe has no fond memories of her mother whatsoever. Both agree that their mother was an alcoholic, but Margaret claims it "wasn't an issue" in her early years as it was for Phoebe. "Phoebe feels my mother was jealous of her," explains Margaret. "But Mother couldn't have been, she had hundreds of friends, she had a southern charm about her and a tremendous verbal ability. Actually, Phoebe and Mother are very much alike, but they wouldn't have seen each other that way. Phoebe is more sultry with black hair, Mother was blond with a Gibson look."

I suggest that perhaps their mother was jealous of all the attention the father was giving Phoebe. But Margaret only observes that Phoebe looked like her father, and Margaret like her mother. "Father joked and teased us all the time, I hated it. Phoebe adored him, but I can't believe that he was the way that she remembers. She thinks he was a saint, I think he had problems like everyone else. He, too, was very popular, people loved him, he was always pleasant, cheerful, and very successful in his business. But he never connected with us at all, he was removed. Phoebe just doesn't remember him that way."

Much of the tension revolves around the history of the father's drinking problems. Margaret thinks he may have been an alcoholic also, Phoebe won't agree, keeping her father's memory sacred. The two sisters avoid the topic as much as possible. Less intimidating are their memories from high school when they competed for boyfriends. Phoebe dated the older boys in Margaret's class, a "constant threat" to her sister. "Also, our rules were different," says Margaret. "She bucked them, I didn't. I was so conscientious that one weekend when I was going away to see a football game, I was compelled to take a chaperon because I was crossing the state line . . . and Phoebe went to Florida to visit a guy whom my parents never met."

The "bitter pill to swallow" was when Margaret's parents told her they couldn't afford to have her go away to college and that she would have to attend a local university. "I knew they had the money; the real reason was that Mother couldn't separate." Margaret says she had no choice but to comply. A year later Phoebe was allowed to go out of town to the state university. Margaret was told she could join her, but she was so angry and hurt, she refused, saying that her sister's choice of schools "wasn't challenging enough."

Margaret has now been married twenty-six years and has two children; Phoebe was married and divorced, and is now remarried with one child. Relocating several times because of their husbands' professions, the sisters have been more separated physically and emotionally than they would care to be. "There were times when we lived in the same city and didn't speak to each other, once for six months, another time, three months," says Margaret, amazed that she can't even recall what the issues were. "Today we talk once a week. We are all we have."

And yet there is still that "tricky, treacherous relationship." Why is that? I ask her.

"There is this continual competition, but there is also love. I remember when we were little, how we used to go camping in this large closet we had under the staircase. We spent the night in there eating and talking with candlelight, it was a wonderful feeling of togetherness.

"Now it's very hard for me when she is visiting back here. I feel very inadequate and she feels the same way. We have a wonderful time together, but the relationship jockeys back and forth, there are times when one is on top of the other.

"It rings in my ears all the time, what people used to say, 'She's so beautiful, and you must be the smart one.' I'm best when she's not here."

In the dramatic light-and-dark world of sisters we again see the resilience and energy of the feminine connection. But in all these scenarios of contrasts, from the sexy to the proper, from the responsible to the irresponsible, it is clear that there is no tension over the differences unless they are embedded and based on deeper, early-born feelings of envy and inequality. Marilyn hated to hear about her sister's lovers, not just because she was unhappy in her own marriage, but because ever since she was a young girl she felt her sister had more choices and freedom in her life. Carey was so wrapped up in her sister's ease at getting pregnant because, as she said, she is still carrying the feelings of competition she had as a child. Pamela is overburdened, but she is also desperately hanging on to her legacy of being the favored child. Most of us can relate to sisters like Margaret and Phoebe, where the feeling of inequality is perhaps more subtle and yet bogged down with an ambivalent, confused, emotional love. What keeps us from comfortably enjoying each other is not really the contrast between our choice of life-style, it lies more in the murky shadows of that "tricky business," the unresolved, unspoken *competition* that has been with us since childhood when we vied for our parents' attention or our special place among the siblings. If we want to understand fully the complexity of sisterhood, and appreciate our feminine connection, we next have to capture and further reflect on the elusive sense of inequality and envy among women as sisters and females.

4

$\triangledown$

Releasing Our
Competitive Spirit

IT WAS A HOT, sticky morning when a young couple came over to our yard to ask if they could check out an addition we had put on the house several years ago. Their two daughters, Heather, three, and Annie, two, were studies in opposition. Heather, the quiet one, stayed just inches away from her mother's skirt, keeping a serious eye on Annie, who was running between our basset hound and her parents, having a wonderful time distracting us with her giggles and flirtations. I had only to look at my husband to know that he, too, was feeling sentimental with this unexpected time warp. These two little girls were much like our two oldest daughters: a year apart, yet mirrored contrasts in personality as they each in their own style, circled their young parents for attention. Eventually, Annie went over to the rope hammock, checked it out carefully, then placed her precious "bankie"—a tattered baby blanket she carries at all times—in the hammock right up to the edge close to her fat tummy. Gently, Annie began to swing her bankie, her make-believe precious baby. Smoothly and silently, Heather came up behind her, whisked the blanket far outside Annie's reach, and began to swing the hammock furiously, threatening the invisible baby's very life. Annie howled in horror, her mother leaped to the rescue, slowing the hammock and returning the bankie to its safe spot close to Annie. Mother mildly scolded Heather, who sulked by the tree and eyed Annie with a sad, embittered gaze sisters have all held or received at one time or another.

Chances are that when Annie and Heather are adults they won't have any lasting memory of the hammock and the bankie. But the competitive incident won't be lost to time, it has been absorbed by the experience of each child. It becomes part of Annie, part of Heather, and it gradually builds up to an attitude, a feeling between them that is rarely identical or even similar.

"No, I Never Compete with My Sister"

Early in my interviews I kept running into blind alleys when I asked the question "Do you compete with your sister?" Over and over again, I heard the finite, impassioned answer, "No," or "Never," or, at the very most, "That was over a long time ago." I could have accepted those answers at face value except that in most of the cases, with few exceptions, the women went on to describe childhoods filled with competition and adult years laced with covert envy. After one woman told me, "No, we don't compete," she immediately spun a list of her sister's "advantages" that she "wished" she shared, everything from being more popular to having a better education. Another woman claimed that she and her three sisters never harbored any rivalry, but then described how they called one of the sisters "moo-cow" because "she was so bossy," and that the sisters drew lines of demarcation in their bedrooms.

I soon realized that such words as "rivalry," "envy,"

60

"competition," and "jealousy" suggest immaturity or insecurity, so they are best avoided. After all, sensitive, intelligent women don't compete, they "get along" with their sisters. I learned to rephrase my questions to "Who is the smartest?" "The prettiest?" "The most talented?" "Who was your mother's favorite?" "Your father's favorite?" The answers opened up a far different and more honest dialogue on competition. The majority of women talked about feeling inferior to their sister at some period in their development. Even the women who acknowledged that in their childhood they were favored by their parents, or had better grades, or were more attractive, whatever the gain might have been, they often felt guilty that they had the edge in the game of competition.

Sophisticated Competition

Dr. Natalie Low from Cambridge Hospital in Boston interviewed thirty women who had sisters for a study on attachment. In the *Radcliffe Quarterly*, Low reports that it was "surprising" that sister-to-sister jealousy was expressed by relatively few of the women. "While jealousy is popularly thought to be a major feeling between sisters," writes Low, ". . . it may be that sibling rivalry belongs more to childhood, when sisters are developmentally less able to share and when the competition for parents is more salient in daily life."[1]

Low describes the women in her study as "highly educated, many with advanced degrees . . . mainly in their 30s and 40s."[2] I would suggest that these astute women know better than to admit to competition and jealousy. Or, it may be that the competition is sublimated and displaced, so that it is no longer targeted at sisters, but rather at colleagues in the workplace or friends, or even at husbands or lovers. Low told me that she knows "competition is out there, because I hear women talking about it." But as a psychologist

61

interested in women's psychology, she contends that men "created" the stereotype of the competitive sisters because they "miss the attachment" between women. "They can only concentrate on the competitive issue."

In my survey I met several women who had had years of therapy or were therapists themselves, or were simply so psychologically informed that they had intellectualized their competition. Christine is an artist and former psychiatric social worker, who mindfully cares for her ailing mother while her younger sister Diane has felt free to come and go as she pleases, no matter what the needs of the elderly parents and Christine's family. It was difficult for me to discern if Christine was intellectualizing her feelings of envy of Diane's freedom, or if she had actually come to grips with their different perspectives. Her story was full of conflicts with her sister which would have driven most of us into a jealous rage, and yet she spoke so fairly about Diane. When I asked her where her angry feelings were, she first spoke as a therapist: "There is no denial from me that there were these bifurcated feelings about my sister, but I don't want to alienate my relationship with her." Then, speaking as a sister: "I really like her. She's obviously my part of myself I haven't been able to express, the wanderlust. She's interesting, has a wide span of interests in business, exports and imports. She can function on her own in the middle of Burma. There's an interest about her that the rest of us don't necessarily have. She also recognizes my talent and business as an artist."

Blind Competition

Christine seems comfortable with her competition with her sister, an enviable but unfeasible position for most of us. Three months after I interviewed Margaret (see Chapter 3),

I heard from her that she had talked to her sister, Phoebe, about their competition and Phoebe was "surprised" that Margaret thought they competed. "I never compete with you," Phoebe insisted. "I was so confused," said Margaret. "I asked two of our mutual friends who know us well what they thought, and they said we both competed and that one of Phoebe's strongest characteristics is her being competitive. I can't believe Phoebe doesn't see that."

Margaret's story intrigued me because the same thing had happened when I broached the subject with my sister Mary when we met for dinner at a hotel where she was attending a conference. She, too, said she doesn't compete with me: "I'm *proud* of you, but I don't compete with you" were her exact words. I felt like a two-year-old getting a pat on the head. An hour later she introduced me to a good-looking man whom she had been dating. "This is my oldest sister," she said teasingly. I was devastated. It was the day before my birthday and I had just confided to her how I didn't like "feeling old." Her friend fortunately had a sense of humor. "Does she always introduce you like that?" he chided. "How are you going to get even with her?" I told him I was going to put it in my book. We all laughed, including Mary. I know and the family knows that Mary is a very competitive person. Indeed, *both* of us are and that is an essential part of our relationship. But why is it so terribly hard for both of us to admit to?

Gaining a Good Name for "Competition"

"It isn't that women don't have competitive feelings, only that they have much more difficulty in acknowledging them, therefore in acting on them,"[3] says Lillian B. Rubin in *Just Friends*. She is speaking about all women—sisters, mothers, aunts, cousins, and friends. Unlike little boys, little girls were raised not to compete but to cooperate and get along, sometimes at all costs, such as sacrificing their individuality or their principles. The Annie-and-Heather scenario would probably have gone differently between two little boys. Mother might not have run to the rescue so quickly, and both parents may have proudly watched as the boys fought it out in the grass. The female lessons of being cooperative and sensitive to relationships is so inherent to a woman's upbringing and so continually fed by society that women don't see how they need that competitive spirit to survive until they are burned or so hurt that they feel defenseless against the emotion. But it's okay to feel competitive. It is the energy of envy. Nancy Friday wrote that she "would like to give a good name to competition."[4] Well, I am giving it a good name. Competition picks us up off the ground and says, "I am just as good as you are." It shouts, "Let me try this! I'm sure I can do it! Maybe I can do better."

"Competition spurs the process of differentiation. It is an act of self-hood,"[5] says psychologists Luise Eichenbaum and Susie Orbach in *Between Women*. It is in the spirit of this healthy competition that I choose women friends who are bright and interesting, just as all my sisters are bright and interesting. I want to learn from my friends, and I take great pleasure in their success, but unquestionably I am at times competing with them in an unspoken but acceptable manner. It may be over how we raise our children, or manage our jobs, or keep our figures, but the challenge is there, and when I feel good about myself, I love it.

"Envy has a sadness and some shame to it," Martha Gallahue told me, "but by the time you get through envy, jealousy, and rivalry, competition can really be fun. Competition can mean people helping each other."

When we sublimate deep, uncomfortable feelings of competition with our sisters, it is likely that we will act out with our women friends, or with our children or husbands when they reflect the unresolved threat or attitude of our sisters. It is the unhealthy, consuming competition, typically covert in its style, that obstructs and threatens promises of bonding. As Rubin explains, "It is precisely because women have, for so long, been constrained from expressing their competitive strivings cleanly and clearly that they can become distorted into the kind of petty rivalries, jealousies and envy that sometimes infect their relationships with each other."[6]

Distinguishing the Different Shades of Green

Some of the confusion about competition between sisters can be alleviated if we first define the terms of rivalry. *Envy* is when one person wants to have what another person has. It could be good looks or a gown, a job or a friendly disposition; whatever it is, you are envious of others' achievements or possessions. For example: "I envy my sister's thick hair." "I envy her job." Eichenbaum and Orbach point out that because it is so difficult for women to express such negative feelings as envy, they often turn to the "psychological outlet of self-criticism."[7] I often heard women disguise their envy with comments like "My sister is wonderful with people, I don't have the patience she has."

Jealousy is when you perceive someone as a threat to a meaningful relationship between you and another person. We typically associate jealousy with romantic or sexual relationships, but it can be applied to family, business, and friendship triangles as well. For example: "I was jealous when my boss took the new associate to an expensive restaurant." "I feel so jealous whenever Dad spends more time with my sister than he does with me."

Competition is the action resulting from envy and jealousy. It is the reaction to feeling lesser than someone else, or to gain what someone has. There is covert competition where we don't express our desire to do as well as or better than the other person, but we intensely feel the pain of rejection and we act out accordingly. You compete covertly (and negatively), for example, when you gossip or spread rumors about the person you are envious or jealous of. And there is the external competition where we openly express or act out our need to look, feel, or perform equally or better than the other person. Either way, good or bad, external or covert, you can't have competition without having envy or jealousy, though the original source of envy or jealousy may change or be sublimated over time.

The Birth of Envy

There are several theories on the early source of envy— from Freud's to feminists' psychology. No matter how opposed they are, all these theories indicate that envy initially has nothing to do with our sisters. It is deeply embedded in the child's view of wanting what the parent has, and later, wanting the parent's full attention and approval. Freud defines the Oedipal stage (two and a half to six years) during which the girl develops a "penis envy" that she necessarily converts to a desire to have babies. Her unconscious wish to get rid of Mommy (who didn't give her a penis) and have a baby with Daddy (who has the penis), says Freud, is an essential part of her development.[8] Melanie Klein traces envy to infancy when the baby (boy or girl) is at the breast and "envies" the mother's power and richness to feed.[9] Eichenbaum and Orbach "reinterpret" and adapt Freud's and Klein's theories to show that envy can be better understood in relation to "the early stages of dependence and merged attachments toward separation and selfhood."[10] That is, the young child in trying to be on her own is always in a struggle with separating herself from the power and independence of the mother.

Sisterly Envy: From Day One

Given these early roots of envy between a child and her parents, the stage is conveniently set for *sisterly envy*. It could take hold the very day baby sister comes home, or even earlier when Mother is pregnant. As one woman recalls, "I was hurt because my mother couldn't lean over and pick me up because her tummy was so big." It was not unusual to hear a woman lament how she was "sent away" to Grandmother's or to an aunt's house when her sister was born, as if her sister were responsible for the banishment, or had betrayed her from the start of their relationship.

Valery was five and living in Detroit in 1963 when her mother, who was five months pregnant, learned she was carrying twins. At first the news was exciting, but then it turned into a problem for Valery, who had always held center stage with her parents. Because her mother needed special care it was decided that for the duration of the pregnancy she should move to her mother's home in Alabama, leaving Valery in Detroit in her aunt's care. Much as her father wanted to keep Valery with him, he had to work rotating shifts as a bus driver, so it was best that she move in with her aunt, who was home all day. "She saw to it that I got to school and my father came to see me every day or at least every other day." Those four months without her mother were lonely for Valery, but at the same time very special because she got so much attention from her father. Valery can vividly remember how after they got the call that the twin girls were born, her father picked her up at her aunt's home and the two of them headed out on a starry night to drive the long car ride to Alabama. "I was his navigator," says Valery proudly. From that time on, Valery considered herself the number one daughter in her father's eyes. While she describes her relationship with her twin sisters as "normally competitive," she maintained her favored place right next to Daddy.

Daddy's Little Girls

In the Freudian tradition, the daughter competes with her mother for the father's attentions. As I will demonstrate in the next chapter, sisters *mainly* compete with each other for the attentions of the mother, just as in their adult life they mainly compete for the attention and approval of other women. But for some women, such as myself, the vying for father's love is paramount in the makeup of the sister-to-sister competition. A woman in her late fifties tells me that she realized after her father's death how she had spent her entire life looking for "the kind of love my father never gave me." Spurred on by her feeling that her father favored her older sister, she spent much of her childhood "looking at my father always through the eyes of trying to discern what can I do to make this man love me more than my sister." Abandoned by her first husband and now troubled in her second marriage, she is wised up to how her jealousy of her sister and neediness for a father has continued to affect her relationships with men.

A Poignant Entry: Anne Frank

Anne Frank was only thirteen when she began her diary in Amsterdam, in 1942. Anne could write what most young girls feel but are afraid to express. She had a freedom of style and honesty that required tremendous emotional sophistication and insight. When Anne wrote the following entry, she was deeply upset because her father and mother had just favored her older sister, Margot, during a quarrel over a book that Anne had "taken" from Margot, seemingly without her permission. After confiding to her diary that the problems between her and her mother were to be expected because the two were always quarreling, she writes:

> With Daddy it's different, if he holds Margot up as an example, approves of what she does, praises and caresses her, then something gnaws at me inside because I adore Daddy, he is the one I look up to, I don't love anyone in the world but him. He doesn't notice that he treats Margot differently from me: now Margot is the prettiest, sweetest, most beautiful girl in the world. But all the same I feel I have some right to be taken seriously too; I have always been the dunce, the ne'er-do-well of the family, I've always had to pay double for my deeds; first with the scolding and then again because of the way my feelings are hurt. Now I'm not satisfied with this apparent favoritism anymore. I want something from Daddy that he is not able to give.
>
> I'm not jealous of Margot, never have been. I don't envy her good looks or her beauty. It is only that I long for Daddy's real love: not only as his child but for me— Anne, myself. I cling to Daddy because each day I look upon Mummy with more contempt and because it is

69

only through him that I am able to retain the remnant of family feeling.[11]

Poor Anne, in her adolescent passion she could recognize that she wanted "something from Daddy that he is not able to give," but she couldn't own up to her jealousy of Margot. It may have been too frightening or threatening to admit to Margot's power over her. It is much easier in her rebellious stage of adolescence to point to her mother as the culprit. As a young teenager, she needed to break away to find the definition of her self, but as a young woman, she can't totally disown the family, thus she allows for her sister, complains of her mother, and clings to her father.

Daddy's Note: Beverly, Liz, and Jenny

Beverly was rushed and frustrated because her schedule for the day had been disrupted by a change in her children's carpool. An attractive, bright woman, Beverly "talks" with her hands and facial expressions, and speaks at an amazingly fast pace, jumping from subject to subject. Frequently, she would leave her thoughts unfinished, and yet she would stop and ask if she was "saying too much."

Beverly is the oldest of four sisters in a family of five children who grew up in a comfortable Midwestern suburb. All her life she has mainly fought or competed with her sister Liz, who is seventeen months younger. Both girls were very athletic and were competitive on the hockey field and basketball courts, but they also fought about their rooms, clothes, chores, and friends. By the time they reached college, their bickering lessened but there was obvious tension over their diverse life-styles. Beverly dated college boys at her small liberal arts school on the East Coast and Liz preferred to date "boys in the army" while she went to a "large state school on the West Coast." There is a touch of snobbery about Beverly when she says this, but I concede that she is being honest about her feelings. Now, at thirty-eight, she realizes that the competition between them is "letting up" because Liz is now asking for help and advice.

"She has two small children and is semi-separated from her husband," says Beverly, indicating with her tone of voice and expression that she would never be put in such an uncomfortable position. "She is so nice to me and she writes to me as if I'm supermom. She appreciates who I am and what I do much more, maybe because the picture is bigger for her now, she used to be so self-absorbed." When I ask if she and Liz ever competed for their father's attention, Beverly responds with sarcasm in her voice, "I *know* Liz has been in therapy and I haven't, and my father is a major element in our competition in *her* perception, but I was certainly not conscious of it at that age. To this day he is a fabulous father and very supportive of us. He was not around a lot. Very busy."

That leads her to think about Jenny, her youngest sister, Jenny, the "shy, insecure, beautiful one." Ever since Jenny moved to the East Coast to go to graduate school, she has been Beverly's "closest sister" and confidante. She has also been a new source of envy. Now Daddy does come into the picture.

"There was an incident with Jenny and my father that hurt me terribly. Jenny was here and I was pushing her to go to law school. She had applied several places and gotten on a waiting list, but was rejected from the one school she really wanted to get into. So she called up and demanded an appointment to discuss this. It turned out that the interviewer was a graduate from her college!" says Beverly incredulously. Without words, she gestures to suggest that her sister's good looks had something to do with her good luck. "Here is someone who is outright rejected and then gets in. She got in around the time I had my second child. He was the first grandson. He was born in May, right before that I had finished my master's degree. It took me five years, I had worked very hard. I defended my thesis the week before he was born. I don't know if my parents were even aware of that. Certainly to them a master's in English didn't carry the glory of going to a top law school. I can remember talking to my father from the hospital after my son was born and he said, 'Congratulations, this is great! A grandson!' It's not that he didn't say those things, but I swear he then went on and on about Jenny getting into the law school. It was unbelievable, he was just so excited about it. I was so hurt. And he paid for her education. I had done it on my own. When Jenny graduated from law school my parents came out and gave this party. I must have expressed all this to my mother. . . ." Beverly stops her story, saying she's afraid that talking about this is going to make her cry. We sit quietly for the first time since she came into the room.

"My father got the word and he just wrote me this beautiful note about how proud he was, and the fact that he had never given me a graduation gift and the nice check . . . the money never had anything to do with it." Beverly is now crying openly, her cheeks streaked with tears. "But this note from him was just unbelievable, he wrote about all the things that I had done."

Beverly's envy of her sisters is clearly traced to competition for her father's approval, though she won't recognize it. As a child, she and her sisters competed in sports, like their father, and as an adult she tried to please him in her education and choice of career. Despite her success, Beverly constantly puts herself and her sisters down, all the while assuming that her father "probably appreciates" her sister

Jenny's accomplishments more. When Beverly talked about the birth of her second child she never told me his name, throughout the interview she would refer to him as "the first grandson," repeatedly mentioning how he was born when she had just finished her master's degree. Even this child, unnamed, but a "grandson," is the symbol of her industrious, hapless attempts to gain her father's approval and love.

"Lord Help the Sister Who Comes Between Me and My Mister"

The love triangle between father and sisters is often the prototype for our romantic/sexual jealousies in our adult life. Father may stay in the triangle or be replaced by husband or lover, just as one sister may leave the triangle or be replaced by any woman who resembles her as a threat.

In Jane Smiley's novel *A Thousand Acres*, the oldest and most levelheaded of three sisters, Ginny, is driven into a silent, frenzied plan to murder her middle sister, Rose, who has stolen her lover. Both sisters are so closely enmeshed that they live in the same farm compound and share everything from coffee in the morning to making their father's meals. Despite their lifelong stick-togetherness, they hold back from claiming their unhappy married lives and their sordid past with a sexually abusive father. It is no coincidence that Rose's disclosure of the incest, and Ginny's reluctant recognition of the father's crime, bring the two women to a stand-off over their lover. For Ginny and Rose, each in their own ghastly style, the past incestuous triangle becomes confused with the present romantic triangle. As jealousy consumes Ginny and she gingerly prepares the poisoned food she intends to give her sister, she feels no remorse whatsoever. It is frightening to see how powerful jealousy is, and how it is bred in the bone.[12]

In real life I fortunately heard no testimony of poisoning or even attempted murder, but I did hear the deep hurt and fury when a sister did "more than flirt" with another sister's husband or boyfriend. One woman in her late twenties angrily told me that her ex-husband "always fooled around" with her younger sister right in front of her. They both knew this upset her, and now that she is divorced, her younger sister criticizes her for still being "uptight" and chooses not to talk to her about her dating life "for fear of a scene."

A forty-year-old woman who changed her mind about being interviewed told me later that her younger sister had tried to seduce her husband many years ago when they were first married. She was afraid that the sister would recognize her story in the book. It is still a painful issue for this woman, but to this day, neither she nor her sister ever speak of it.

There is no way of estimating how frequent this kind of competition occurs between sisters. But I do know from the survey that it exists, and for some a sister seduction is innocent and long-time forgotten, while for others it is deliberate and the jealousy is devastating. I found both of these reactions within one set of sisters. "One time when my younger sister Kate and I were in high school we got stoned together, and she accused me of trying to steal her boyfriend; there was a terrible scene," recalls forty-year-old Maggie, the middle child in a family of four daughters and one son. Later, Kate slept with the lover of her oldest sister, Irene. To this day Irene hasn't forgiven Kate, while Maggie, who is less involved, glibly sums it up with "This was years and years ago, Kate wouldn't do that kind of stuff now."

Like all important issues between sisters, sexual jealousy is a matter of perspective and history. A married sister recalls how five years ago at a family wedding she perceived her husband's drinking and flirting with her older, single sister as "threatening and upsetting." Apparently the single sister saw the whole evening as nothing more than "a good time," and the subject has never been brought up by either sister. But the married sister told me that when she recently ran across a photo of her sister and husband with their arms around each other at the wedding, it confirmed her suspicions that they were having a flirtation and she "furiously ripped it up" because she couldn't bear to look at it.

Ginger is forty-one, her sister June is almost three years younger; the two say they have "forgotten" all the differences and quarrels of childhood and are now openly loving and supportive. Both sisters regret the fact that they live nine hundred miles apart; they like to joke that someday when old and gray, they may live together. A remnant of the past rivalry, however, came up during Ginger's interview as she recalled a time when she came home from college and discovered that her sister was dating a boy she had recently dated herself and had been corresponding with.

"I was devastated, crushed, it was very hard for me to accept. I wept a lot," says Ginger, sounding as if she were still grieving. "I didn't blame June overtly. She was having problems at the time and this was at least making her happy, so I didn't know what to do. Looking back, it seems minor, but at the time it was horrible."

Later when I interviewed June, her story and attitude were quite different from her sister's. "The first person that I really fell in love with was someone Ginger had been dating," says June offhandedly. "But she was engaged at the time, so it wasn't a problem." End of discussion. I didn't point out the discrepancy to June because I had interviewed this particular pair of sisters separately, and I felt I shouldn't share any information or confidences but should, rather, record their different perspectives. Four months later June telephoned me to say that she hoped I remembered her, and she would "like to change" what she said about dating her sister's friend.

"I didn't realize that it really was very upsetting to her," she told me solemnly. I asked her what had changed her mind. There was silence. "Did you talk to Ginger about it?" I asked gently.

"Yes," she said. "Honestly, I had no idea that the incident meant so much to Ginger. She told me she didn't mind so much what I had done, but she minded because of the boy's behavior."

I felt that June knew her sister really was deeply hurt by the flirtation, otherwise why would June have called me back to claim her part in it? But Ginger apparently couldn't fully claim her feelings. Like Anne Frank, who blamed her mother, Ginger told June that she blames the boy's behavior. It's often easier for sisters to blame the other guy than to confront each other.

A friend of mine, who has one sister, believes the seductive plays between sisters and their loved ones is very much a reality, but rarely expressed openly. "There seems to be a current between me and my sister's husband, even though I'm not attracted to him physically or sexually. But there is this silent play going on. Maybe it's because it is so forbidden."

At this writing there are several television comedies and dramas about sisters. Most of them touch on or revolve around the he-took-my-man theme, but with little thought as to how sisters actually relate. In one improbable scene in *Sisters,* for example, Teddy, the foiled sister, paints the word "slut" on her younger sister Frankie's car when she realizes Frankie has stolen her ex-husband. That's just for starters— there are enough barbs and hotheaded scenes between Teddy and Frankie to neatly break up two generations of family. But all is forgiven and forgotten—for the time being—when they band together to support Georgie, another sister, whose young son is diagnosed with leukemia.

A more likely depiction of "sister adultery" is in Woody Allen's *Hannah and Her Sisters*. Here the heinous crime of one sister's sleeping with another sister's husband is hidden and racked with guilt, and yet there is no open or climactic confrontation. The sisters skirt the issue as they gingerly quarrel about other things. The only piece of film fancy comes with a happy ending—the affair is ended with no one hurt and everyone wiser.

The Legacy of Jealousy

Our sisters don't have to be involved in the love triangle, they can be a thousand miles away from our lovers and still make their mark. If our jealousy is unresolved from childhood, it is highly likely that we repeat the pattern of jealousy when women like our sisters are perceived as threatening to a sexual relationship.

Colleen admits that she was "always suspicious" of her husband, Charlie, having an affair. When they went out socially, after a few drinks Charlie would always turn on the charm to whichever woman struck his fancy, ignoring Colleen for the rest of the evening. Afterward there was usually a scene with Colleen crying and Charlie angrily denying her accusations. After the birth of their third child, Colleen discovered that Charlie had been having an affair for two years. At first she was devastated and angry, but she also felt uneasy that she had partly caused the problem by being so suspicious and jealous for so long. Emotionally and financially dependent on her husband, Colleen stayed in her marriage, which now limps along with distrust. But all isn't lost. With therapy, Colleen was able to build her self-esteem.

Equally important, she has come to understand the origins of her suspicions and jealousy.

"My therapist and I kept talking about my relationship with my father and mother, but it wasn't until later when I started recalling the way my father treated my little sister that I could make the connection about how I have always distrusted my husband. I could actually *feel* the way I had about my sister taking my place with my father, it's right in the pit of my stomach," said Colleen while pressing into her stomach and wincing. "I must have hated her so deeply and couldn't tell anyone. We all knew that Daddy loved intelligent women, and my sister was always considered more intelligent than me. To this day when I meet a woman who is successful in her field I see green, then red, it goes right to my stomach. When we go out, I can spot the women my husband will be drawn to . . . she's usually very pretty, very aggressive, and always very smart, just like my sister."

Now in her middle forties, Colleen has uncovered facts from her family history that have helped her realize that she had more than just cause for her early reactions. Indeed, her father was a womanizer and had had several affairs, which were supposedly kept secret from the two sisters but had caused much anguish in her parents' marriage. That "sense" that her father was cheating on her, which Colleen felt physically with a sick stomach, was probably what her mother felt about her own dilemma, and what Colleen sympathetically adopted. Colleen also learned that when she was born, her father was away a great deal of the time setting up a new business, but three years later when her sister was born, her mother was ill and the father rallied to care for the baby. The father and daughter's early and unusual relationship grew into a companionship, and Colleen often felt excluded from their walks and "special times."

If Colleen had had more self-esteem, none of this would

have been as destructive and invasive as it was. But with a father so involved in his affairs and uninvolved with a failing marriage, and a mother equally caught up in the fray, Colleen found little support for her value as a person. The target then became her sister; as the beautiful and intelligent culprit who in time represented all beautiful and intelligent women who "steal" men. Attracted and married to Charlie, a man like her father, Colleen always felt locked into jealous triangles.

"The only way I've been able to get over my jealousy with my husband," said Colleen, "is to build my own life and work on my self-esteem. Knowing about my father has helped me immensely, though I don't know why. It dilutes the feelings. I'm even getting to like my sister."

It's All in Our Looks

We can usually trace the adult issues of competition to what was once considered important in the family during childhood. With little girls, no matter how intelligent or talented they may be, the burning issue that typically gives them a sense of worth is their *appearance*. Simone de Beauvoir leaves little room for doubt about what little girls are up against: "By means of compliments and scoldings, through images and words, she learns the meaning of the terms *pretty* and *homely*, she soon learns in order to be pleasing she must be 'pretty as a picture'; she tries to make herself look like a picture, she puts on fancy clothes, she studies herself in a mirror, she compares herself with princesses and fairies."[13]

Several women told me that there was "too much emphasis" on appearance when they were growing up. To this day, these same women weigh the success of an evening on how many compliments they received, not especially from men but from other women—just as they once hoped to please their mothers for the way they kept their bows straight and their slips from showing.

But there can be a relaxed and healthy side to sisters who compete over their complexions or wardrobes. Many women testified that they loved to shop with their sister. They also liked to do each other's hair, help with makeup, share clothes and jewelry, and generally collect ideas on how to look good. "If my sister doesn't look beautiful, I don't feel beautiful," remarks a woman who "routinely" swaps outfits with her sister. One young woman said she buys her sister clothes when she sees something she knows would look fantastic on her. Another woman described how her mother deliberately "dresses trashy" in contrast with her sister, who is always up-to-date with the latest in fashion. The two women have been playing this game of outrageous contrast for more than sixty years, apparently loving every minute of it.

How Siblings Establish and Maintain Competition

Siblings are perfectly capable of creating and maintaining competition *within the management of their relationship* with no help from parents whatsoever. Beverly was quite open about the fact that she is jealous when two or three of her sisters "go off" by themselves. "I don't like to be the outsider, I feel like I'm missing something. I feel badly, I feel hurt." She especially has a hard time when the sisters who live near each other share holidays with their husbands and children. Feeling a million miles away as her sisters are celebrating together, all she can do is make that precious long-distance call, which often just leaves her teary and feeling empty. "I just wish I could be a part of it," she says remorsefully.

As Claire, the oldest of three sisters, told me: "We go

through periods of being close or not close. But now we are going through a period where I'm close to both my sisters, so there is almost a point of jealousy over who I am spending time with or where I am staying when visiting."

I think one of the cruelest things I ever said to my sister Mary was in an incident over "sharing" sisters. I had made plans to visit my mother in northern Wisconsin. I was going to fly to Milwaukee and meet Ruth, and together we were going to drive up north. On the second day at Mother's, Janet, who lives near Mother, was going to join us for a day of visiting. It wasn't a planned sister reunion, it was strictly a short visit with my mother. Mary called me from Tucson a week before my trip, which she had heard about from Mother.

"I tried to change my schedule so I could be with you next week," she offered.

"Why?" I said, sounding like the ice queen.

"Because you are going to be together, I want to be there."

"It's no big deal, I had no intention of making this a sister time," I told her offhandedly.

I didn't sleep that night. Why couldn't I have said with *some* warmth in my voice, "I'm sorry you can't join us also"? Instead, I cut her off with my covert rivalry. I realized I was getting back at her for a similar mistake the previous Christmas when she planned a family gathering without telling me because she (rightfully) assumed I couldn't make it. When I got upset, she at least had the decency to apologize to me.

I never have such rivalrous moments with my other sisters as I do with Mary. As Walter Toman points out, "A child can accept [her] second-youngest or third-youngest sibling more easily than the sibling immediately succeeding [her]. In their affinities and affections ... siblings are *sometimes* inclined to skip the closest in age among the younger ones."[14]

Several women spoke of the targeted jealousy with the sister closest in age. Often the older sister would say that she had no problem with her youngest or "baby" sister because she "took care of her," but the tension lay between her and the middle sister. Toman's theory is supported by the fact that nearly all middle sisters I spoke to were troubled by the youngest sister, not the oldest. It is the sister who takes our place who seeds the jealousy.

The Bright Side

The early issues of competition between toddler sisters spread into their childhood and adolescence, taking on new forms such as grades, friendships, athletics, and appearance. As adults, sisters are comparing and competing with one another's life-styles—their choices of career, their spouses, and how they raise their families. While I heard many stories about competition in school and performance, I was particularly struck with how most women in the survey, even those who were highly envious of their sisters, were openly proud of their sisters' careers and achievements. This is the good name of competition; it is also the positive product of the postfeminist era. Even in instances where the sisters were estranged there was a familial and feminine pride in what the sisters accomplished, professionally. A thirty-eight-year-old woman, who first competed with her sister in her professional field in academia and then went on to choose another career in business, admitted comfortably that her sister was "the best" at what she does.

Healthy competition thrives in families where there is love and respect for the children. If a child feels supported by a parent but is surrounded by charming, talented siblings, of course she will feel *energized* to come forward with her own identity. My good friend Anne tells me that when she was nine she stood naked in front of her mother's mirror and said aloud, "You're no beauty or brain like your sister Mary, so you better work on your personality." Those of us who know both Anne and Mary see them as intelligent and attractive women, but Anne is convinced that she had to carve a separate nook for herself, and she has done so beautifully.

Rosemary comes from a talented family in which three of the four sisters are professional musicians. All four sisters, who are now in their sixties and seventies, are Phi Beta Kappa, as was their mother. Rosemary and her sisters exemplify the healthy competition that thrives in childhood and energizes adulthood. In their youth, the two oldest sisters played their instruments to please their father, a teacher and musician in his own right. When Bea realized that she didn't have the talent to play as beautifully as her sisters, she decided to put all her efforts into her studies. "She was very active in school, and probably the brightest of the four sisters," says Rosemary. "But she told me it wasn't Mother who made her achieve in her studies, it was the example of her three older sisters."

As for Rosemary, initially her parents didn't even think she had talent or any interest in music. "I wanted so badly to play like my sisters," she recalls. "Long before I started my music lessons, I used to lie in bed at night with the door cracked open and listen to my sisters practicing. I can still remember the melodies." Finally her grandmother, with whom she was very close, demanded that her parents give Rosemary the same opportunity her sisters were receiving. Her lessons started immediately. If her grandmother hadn't stepped in, Rosemary wouldn't be the musician she is today.

A Family History of Envy: Marion, Pat, and Lesli

This leads me to think about how grandmothers or other extended family members can unwittingly feed or affect our childhood competitions. Not all stories end as happily as Rosemary's. For forty-four-year-old Marion, her grandmother's influence proved to be the core of competition between her and her sisters Pat, forty-nine, and Lesli, thirty-eight. Marion told her story with no reservations or apologies. She is passionately competitive with her sisters, especially with Pat. The sisters call each other only two or three times a year and meet once a year at a family beach house. This sparse schedule doesn't mean that they are not involved. Marion is obsessed with the tension among the sisters, talking as if they still live in the same house and confront each other daily. She is also convinced that the two sisters probably talk about her when she isn't there to defend herself.

The issues are major—money, career versus children, and religion. Marion is a lawyer who works on a time-share basis so she can be with her children. But neither of her sisters has any money and both feel that a mother should stay at home with her children, so Marion claims that she always feels uncomfortable when around them. "I feel guilty for working and I feel as though I should be giving them things. I don't express my anger to my sisters, just like I hold back with my friends—I don't tell them when they make me mad."

The "biggest problem" for Marion is that Pat is a born-again Christian, who proselytizes to the point of not letting anyone have a good time when they gather at the beach. "I don't like her husband, and I don't like the constant religion thing, the hypocrisy. We are told we can't drink and he pours it [alcohol] in a cup you can't see through."

The problems go way beyond religious conversion and careers. It all began forty-nine years ago in a New York tenement, where shortly after Pat was born, she and her mother moved in with the grandmother while Pat's father went overseas to fight in World War II. During the war years Pat developed a close and special relationship with her grandmother. After the father's return, the family moved into the apartment just across the hall from the grandmother, and two years later Marion was born. "I have a very good relationship with my father that my sister doesn't have," Marion says with obvious pleasure, then adds in a far more serious tone, "Grandmother took my sister, my father took me. I was jealous of all the attention Pat got. Grandmother took her on vacations and never took me anywhere. It was clear that she was special. My grandmother unwittingly set us up for life."

In grade school, even though they were four grades apart, Marion kept track of everything Pat did. The memory of her obsessive envy is fresh. "I kept one of her report cards and put it under the blotter of my desk. My mother was very upset by this and told me I shouldn't be comparing myself. But I was determined to do at least as well. And I did, and I think Pat resented it. My little sister, Lesli, just dropped out of the competition and developed something else. Her personality and wit make her less of a threat. She has a self-deprecating humor; she will say about herself, 'I'm stupid.' We can laugh about things, especially when we are at the beach. My therapist suggests that I focus more on the positive and the importance of Lesli, and let her know that I like her. I'm working on it."

Mother's (and Your) Ongoing Contest with Her Sister

If a mother's competition with her sister(s) is left unresolved, chances are high that it will eventually involve their children as well. "The Battle of the Girl Cousins," as one woman put it succinctly, is often an overt expression of competition between our mothers and aunts that is usually unbearable or uncomfortable for a relatively short period of time in our childhood and adolescence. Recall Valery, the "navigator" for her father when they drove to Alabama for the birth of her twin sisters—she told me that eventually her family moved to South Philadelphia, where Valery's mother's sister and her children lived just down the street. "My mother and aunt were always comparing our grades and how we were doing with our music recitals. My cousins were smarter, they were always getting A's. But my sisters and I did better in our careers," smiles Valery, "so my mother feels she won."

Amy Tan in *The Joy Luck Club* captures the endless competition between Auntie Lin and Auntie Suyuan (two inseparable "chosen sisters") and their blind appraisal of their prized daughters Waverly and June. "From the time we were babies," June complains,

> our mothers compared the creases in our belly buttons, how shapely our earlobes were, how fast we healed when we scraped our knees, how thick and dark our hair ... and later, how smart Waverly was at playing chess, how many trophies she had won last month, how many newspapers had printed her name.... When I failed to become a concert pianist, or even an accompanist for the church youth choir [my mother] finally explained that I was late-blooming, like Einstein, who

everyone thought was retarded until he discovered a bomb.[15]

If our mothers have competed through their children, we are likely to carry on the tradition. Several women testified that they felt their sisters competed with them over their children's accomplishments to the point where one sister couldn't be honest with another sister over her child's good grades or sports awards. "It causes too much tension, so I don't bother," says one woman whose only daughter excels in the classroom while her sister's two daughters do not. Another woman tells me that she had never competed with her sister "until we had children and it opened up a whole can of worms." Because the competition was so destructive, these two sisters, who treasure their relationship, decided to enter short-term therapy together and work it out.

Others expressed a different form of competition by noting that they were determined to "not make the same mistakes" their sisters made in raising their children. A sixty-two-year-old woman with three sisters looks back and evaluates how all four raised their children in response to the other. "My oldest sister couldn't say no to her children, she has had a lot of problems ever since; one child is an adult now living hand to mouth and she seems to have a dark side to her. The next sister saw this and she went the other way and was very strict with her children. I think my youngest sister and I sort of tempered all this. Neither one of us made threats we couldn't keep and I've been very open with my children."

Changing from Envy to the Competitive Spirit

Once the envy between sisters is acknowledged as destructive or useless, the incentive to change is stronger. Unfortunately, because the feelings are so deeply rooted, the process of changing our jealous reactions is a conscious, difficult exercise that takes more than a healthy dose of self-esteem. One woman told me that she has been working hard on not overreacting to her older sister, but whenever her sister "brags," it triggers the old green-eyed fury. One method she uses is to imagine that her sister is one of her friends, then she doesn't have as violent a reaction to what she is saying. Several women claimed to have "mellowed" in their jealousies with their sisters; they had no formula for this change of heart, but they all said they thought it was because they were "aging," and learning to accept each other. I suggested to them that it was also because they had grown in their own self-esteem. There is no need to feel the *sting*, the bleak side of competition, if you feel good about yourself.

"A Competitive Love Squeeze": Joan and Alice

Joan cannot totally give up her feeling of comparison with her older sister Alice, and yet considers her relationship with her "loving and very close." These two sisters defy the myth that sisters who are far apart in age—Joan is forty-three and Alice is fifty-three—aren't competitive or intimate, but they also demonstrate how functional competition between sisters can be even when it takes a long time and hard work to make it happen. Joan and Alice were raised in an observant Jewish home. Their father was a jeweler, their mother taught religious school and was at home full-time;

the sisters also have a forty-eight-year-old brother, Steve, who with his "spontaneous life-style" is close only to Joan.

"My most vivid memory of growing up with Alice was when she was seventeen and I was seven," says Joan. "I would sit on the edge of the tub watching her put on her makeup; when the doorbell rang it was my job to go check out the boy and come back and tell her what size heel she should wear." There were other special times, such as when the two girls were in overnight camp and Alice comforted her sister through her homesickness. But that is where the childhood memories end. When Joan was ten years old, her sister married; from then on her presence was revered and maintained by their mother, who never let Joan forget what a wonderful sister she had.

" 'From Alice to Alice there is no one like Alice.' My mother's phrase," recites Joan in her mother's voice. "This put me in her shadow. I have felt inferior to her—in every area, she has won a prize. And I have held some very strong myths, such as 'Alice was a social butterfly, very popular.' That was probably true. My parents say she was very strong-willed, bright, achieving, and she is that way now. My mother is the verbal one who carries the myth or images, my father is not that kind of person, he doesn't make legends out of people."

After years of working through the myth and dealing with the reality of their life-styles and personalities, Joan views her sister as her total antithesis. Intense, compulsive, a perfectionist who insists on doing all family dinners herself, even when ill, Alice is known by her family and friends as an overplanner and overachiever who savors every moment of her tasks and self-imposed tight schedules. "I admire her drive in all that she has accomplished," says Joan, referring more to Alice's career than to her dinner parties. Alice hadn't completed her education when she married at age twenty; after her two girls were born, she went back to school

89

under her mother's advice, and got both a bachelor's and a master's degree. She is now principal of a large school. From her home, Joan runs a small public relations firm that promotes health professionals. Preferring to work by herself and at a pace determined greatly by her two children's school schedule, Joan says she is the type who would just as soon sit around in her robe all day Sunday.

No matter what their work load, the sisters religiously talk on the phone twice a month for an hour at a time. "It's cheaper than therapy," remarks Joan (a comment I heard often from sisters about their lengthy long-distance calls). Despite the calls, the differences and competition come out more when the sisters visit each other and Alice wants to take control of the day's itinerary. Joan, who tends to keep things to herself, "gets annoyed" with having to run from museum to museum when all she wants to do is sit and read a book, but she doesn't say anything because "it's not worth the bother." A more serious issue is their eating habits. Alice eats little because she is always trying to keep her weight down, but Joan, who is petite, has a blood sugar problem and has to eat frequently. Only recently during a madcap visit, Joan finally learned to express her needs so they would stop and eat small meals.

While Joan is more analytical and tends to be introspective, her sister prefers to "stay away from therapy talk."

"Alice and I have gotten close in the past ten years since I have learned that she doesn't operate on feelings first, like I do. I have been helpful to her to learn how to do that. When I have problems I go to her, but I am not the first one she would call. Actually I'm not sure she would call anyone, though I notice that she is calling me a little more frequently. Remember she is like a machine, she doesn't want to be shown as human or vulnerable. When she falls asleep in the living room that is the only time I see her wind down."

* * *

A mother of two teenage boys scolded her sons for their constant fighting over "grades, girls, and basketball."

"I told them they shouldn't be so cruel to each other because someday they would need each other as a friend. They looked at me as if I were crazy." Days later, while we were talking about sisters, the woman realized that when she had warned her sons that their fighting and competition was dangerous, she was "thinking as a woman. No wonder they didn't respond." Girls, like boys, can compete for their father's, mother's, or sibling's attentions, but eventually their competition is suppressed in the nurturing makeup of womanhood. When suppressed competition is coupled (and managed) with a sense of low self-esteem, it can fester and spread into adult relationships with our sisters, daughters, women friends, and colleagues. Fortunately, we can change the nature of the competition from "hidden" to "good." When Joan "looked at the reality" of her parents' myths about her sister, Alice, she was released from a long-held jealousy and is now able to assert herself and her own needs. And when Colleen discovered the early origins of her competition with her sister, and her father's unfaithfulness to her mother, she was able to feel more secure within her marriage and in relationships with other women. In such cases, the resolve came not because the competition was discussed between the sisters, but rather because it was acknowledged and released. There was a strong desire on both Colleen's and Joan's part to change the harsh judgments they had been placing on themselves. As we shall see in the following chapter, the young girl compares herself to her sister through her mother's eyes. But it is also through the mother with whom she shares her gender that she is inspired to reconnect and change.

91

5

▽

Sisters in
Their Mother's Eyes

MOTHER IS ENDEMIC to the relationship between sisters. Even in the most patriarchal families, Mother is *the* most important person in determining how sisters relate to each other. Whether the sisters number two or eight, Mother is central to their dynamics. Whether Mother dies in childbirth or outlives her daughters, she is omnipresent. Whether Mother was loving or emotionally absent, she leaves her lasting impression on her daughters, individually and together. For Mother is the role model of the sisters' feminine identity. Yet she is rarely seen or perceived identically by her daughters, nor is she reenacted identically in their roles.

In Terri Apter's work on adolescent daughters and mothers, *Altered Loves*, she tells us: "However strongly one sister influences another, the influence is not simply from sister to sister but from mother/sister to mother/sister/sister. The girl is influenced not simply by what the sister is or does, but also [by] how the mother responds to her sister's behavior, and how she contrasts this response to her mother's responses to her."[1]

To understand the significance of the mother/sister/sister

dynamic, we first have to isolate and understand the origins of the mother/daughter relationship. How is it developed? What impact does it have on our adult life?

A Magical Attachment from the Start

In early infancy, for boys and girls alike, the mother is symbiotically attached to her infant. It is the mother who represents the world, and it is through the attachment to the mother and the wish to detach that the child will later discover himself or herself and the outside world. Few of us can remember the sensations of "seeing" the world through our mothers, the touch of her skin, the warmth of being held, a smile or frown that encircled our being. Yet somehow it infused in us not only joy and comfort but also, later, the fear that we would be left without it. From three to twenty-four months, the mother continues to be the love object, but at thirty-six months the child develops object constancy—that is, the mother is viewed as a whole person, both good and bad—and can experience *ambivalence*, that is, both good and bad feelings toward the mother. It is also at this time that the child feels she or he cannot receive enough love from this powerful person, Mother. This early stage, called pre-Oedipal, is longer and more intense for girls than for boys because the mother is less likely to think of her daughter as different or separate from herself. If the child is a boy, the mother is already promoting and preparing for his coming autonomy and independence.

The Oedipal Stage and Gender Identity

From two and one-half years to approximately six years of age, the child is in the Oedipal stage, when he or she is attracted to the parent of the opposite sex, thinking of the parent of the same sex as the rival and wanting that parent out of the way.

(In Chapter 4 we discussed the Oedipal stage in relation to the origin and development of envy. The Oedipal stage, a time that occurs for all children but need not be identifiable, is multifaceted in its effect on children: here we need to reexamine it in relation to forming our gender identity.)

Ever since Freud defined the Oedipus complex, there has been a continuous debate over how the boy and girl go through the same attraction process to a parent and yet come out differently. According to the classical account, the boy is attracted to his mother, but in fear of his father (castration complex) he gives up his love for his mother and thus *differentiates* or learns autonomy. The girl is first angry with her mother for not giving her a penis, so she rejects her mother and looks to her father—since he can't "share" his penis, she decides on an alternative plan to have a baby from him. Fearful of rejecting the mother, her love object, she decides to become like her mother, thus she *identifies* with her. According to Freud, "Identification with her mother takes the place of attachment to her mother. The little daughter puts herself in her mother's place, as she has always done in her games; she tries to take her mother's place with her father, and begins to hate the mother she used to love, and from two motives; from jealousy, as well as from mortification over the penis she has been denied."[2]

A Woman's View of Oedipus

Contemporary theorists of feminine psychology, such as Nancy Chodorow, dispute the classical interpretation, because it bases feminine psychology on masculine terms (penis envy) and implies that in the process of resolution, the daughter *totally* rejects her mother. I concur with her theory because it is supported by what I and others have observed in raising daughters. Because the symbiotic union between daughter and mother is so strong and intense in the pre-Oedipal stage, Chodorow says, it is different for the daughter than for the son when it comes time for rejection and repression. While loving her father, the little girl keeps "looking back" to see if her mother still loves her—just as she also looks back to see if she has succeeded in making her angry. "A girl never gives up her mother as an internal or external love object. . . . A girl's love for her father and rivalry with her mother is always tempered by love for her mother, even against her will."[3]

A boy is faced with the choice of giving up his penis and giving up his object of love, Mother. In both instances, notes Chodorow, he makes the choice fast; usually he opts for saving his penis, which means he still opts for mother over father, but he represses his feelings thoroughly, so that he will not be subject to castration by his father. "For a girl, however, there is no single oedipal mode or quick oedipal resolution, and there is no absolute 'change of object.' "[4]

Remember, the girl doesn't come out of this with a pure and steady love for Mother. Instead, she continues to carry an ambivalent love, just as it was in infancy when she felt the early need to separate from this omnipotent person who couldn't provide enough consuming love.

An Ambivalent and Reflective Love

Because we are inextricably bound to our mothers in our feminine qualities, so, too, are we bound with our sisters. In the seventy-five stories told to me, every single woman *volun-*

teered testimony on how she and her sister felt about their mother and how it affected their relationship. The same was not always true for information on fathers or other important members of the family, such as grandparents or brothers. Often, I had to ask a woman how those relationships affected her sisterhood; her testimony was typically less involved than what she had to say about her mother.

Rarely did the sisters in one family feel identically toward their mother. But no matter if they reacted to her with love, pride, empathy, anger, frustration, or sadness, there was a strong need to express it in relation to their sisterhood. "My mother and my sister Dale are a team over here," gestures Melinda with a sweep of her arm, "and I'm way over here. They are both very bright but they have a different style from mine. Mother uses anger, but she doesn't act angry, she's a martyr. No, that's not entirely fair, she can be angry openly but it is very, very rare and you have got to be weaker than she is to get it. And Dale is just like mother, they both go cold. Icy, icy cold. They shut you out." Melinda's wide gesturing was aptly symbolic of how she has always viewed her place with her mother and sister. As we talked more, she revealed that she felt she had the same "spunk" as her mother, and her sister Dale didn't. She owned up to the qualities she admired in her mother, and dished out the least admirable qualities to Dale. I was not surprised to learn that her mother had been very ill and isolated during her pregnancy with Dale, and after the arrival of the baby she had little energy or inclination to be with Melinda.

Caroline explained her role as the responsible sister, not just because her personality is so similar to her mother's, but because her sister's is markedly dissimilar. "Mother is a tough woman, selfless, everything is for her family. There were times when it was extremely difficult to be her daughter because of how demanding she was. And partly because

97

I'm extremely stubborn myself. When I was a teenager, I know I gave her merry hell. It was normal, but it wasn't a fun time. My sister Amanda didn't have the same experience. She would tell my mother she would do her chores, but then she didn't do them and she would get away with it. By the time I was eight, I was fixing dinner for the family. Mom came home at six and wanted the dinner on the table. Amanda didn't have to do that until she was in high school."

How often I heard age-old complaints that one sister didn't have to do as much or as difficult chores as the other. Traditionally, we expected the daughters to be the little mothers and housekeepers, but there can only be so many housewives in one kitchen. If the oldest or most available daughter in line was assigned meal and baby duty, it makes sense that the next daughter in line would have fewer responsibilities (unless there are many more babies to come) or would certainly learn from her sister's exhausted state of servitude. Some of this early nurturing is very self-imposed. Several women recalled how they "adored" taking care of their baby siblings and they took great pride in being the sister who cooked the meals or pushed the baby in the carriage. The complaints often came because the situation was too overwhelming for the child, and/or there wasn't enough feedback and appreciation from the mother.

Not all sisters see themselves as contrasts to their other sisters in relation to their mothers. A few women spoke of the bond between the sister and the mutual alienation of the mother. Author Jane Howard muses over why she and her sister Ann are so close, and yet so comfortably distant from their mother, known by her friends and kinfolk as "The Blithe Spirit."

> With Ann and me, our mother was not often blithe, nor were we with her. It's odd. We were thought in our

circles to be amusing, and so was she in hers, but regrettably seldom did we laugh together. We never developed enough rapport. Sometimes mothers and daughters do have strong rapport; I have seen it. But in those cases, the daughters seem less close to each other. . . . Can this be some new maxim of human nature, or is it somewhere written that you can have real, ready access to your parents or else to your siblings, but not to both?[5]

Sharing Mommy with Sister: Early Memories

Cynthia Glauber quotes her sister, Adrienne Rich, as saying: "When my sister was born, it was like losing the Garden of Eden."[6] Her words ring true with most of the women I interviewed. Carey (see Chapter 3) complained to me that her sister Chris was born on her third birthday. "It was a present which didn't charm me. I remember it all clearly. The morning of my birthday I had roseola. I woke up feverish and went into my parents' bedroom, feeling awful and wanting my present. My mother was getting ready to go to the hospital and told me my present was on the dresser. I could barely reach it, but finally I did . . . it was a Tiny Tears doll." With her emphasis on how she had to reach her present herself, and the disappointment in her voice, I silently wondered if the tearful baby doll more aptly represented her and not the baby sister her parents intended her to play "mommy" with. Whatever, the stage was set for a lifetime of competition. These two little girls civilly shared the same birthday, but not their mother. Carey got the most attention from her mother through her hot temper. After she and her mother had screaming, emotional arguments, she would somehow take it out on her sister Chris, who didn't fight back.

Another woman recalls how when she was four she was waiting on the porch for her mother to come home from the hospital, when "suddenly the big white ambulance turned the corner and quietly came to a halt before the house." (In the 1940s, new mothers were routinely delivered home by ambulance.) As if in slow motion, her mother emerged from the ambulance with the baby wrapped in layers of pink blankets. In that solemn moment, she saw her mother as a queen carrying a princess. "Life has not been the same since that day," she quips.

Heidi was six when she unexpectedly "gained" three sisters—triplets. "How can you compete with that? They were a sideshow. A white wicker stroller that took up the whole sidewalk," says Heidi with the glib humor that she has relied on all her life. "It was pretty hellish. One would get sick and they would all get sick, and my mom would yell at me a lot when things didn't go right. I was an active, bright, interesting kid and when they came along, she had nothing left for me." Determined to establish an identity of her own, Heidi started lying about her name. "I told my friends at school and in the neighborhood that I was Gene Autry's daughter, Elizabeth Marie Autry. When my mother found out she made me tell them the truth. But my dream was to escape these triplets. Everybody started calling me 'the triplets' sister.' I had lost my name in the process."

As we get older and the pain of jealousy is more concealed, we still continue to vie for mother's love, but with a more critical and so-called sophisticated view. When the adolescent daughter sees that she has to share her mother with her sister, there is a part of her that cannot help but think: What about me? Don't I matter? Why didn't Mother believe that I could be responsible just once? Why did she put her energy into my sister's schoolwork and not mine?

100

One woman laments how her mother could always "laugh and have fun" with her younger sisters, but not with her. "I have to be the serious one all the time."

As girls or young women, we are tuned in to every nuance, every whisper between our mothers and sisters. We search for the tiniest of clues to help us through this struggle of loving our mothers and wanting to grow apart, yet not wanting to share our mothers with another like ourselves— sisters. Several women noted that their mothers "talk differently" to them than they do to their sisters. "My mother talks to me as if I'm a child, and she never does that to my sister," said one woman who was deeply hurt by her mother's "obvious fondness" for the older sister.

At eighty-six, Lily is the only surviving sibling in a family of four. Now living in a nursing home, she is weighed down by the past and her unresolved bitterness over her mother's favoritism toward her older sister Edith. Alone with her memories, Lily relentlessly picks at scenes from her childhood. "My mother always let Edith have her girlfriends overnight. I never had any of that. No music lessons, no dancing lessons, nothin'. When Edith would go out with her friends and play tennis, she would come home and not do her chores, I would do them. In my mother's eyes, I had nothing going for me at all, no looks, no nothin'."

Even though Edith was the preferred daughter, it was Lily who took care of her mother in her declining years. Edith managed to rebel and declare her independence early in her young adulthood, while Lily, who was always looking for approval and affection, later felt it was her duty to live with her ailing mother and put up with her constant criticism and demands. "It's funny," said Lily without smiling, "I have never been able to understand why I was so crazy about my mother when she really didn't care too much about me . . .

she cared more for my sister. I still haven't figured that out. It was a love–hate relationship. I adored my mother, I don't know why."

Sisters Are Great Guinea Pigs

In *Altered Loves*, Apter recalls how in her adolescence she cleverly learned to handle her mother by watching her sister's mistakes: "With the secrecy of deliberation, I grew to feel a kind of superiority, since it was she (my sister) who in adolescence knocked so clumsily against my mother. I took notes, learned lessons, and steered clear of my mother in certain areas, learned how to keep things private— especially sexual feelings, or feelings of admiration and adoration of others, which my mother was so adept at reducing."[7]

Many of the women I interviewed remarked that when they were young, they rebelled against their mother, but their sister didn't, or vice versa. We shouldn't assume that the oldest goes through adolescent rebellion and the youngest learns to hold back in order to stay on the good side. Often the oldest didn't rebel because she felt a responsibility not to. "I was the good girl," says Marty, who comes from a family where the father was a stronger but more intimidating figure than the mother. "My father was a difficult person, there had to be some peace in the household. My sister wasn't afraid to fight." Another oldest sister reflects: "I was the one that did what you were supposed to do and yet I envied my sister being the one who got all the attention, though I didn't envy her pain of feeling rejected by my mother."

The Many Sides of Mother

In her work on understanding early childhood, Selma Fraiberg tells us that the child's earliest imitations of her parent "lay the groundwork for a solid identification with that parent" and eventually those "certain qualities" are taken over and made a permanent part of the child's personality. Undoubtedly, those early imitations delight parents as they recognize a "little mother" in their daughter's "sweet stubbornness," or the way she lowers her eyes when she wants attention, or her penchant to cuddle her doll against her chest. Invariably and unwittingly the young girl follows her mother's role and integrates it with her constant evolving sense of self.[8]

But if the mother is the role model, how does she produce two daughters—or more—who are so different from each other? In the preceding chapters we discussed all the factors that contribute to our sibling differences, so we know there are numerous influences that affect our personalities; but we also need to recognize the immeasurable and powerful influence of the mother's *developed and undeveloped* self on her daughters.

Emily, an English teacher in her early sixties, compared her bifurcated experience with her mother and sister to that of the sisters in Gail Godwin's novel *A Mother and Two Daughters*, where the mother splits her two girls between the two aspects of her personality—the dramatic and the conventional. "In the book it is almost preconceived, calculated, it's not sublimated, almost conscious. It certainly was the same in my family."

According to Emily, her mother was an independent flapper from the 1920s who was unhappy as a housewife. "She was an unactualized woman. She died an alcoholic, cirrhosis of the liver. I saw that as symbolic as being unable to resolve her independence. Though she resolved it in some way by producing two different women. I'm the independent, bossy one. I'm my mother's passionate side, exotic, brash, the rule breaker. I take risks and I look for stress. My sister took on a lot of the repressed, the socialized, the weak person. Then later my sister became an alcoholic."

In Chapter 9 we shall see how Emily and Bea have accepted each other since their mother's death and Bea's recovery. But for this discussion, note that one of the contributing factors to sisters' different personalities is that children absorb their mothers' (and fathers') wishes and projections.[9] That is, the mother may raise one child as she is, and another child as she wishes to be, or another as how she fears she could be. Bea's mother may have seen herself in her younger daughter's eyes and projected her insecurities with friends and husband. When I met with Bea, she claimed her childhood was wonderfully happy with her closeness to her mother. Her mother's fears and insecurities, as described by Emily, weren't apparent to Bea until she was in high school. That doesn't mean that they didn't exist before then, rather that Bea was only "newly aware" of them during her adolescence.

Dreading to Be Like Mom

"I swore I would never be a martyr like my mother; my sister is the martyr."

From early adolescence well through adulthood, women expend a lot of emotional energy trying not to be like their mothers. Despite our concentrated efforts, and our mothers' pleas not to repeat their mistakes ("Don't ever try to do it all, like I did." "Whatever you do, put yourself first"), we uncannily find in ourselves the distinct traces of our mothers' most undesirable traits. A woman whose mother was manipulative, realizes she is manipulative with her husband, her children, even her friends. How could this happen? she cries. "I hated that in my mother."

I contend that the mother's different traits—those we dread and those we admire—are not necessarily exclusively adopted by each of her daughters but, rather, are shared or spread to some degree among and between all the daughters. For example, if an aggressive mother has three daughters, one may be dominantly aggressive and the other two may have the potential for aggression, but not have it as a discerning characteristic.

We are by no means innocent receivers of our mother's influence. Most of us consciously and unconsciously select what we want from her or what appeals to us at the time of our development. As adults, it is easier to discern which of our mother's characteristics we have enveloped and which we have rejected, and often we are surprised at our unconscious absorption—and even more surprised at how our sisters selected differently. Many of the women I met felt fortunate that they had adopted their mothers' drive for independence and initiative, even though their mothers may not have been able to realize fully their own potentials. Since most women's mothers lived and raised their families in "unliberated" times, they claimed their mothers had been denied education and career opportunities. And yet, they knew how capable their mothers were and were grateful that their mothers wanted better for them.

"My mother had very high expectations of me," explains Elsie, who, unlike her two sisters, holds a graduate degree and a highly stressful job. "I didn't get a lot of feedback, Mother was a very closemouthed person, more Norwegian than Irish, but she always expected me to do more. My next sister was artistic, so Mother had different expectations. My mother may have been trying to live out some of her wishes by pushing me. I never realized this before, but after my mother died (in her late forties), my father told me that Mother had to quit college after a year and a half because her father had died. I realize now for the first time, she wanted more for me."

Susan, the successful science editor (see Chapter 2), notes: "My mother did not prepare her three daughters for marriage, rather not to get married, always emphasizing that you needed to support yourself and be independent. Even at age seventy she was an independent soul, helping others."

Wendy's mother is fifty-three and living her life to the fullest, a source of pride to her two daughters, who have always had a close and supportive sister relationship, particularly through their parents' divorce when they were in their teens. "My mother was an only child," says Wendy, "so she doesn't cling to us, she is very independent. She was always smart, always doing something. When my sister and I went to Sweden and Poland together, my mother was thrilled that we could be together, even though she couldn't join us. She was just as thrilled when my sister went to Senegal to study. My mother always shares in her travels, she takes me on one trip and my sister on the next one."

"My mom calls me her gypsy daughter," says Jo (see Chapter 3) who has switched jobs and cities more than a dozen times in several years. "She sees the world because of me and she tries to travel to wherever I go. She always says, 'Take your time, don't be in a hurry to get married.' My mother married young. My grandmother says the same thing . . . it's wonderful."

A considerable number of the women I met said that they learned from their mother's mistakes or unhappiness, rather than from her strengths or encouragement. These women described their mother as "bored" or "miserable" and feared they would someday grow up and be as she was. With both the "gypsy" daughter and the many daughters who reacted to their mothers' being "bored" or miserable, it was interesting that their sisters didn't necessarily react the same way. Just as the mother raises her daughters in the double image of herself, they respond in reverse or in reaction to each other. These different responses are also a product of birth order and the parental influence.

The Little Mother Syndrome

As I pointed out earlier in Melinda's story, the most frequently mentioned phenomenon in the mother/sister/sister dynamic was that one of the sisters was the surrogate mother, and one was the needy child. This was true for families where the mother was home full-time and went out only for church and the groceries, as well as where the mother worked full-time out of the home. The external causes for surrogate mothering were numerous: the mother had more children than she could handle, or she was at a stage in the family when most of the children were grown and she could rely on their help with the last baby; the mother was dysfunctional because of depression, alcoholism, or other illness; the mother had other duties, such as caring for her elderly mother. Whatever the cause, her daughter, usually the oldest in line, took over the mother's responsibilities as best she could, and her siblings responded willingly.

Ronny's mother was a drug addict who emotionally and physically abandoned her three daughters. Now in their forties, Ronny and her sisters are doing very well in putting their lives back together, but Ronny still feels as if she is responsible for her sisters' happiness.

"I grew up as the classic caretaker," Ronny told me when she was explaining why she feels obligated always to return her younger sister's calls even when she doesn't want to, because she "needs constant reinforcement."

"I recently found a letter that I had written to my parents when I was young and I had taken my two sisters on a train. The letter made me weep because I was only about nine, but it was a mother's letter. I had gotten their lunch and I was so worried that we wouldn't get off at the right stop. I still feel this way now. I love my sister and I care for her and I admire her enormously for what she has done with herself in her life.

"Interestingly enough, my mother takes credit for that. Would you believe it?"

It isn't possible for any child, no matter how mature, to fill a parental role adequately, thus there are often problems of disappointment and an imbalance of affection in the later years. Several older sisters were confused because the younger sisters they took care of were no longer responsive or available to them.

Vicky talked with much bravado about how she didn't want to marry and have children.

"I always saw my mother as stuck, stuck with her husband and children. I'm not going to make that same mistake." Vicky at forty-eight is attractive and single, with a busy career in Washington, D.C. Her job takes her all over the United States and Europe, another reason for not wanting any extra commitments. Her story could be sad, but she delivers it with such bravado that there is no room for tears. With little emotion she notes that her younger brother committed suicide when he was fourteen and she was twenty-three and living away from home, and that same year her father died of a massive heart attack. "One hell of a year," snaps Vicky. Because her mother "could no longer function as a parent," Vicky returned to take over as a surrogate parent, a role she had been conditioned for since she was three years old, when she inexplicably felt responsible for her baby sister's safety.

"My mother was only twenty-one when I was born and she wasn't very mature herself. I played mother to my mother. My mother didn't like my father. I don't like my father. I think I was also a parent to my two sisters. Jill is two years younger than me, Cindy is five years younger. They were real adorable kids, blond, chubby, real cute." Despite her obvious love for her little sisters, Vicky mostly remembers feeling overwhelmed with their care and her mother's emotional absence. "One time when Jill was three we were on the back porch of our apartment building and the milkman warned me to watch her so she wouldn't fall down the steps. I said, 'No, she won't fall.' And with that, of course, she did fall down the steps, cut open her head, and there was all this blood. I just felt so responsible, I didn't really know it was a possibility. My mother must have been really crazy to have me back there watching her, or she should have warned me. Either I was a very responsible kid, or she put this role on me."

Then there was the time when Vicky was seven and two-year-old Cindy was sick in bed with the flu. "I was reading her a story when Cindy started to convulse. I went and got my mom, who got hysterical and sent me to get a neighbor who was a nurse. By the time we got back, Cindy had passed out. A day later my mother asked me to go tell the neighborhood kids to be quiet because my sister was sick. I anguished over telling my friends to be quiet. Why didn't she do it?

"I don't think my mother knew how to mother," says Vicky. "She was certainly depressed. And she and my father were two people with no financial responsibility. They were always in debt. My father always made my mother cry. There would be yelling and picking at each other, and she would always cry. I decided very young, before I was a teenager, that I would be the antithesis of what my mother was and consequently wouldn't allow myself to get into any relationship that would lead to marriage. My sisters didn't see it that way. But they didn't have to play mother at such an early age."

Behind her bravado, Vicky is very disappointed that she can't be as close to her two youngest sisters. Both of her sisters are happily married and both have two young children. While these two are close to each other—they live nearby on the West Coast—they still have an ambivalent relationship with Vicky, whom they necessarily see less frequently. Even if they all lived in the same city, it may be hard for these two younger sisters to give the total feeling of intimacy that Vicky requires and misses. Vicky played mother when she wasn't ready and still needed more care from her own mother; in turn, she wants a mother–child response from her sisters. Her sisters, meanwhile, may be carrying feelings of disappointment, even anger, toward Vicky, who didn't fit the bill of the all-caring mother.

Mother Comes with a Past

Simone de Beauvoir speaks of the load a mother necessarily brings to her offspring: "The mother's relations with her children takes form within the totality of her life; it depends upon her relations with her husband, her past, her occupation, herself."[10] The whole dynamic of the mother–daughter relationship is not singular or privately confined or one-generational. The mother comes with a history, she moves, thinks, and responds *in reaction* to those around her and before her, because she is a woman emotionally connected to others from the time of her early childhood. Unquestionably, and invariably, she carries that history to her daughters, who in turn react to each other.

A woman whose mother clung to her own childhood while raising her family, now maintains a strained relationship with her younger sister, whom she never wanted to share with her mother. "My mother was the youngest of twelve in a British family, with live-in help," she explains. "She is a nervous person and a worrier. She and her mother were close friends. In fact, they would go to lunch every day. I remember crying when she would leave me alone with a nursemaid."

Nora and Judith's Story

"Every mother carries with her a bit of her 'unmastered past,'" writes Alice Miller. Without question, our mothers respond to their daughters while wearing the "invisible chains" of their own history.[11]

I think one of the most fascinating "mother histories" I heard was from two sisters in one family who met with me separately. Nora, fifty-two, is a family therapist, who speaks with a quiet objective wisdom about all her family has been through. Judith, forty-five, is a singer and teacher who has a more intuitive, dramatic sense of the sisters' special relationship with their mother.

Their story begins long before they were born and before their mother, Carolyn, even met their father, Peter. A handsome, athletic young man, Peter was a promising musician and headmaster of a boys' school when he fell deeply in love and married his first wife, Nora, a very beautiful woman. Shortly after their first year of marriage, Nora died in childbirth, as did the twin babies. Nora's mother soon introduced her grieving son-in-law to Nora's best friend since childhood, Carolyn, a tall, lean, dark-haired young woman who

111

was always given the "pants" part in school productions. With Nora's parents' blessings, Carolyn and Peter married. In time, two sons were born, then finally their first daughter, Nora, named after the dead wife. Seven years later came Judith, and then another boy. According to Nora and Judith, this was and is still a vital family of ambitious, intelligent children who lived for many years in the "sanctified legend of the first dead wife."

"My mother was jealous of the dead wife and I was 'adopted' by her parents as their grandchild. So there was a continuing issue with me and my mother and the dead woman," explains Nora. "She allowed my father to name me after Nora because she was ambivalent, after all they went to school together, grew up together. But Nora was the perfect woman. It was so hard for my mother to live in her shadow ... my father always kept Nora's picture right beside his bedside."

When Judith was born, a relieved Carolyn directed her attentions to her second daughter, who brought no memory of the past. Inevitably, a triangular relationship evolved between the two daughters and the mother. "But not to the extent of conflict," says Nora, who apparently curtailed potential jealousies because she received strong support from her father and grandparents. "My mother was obviously interested in the things I did, and yet was constantly having to battle this other identity. It's only in recent years that I felt myself to be fully her daughter."

Judith has always felt fully her mother's daughter, and has been particularly close to her in the past fifteen years, during which, after her father's death, her mother "blossomed" into a strong-willed, independent woman electing to travel around the world and pursue her lifelong interest in music. "She was a flexible woman, but far more flexible in her eighties than in her thirties," says Judith proudly.

"She played the violin, she was more musical than my father. We used to have wonderful family hymn sings, with madrigals and all." Despite the healthy change in her mother, Judith still reflects some of her mother's early insecurities. "My fantasy as a child always was that if I had been my father and his first wife's child, I would have had skinny legs and I would have been perfect. My mother was actually very beautiful, but she never thought it, so no one else did either. All the attention was given to the first wife and to my father for being the athlete, the handsome man. You look back at my mother in her pictures and you can see how lovely she was. I think my mother thought it was a kind of gift to my father to name my sister after his first wife. I don't think she had enough self-esteem to say, 'Hey, you can't do that.'"

With all this tension between the mother and two daughters, how did Nora and Judith keep from tearing each other apart? There are several reasons, says Judith. "As weird as this whole history was, my parents didn't actually play favorites. They finally allowed each one of us to be our own person." Also, each sister was close to one of the brothers, which helped to diffuse the tension, says Judith. And finally and ironically, the most compelling reason was that Nora became Judith's adviser and disciplinarian at a very young age. "I don't have a lot of early memories of my sister," says Judith, "nor do I have memories of her acting as the bossy parent to me. I know she says she did, and it obviously affected how we related together. I still get upset with her, but I think I can say things more to her now than I could before. I was a difficult child—my parents couldn't always handle me, and my mother was so busy with all the children, so they would ask Nora to get me in line. That same relationship continues, though I think it fluctuates. I still look to her partly because of the profession that she has gone into, as somebody I can get advice from, and when I do that, it definitely keeps her in the big-sister position."

Whatever conflicts there were between the sisters, the "railing" stopped when Judith was going through a difficult divorce and she relied heavily on Nora for advice and support. Nora, meanwhile, had been working for years on her strained relationship with her mother and had come to accept how the dead wife's legend had deeply affected them. Less than a year before I met Nora and Judith, they had expressed their ultimate love as they jointly tended to their dying mother. "My mother was visiting my uncle in California when she developed a sudden meningitis and never regained consciousness, but she was alive for about five days," explains Nora. "All of us lived on the East Coast and all of us flew out and were with her those five days. In the process each one of us allowed the other to have a quiet time alone with her. But we were also together with her, we sang Bach chorales to her, read poetry . . . we each talked to her and had a sense of ending our relationship with her, but not in competition with each other. To some extent my sister and I managed that process. It was a wonderful good-bye. We all credit our mother that we could be inspired to do this . . . the music, the poetry. We ultimately had to decide to take her off the life support. If she had died when I was twenty, it would have been much more difficult, I wouldn't have felt as connected to her as now."

Nora and Judith, now remarried, live in different states but talk on a weekly basis and try to spend holidays and vacations together with their husbands and children. "We had a big family gathering at Thanksgiving," says Judith, "it's an awful lot of fun now. But this is the first year that my mother won't be here for Christmas, it's going to be hard. And yet it's nice to know that things continue without my

114

parents. I feel much closer now to my sister than I did as a child. We are lucky, a lot of families don't have that."

We Can Survive Together

She is right, of course, a lot of families don't have that. And yet, I was struck by how many sisters who grew up in totally dysfunctional families were able to maintain a supportive bond. Indeed, my survey shows that when there is a strong dysfunction in the mother, the sisters often commiserate and join forces in order to support each other emotionally. A therapist told me how two of her patients, who were sisters from a family of abuse and alcoholism, *physically* held on to each other throughout their sessions. And yet, physically and emotionally, sister bonding in the midst of a dysfunctioning family is not a given or easy resolve. As one woman testified, she had no idea she was close to her two sisters until twenty years after she left home. "Both my parents were alcoholics, but we never discussed it. After college we all went our separate ways. There was never animosity or even strong feelings between us, but we rarely kept in touch. Then when two of us started having problems with our own marriages, all three of us were drawn together, talking on the phone every Saturday. This all happened gradually, but thank God I have them now."

Gretchen and Olga's Story

Gretchen's childhood was like a Grimms' horror tale, except that it was very real. The youngest of three children, she and her sister, Olga, and their brother were born and raised in Germany. Her mother was an American married to a

115

German Nazi soldier who later served time in prison for crimes in the city where they lived. Living in the States for thirty years, and now settled in California, Gretchen still speaks with a German accent and often hesitates to turn a phrase in the colloquial American way. "My father was only home two years, when I was seven to nine. I have a few memories of a very punishing father. I try to block the memory out. I remember my mother would leave us and bicycle to the prison, where she would try to throw food over the fenced-in area." But Gretchen can't block out the memory of her mother's lover, another soldier, who favored Gretchen but not Olga. "This caused a lot of problems. He would punish Olga by locking her in the bathroom or cutting her hair in the middle of the night when she was sleeping. Olga recently shared this with me. She also shared that Mother has always been an alcoholic, which I didn't know. Olga thought I knew and has resented me. We had both resented each other because we didn't understand what was going on. Now that I know about the alcoholism and why she was abusive to us, for the first time in my life I could tell my sister I love her.

"My sister was never very much liked by my mother. She tried so hard to get her attention, but was abused. No matter what she would do it for my mother." Gretchen is speaking about the adult Olga as well as the child. When the mother divorced, she took her children to the States, but ignored their needs as she became more involved with lovers, two more failed marriages, and her alcoholism. Through all this, Olga "jumped" to her mother's side whenever she wanted anything. "Olga has seen my mother drunk and will drive out of her way to help her," says Gretchen. "I have always lived many miles away, so I wasn't part of them. I don't know if Olga ever succeeded in getting the love and attention she wanted. I don't love my mother." After

Gretchen married, she tried to like her mother, she even took her on a trip to Europe "like good daughters do," and would include her in family celebrations.

But the deciding blow came when Gretchen's twelve-year-old daughter died from an allergic reaction to the anesthetic during routine surgery. Gretchen's mother didn't call and acknowledge the death and Gretchen's grief until three months later, even though she lived three hours away. A year later, Gretchen's husband died of a brain tumor. This time her mother took six months to call. That was seven years ago. Gretchen now calls her mother once or twice a month, to "check in" and attempt forgiveness.

"My sister says, 'Start loving your mother, accept her, you can't change her; maybe it was the war that made her an alcoholic.' Maybe I'm hard, but I think we have a choice in life. I could have been an alcoholic after my daughter died, and I wasn't. I was hoping my mother would have the courage not to get involved in alcohol and involved with so many different men. I hate to say this, but I feel starved for affection from her; since I can't have it, I don't want to be with her."

As Gretchen reclaims her life, she is beginning to understand her sister, and finds herself wanting to be with her. "Olga just married for the fourth time, I'm once married. In her young adult life, Olga hung with blue-collar workers, I mostly went with college people. There is a major difference in how you look at life. Because I married the way I did, I was able to experience the finer things in life and could afford things that she couldn't afford. She has no need or great desire to attend the opera. It's terrible to say, but I feel more privileged than she. Here my husband was a Harvard graduate and my sister is a cleaning lady. When she was seventeen, she was a cook for a wealthy family and I was fortunate to be thirteen and go to a school. She is very bright and I admire that in her, but she has never been interested in education.

117

"My children and my mother-in-law think that Olga is jealous of me, I've had a better life than she. And yet, after my daughter and husband died, I wrote her a long letter. I told her that life is not fair, and it's different for everyone. She has less money, but I have lost people. The purpose of the letter was to feel closer to her. Maybe I was trying to compare our two pictures and to bring them together."

With no prompting from me, Gretchen asks herself: "Why should I care? She is my sister. In time of crisis, if I were to call and say I need you right away, she would take the three-hour trip immediately. She continually says, 'I love you, I love you.' Now I have said it. I don't think she realized how hard it was, or how meaningful."

Looking Beyond My Mother/My Self: Resettling and Acceptance

Ever since Nancy Friday wrote *My Mother/My Self* in 1977, women have fussed and deliberated over their adult need to "break away" from their mother in order to discover their true selves. But as therapist Marianne Walters points out, we need to come away from Friday's dangerous premise and our habit of "mother-blaming" if we want a more realistic and feminine approach to the mother–daughter bond.[12] The intelligent and sensitive task is for the daughter not to separate totally from the mother but to differentiate herself from her mother enough to gain her own identity *and*, in the same process, to accept her mother for who she is.

Emily Hancock tells us: "A turning point in a woman's development of self is the 'resettling' of her relationship with her mother. For some it is a 'wrenching confrontation,' for others it is a subtle psychological process."[13]

I am attracted to the idea of "resettling." That is exactly

118

what the mother/sister/sister process is and should be. If women solely mother-blame and rebel against their mothers, they rarely come out ahead. Mother-blaming is an impractical and insensitive solution, even for those who have been damaged emotionally by dysfunctional mothering. As Erik Erikson persuades us: "The problem of adulthood is how to *take care* of those to whom one finds oneself committed as one emerges from the identity period, and to whom one now owes *their* identity."[14] Feminists would add that the concept of breaking from our mothers is based on male principles. Jill Barber and Rita Watson, authors of *Sisterhood Betrayed*, write that when women rebel against their mothers, they may seem to create a better world, but it is often simply "different" with "different problems against which their daughters will rebel."[15]

The whole process of resettling with our mothers is both complicated and enhanced by the support of sisters in both adolescence and adulthood. Though sisters are bonded in their family history, each one approaches her reconciliation and understanding of her mother in her own way out of her own needs. And yet I know from my personal experience and from these interviews that a woman who has sisters cannot analyze and work out her relationship with her mother *without* also considering the impact of the sisters. If we try to isolate our experiences with our mother and ignore our sisters' histories and perspectives, we are only robbing ourselves of a full understanding.

When adult sisters approach their resettling phase with their mother, a time that has no limits but often comes in one's forties, and flowers in the fifties, it helps to have one another's support and confirmation. Several women confessed they couldn't carry on a phone conversation with their sister without commiserating about their mothers. They turned to each other to confirm their fears, their anger, their confusion, from something their mother said, or did, or didn't say, or didn't do. There is an indefinable solace in not having to spell out fully to your sister what you are feeling about your mother. All it takes is a look, or a few key words, some unfinished sentences, and the two of you are shaking with laughter or with frustration over the woman who is central to your lives. There is also comfort in knowing that you and your sister share in the love and compassion for your mother when she is in need. Nora and Judith, who sang their mother's favorite chorales as she lay dying, reaffirmed their sisterly bond. Today, their stronger relationship lies not just in the mutual mourning of her death, but in the knowledge that they understood and accepted their mother, each in her own way.

6

▽

A Private Language

EACH FAMILY OF SISTERS has a language and a turn of phrase all its own. Sensitive to each other since the day when one sister touched baby sister's cheek or when the two sisters pushed each other down in the sandbox, sisters can speak without words, using their eyes, a gesture, just a turn of the head that tells them enough or even too much within the context of their family. No matter how many years apart or the degree of access, sisters speak of an intuitive communication where they are tuned in to the nuances and emotion behind the words or the look.

All the laughter, the telling silences, the secret codes, the familiar voice, the whine, the "cries and whispers" between sisters, point to their symbiotic union, their feminine connection. Good or bad, distant or apart, sisters are tuned in to each other with an uncanniness that baffles outsiders.

An eighteen-year-old tells me how she gently "kicked" her sister under the table when their father made a remark at the dinner table that she knew wasn't true and that was insensitive to his daughters. "We didn't need to talk about it, we both knew he was off."

*   *   *

In a powder room at a wedding reception, a small group of older women are happily chatting with the young bride and her "little" sister. Suddenly the two sisters just look at each other and firmly grasp each other's hands, then lightly excuse themselves, leaving the women envious of their exclusive language.

Four young sisters, from ages five to fifteen, are seated at their dining room table after school enjoying a snack. For the past half hour they've been enjoying telling me what it's like to have so many sisters and which sister is more likely "to fight" or cause trouble in this closely knit family. As they talk, giggle, and tease each other, I'm drawn to the oldest, who is silently watching her little sisters with a look in her eyes that is unquestionably proud and loving. I have to turn away, for some reason her look brings tears and the memory of how much my two younger sisters once meant to me when I was caring for them.

I ask two sisters, both in their sixties, which one would like to describe further their father's abandonment—a sensitive part of their family history. Seated on a small couch, they look at each other for approximately ten or fifteen seconds at the most (it seems like five minutes to me). I watch closely and can't detect any signal between them, no words, not even a pursed lip. As the eldest turns to me and begins to recount the history, and the younger one comfortably sits back, I realize that somehow they have mutually decided who would speak—and I have missed their private signal.

The Sounds of Sisterhood

Like their contrasting personalities, sisters' voices may have their individual tones, inflections, and pace, but often women told me that they and their sisters "sounded alike" and were frequently mistaken for each other on the telephone. A woman recounts the time her young son was at a camp in Maine and arrangements were made for her sister, who lived nearby, to visit him. "My son burst into tears when they met," she said. "He told me later that he was so homesick, and even though his aunt doesn't look at all like me, her voice sounded just like mine."

Not all sisters were in vocal harmony. One teenager adamantly refused to believe that she sounded like her older sister, from whom she is painfully distant. "We were never around each other when we grew up . . . so why should we sound the same?" she asked me in the exact southern drawl of her sister's.

Measuring Our Words

The amount (not necessarily the depth) of talk between sisters depends on the personality of the sisters, as well as the degree of intimacy, and the circumstance. An outgoing sister going through a divorce claims that she "has to talk" to her sister every day, sometimes twice a day. A twenty-four-year-old sister holding a new job in a strange town calls her older sister for support and gratefully learns that she will come and stay with her during her vacation "just so we can talk." Several women said they talked to their sisters more when they were both raising infants and needed sympathy and support. And as is fully examined later in this book, sisters in their fifties and sixties claim to enjoy more frequent and intimate communication with their sisters than in their earlier years.

Women routinely testified that they "easily" spend a long time talking long-distance to their sisters. One woman said she locks her bedroom door on Saturdays and everyone in the family knows that is the time she has for her sister's phone call. A few women mentioned that their long and regular phone calls "bother" their husbands. "He feels shut out," says one woman, who will stay on the phone with her sister for over an hour, two or three times a month. "He thinks we are talking about our marriage. He doesn't like my telling her so much. I just ignore him."

Many women told me they can laugh harder with their sisters than they can with friends. Humor lets sisters sail back to childhood, when the adults didn't have a clue what was so funny at the dinner table or behind the closed bedroom door. The private jokes put us on equal ground with our sisters; it is also a tremendous release for built-up tensions within the family. "My sisters and I would rather laugh than cry," said the oldest of three sisters, who shared a difficult childhood with the loss of a brother in his teens. The third sister in a family of four sisters tells me that when she and her sisters are together, they "all talk independently and laugh. My husband doesn't understand this, he thinks we don't hear each other. We do."

Another woman who feels "blessed" with a family of five sisters, told me that there are many times when she and some of her sisters are laughing so hard, the tears start to flow and they can't finish their sentences. "No one knows what we are finding so funny. We are just totally out of control. Actually, it bothers my husband when we get like that."

Tell Me About Your Love Life

How much sex talk is there between sisters? I can only speak for the women in my survey, myself and some of my friends, that it is not as much as we might guess. Again, it depends on the personalities involved and the degree of intimacy that preexists between the sisters. It also depends on how the sisters handle their competition, and their fear of judgment or criticism. Women in their twenties and thirties spoke of "sharing" with their sisters the attraction, and the personality, of their lovers, or the quarrels and special times, but most of these sisters kept their actual sex lives private. As one twenty-five-year-old puts it: "When my sister comes home from a date, I would never ask her what she did with her boyfriend . . . whatever they do is their business, whatever I do with my boyfriend is my business."

Older sets of sisters, late forties and above, also hold back in "telling it all" or they allude to their sex life without being too explicit. One woman said she listens for clues about her sister's sex life. The reason she doesn't come right out and ask her is that she fears her sister has a better sex life with her husband than she has with hers. A friend of mine who was involved in an extramarital affair hasn't confided in her two sisters for fear of being judged or criticized. "I feel like I'm being dishonest with them for *not* telling, but I just don't want to put myself in such a vulnerable position."

Talking About Our Marriages and Relationships

Sex may or may not be a touchy subject, but many of the women in the survey claimed to talk about anything and everything else in their marriage life *if* they had a sense of

125

trust and intimacy with their sisters. It is interesting that many women are initially more likely to share intimacies about their marriage with a friend than with their sister. Again, it may be a geographical distinction, with friends typically being closer and more available than sisters.

Lillian Rubin notes that: "generally, women's friendships with each other rest on shared intimacies, self-revelation, nurturance, and emotional support." Rubin contends that women relate easily to other women because it is a "continuation of the early experience" of relating to the mother.[1] In some ways, she says, this continuation is also the process of relating to self, or self-individuation.[2]

If this is so, why then do we hesitate to open up totally to our sisters? The answer lies in the complexity of the relationship. We hold back because of the competition and unresolved issues or the fear of showing our vulnerability, but we also turn to our sisters when faced with crisis and change, or when we have gone through the process of individuation and realize that our sisters are not a threat but a fulfillment of who we are. When we understand the roots of our competition, or when we have such deep needs, whether it be facing breast cancer or a job loss, or simply old age, we turn to someone who is part of our self-identity. Our sisters. We may learn intimacy from our mothers, but few women are fully intimate and totally open with their mothers. The same is true with sisters; yet, because sisters are more *familiar* to each other's experiences—that is, they are from the same generation—they have more potential to share intimacies at some point in their development *if that is what they choose.*

for their
or "out-
ting, to
med to
azy," or
a rem-
sisters
ter of
wen-
two
mes
ted;
ing

ns
n-

ommunication

t outrageous myths of biological
s can express their anger to each
of outspoken sisters doesn't neces-
sisters *resolve* their differences, but
up a fighting spirit, just as they did
e and could pull each other's hair or
The characterization of sisters as pre-
nt upsurge of sister shows on network
of feisty, outspoken, clever women who
ters with whatever pops into their minds,
utting or cruel. If this were true in real life,
d be that the sister-to-sister relationship
ffer. In order to get a truer picture of how
nicate and express themselves, let us first ex-
ey handle their anger, and then how they ap-
r sensitive issues; for these are two distinct
ons in the covert and overt communication be-
rs.

ority of the women I interviewed said they were unable to
eir anger directly to their sisters.

woman said it for most of us: "We fought when we
ttle, but we never fight to each other's face, now."
erally, the women in the survey claimed to "hold back"
tempers, no matter how close their sisterly bond. This
e tempering of tempers prevails among my women
ends and in my own family experience, where adult con-
ontations can be counted on one hand, and recalled to the
ninutest detail.

There were, of course, some exceptions in the survey.
Typically, these were younger sisters in their twenties who
felt little or no reserve for speaking their minds to each

other. These women expressed a lower tolerance
sisters that would occasionally show up in "scraps"
bursts" about anything from the men they were da
their choice of jobs. Fresh from adolescence, they cla
be letting off steam, accusing each other of being "l
"selfish," or "out of it," or "a pain." Their bickering,
nant of childhood, was often short-lived, with the
returning to a neutral or loving stance within a mat
minutes. One mother of two daughters in their middle
ties described how she has to leave the room when the
start "picking at each other." But when the mother co
back twenty minutes later, it's as if nothing has happe
the two young women are usually "just talking or laugh
about some private joke between them."

For most women in the survey, however, confrontatio
and instant makeups with their sisters were nearly no
existent.

> "We almost never get angry with each other; if we do it's
> her [sic] who gets angry with me; from the beginning,
> one and two years old, she was always very protective of
> me." (twenty-four-year-old, the second of three girls,
> speaking of her older sister)

> "I don't know why I don't express my anger toward
> her. I do it toward my husband, children, and friends,
> but not my sister. I could tell my mother how I felt and
> didn't feel I would lose her love. And yet I couldn't
> ever say to my sister, 'You creephead. You've gone off
> without any reason at a time of crisis in our family.
> Couldn't you have come home?' I've not really said
> that, but I'm certain she knows I feel that way." (forty-
> five-year-old older sister who is left with the care of
> ailing mother)

"It takes a lot for me to lose my temper, I've only once or twice done it with my sisters. Sometimes Leona's self-esteem is so low, I don't tell her any criticisms, I cushion those things." (thirty-three-year-old talking about her younger twin sister)

"I'm the one who takes risks, and yet I don't let myself be angry with her, I never let her know when I am upset with her." (fifty-one-year-old, older of two sisters)

The above testimony is not unusual given what we know about women's psychology. Studies abound on the difficulties women have with expressing anger. Good girls aren't supposed to lose their tempers. The fear for the young girl is that if she loses her temper, she may lose Mommy's or Daddy's love, and because autonomy has not been an essential part of her upbringing she finds that possibility far too threatening.

The theory fits as long as it's in the triangular context of the child and the adult. Young siblings, however, do find arenas where they can let themselves loose, and physically and/or verbally fight. Fighting or "scenes" between young sisters may be deemed "unbecoming" in a household, and even strictly punished, but are without the severe, unconscious threat of loss of losing the parents' love. Clearly, the competition between young sisters can be far more passionate and stronger than the fear of any lost affection on their part. For some little girls, particularly those sensitive to their parents' disapproval, fighting with a sister is simply too threatening even to approach. In my survey many of the firstborns, or the sisters who deemed themselves "peacemaker," never or rarely ever allowed themselves the freedom of venting their hostility to their sisters. Whether this was part of their surrogate mother role, or their wish to keep stability in the family, or their need to maintain their parents' approval, they usually voiced some regret at not having a childhood where they could tease or taunt, like other sisters.

As mentioned earlier, I didn't fight with my siblings, though they had their open battles. But when I was nine, I had my own way of vicariously living a temperamental life. On Saturday mornings I would love to sit on my friend Diane's bed and watch her fight with her sister Marilyn, who was a year older than Diane. Their mother was a widow, a rather formidable woman who kept an immaculate and preferably "quiet" house. During the week she worked for an insurance company, and on weekends and evenings she taught piano, so she had little time or patience for Diane and Marilyn's "shenanigans," as she disdainfully called their fights. Somehow those two still managed wonderful weekend bedroom battles while their mother gave piano lessons downstairs. With "The Skaters' Waltz" playing in the background, Marilyn and Diane would grip each other's wrists and leave fingernail marks, or scream "dare yous" smack into each other's face. One of the best fights was when Diane tore the sleeve on Marilyn's white cotton blouse. They both attacked, and they both survived, and their mother never knew—or at least that is what I wanted to believe. (These two sisters are now the best of friends, living two hundred miles apart and sharing the hospice care of their elderly mother and their aunt.)

Most of the women in the survey described their "early fighting years" with good humor. There's little doubt that girls, made of sugar and spice, are quite capable of wreaking havoc with bumps and bruises, black eyes, teeth marks, and "snakebites" on the neck and arms. It was not uncommon for women to mark their earliest memories with their sisters with some physical injury. One remembered being shoved off the piano bench; another recalled how her older sister and a friend had "chased boys" and impatiently "dragged" her along, scraping her knees and legs on the sidewalk.

"I have a scar on my head from when my sister hit me on the head with a shovel," said a forty-seven-year-old woman rather proudly. "I can't tell you what even provoked it. And I remember one of us once hit the other over the head with a chair; it was probably me."

One of my closest friends, Anne, known for her air of serenity and diplomacy in difficult times, revealed that when she was eight, she pushed her older sister off the bed and the sister broke her collarbone. "We were fighting over a doll," she explained to me quite calmly and with a hint of pride.

When little sisters can't physically fight, they can tease, tattle on, or trick each other with a vengeance. With no shame, they lock each other in closets, fail to give crucial phone messages from boyfriends, steal each other's clothes, snub each other in public, and plot or threaten to "lose" each other wherever they go, be it a department store or church picnic. As one young woman, fresh from a bickering childhood with two sisters, puts it, "sisters can be just plain catty and *mean.*"

One woman described how she and her other sister would get even with their youngest sister's being Daddy's favorite by grabbing her security blanket during road trips and hanging it out the back window of the station wagon. With their little sister screaming in terror, their father would finally yell, "What's going on back there?" And the two demon sisters would claim complete innocence.

Legitimate Terror

We are told that siblings can abuse each other physically and psychologically to a degree that is as destructive as adult abuse. My survey was a random one, so I didn't look for such incidents of abuse, but testimonies came from two women who spoke of their deep fears of their sisters, whom they depicted as holding a power over them. One of the women claimed that her sister teased and taunted her to the point of her not being able to make friends or relate to her mother. All this was apparently going on behind the mother's back, so that the mother thought her oldest daughter was simply watching out for the youngest, who was very shy. The other woman, whose full story is told in Chapter 11, was physically abused by her older sister in a family where the children were routinely disciplined physically by the parents. They were raised in the 1940s by European parents, and the act of bruising, spanking, and shoving was not considered "abusive." And yet this woman knew that something was wrong, so she instinctively hid the scratches on her hand, made by her sister, for fear that her mother would punish them all over again.

A Welcome Change in the Temperament

Fortunately, sibling abuse among sisters is rare, and most sisters enter adulthood with their new skills of appeasement. When sisters leave the nest to either attend college or work outside the home, they find that they can see and appreciate each other as individuals and not as enemies vying for their parents' attention. They may still have their "scraps," but many of the women spoke of "coming together" with their

sisters during their early adulthood. Two sisters who fought all through grade school and high school found themselves running up long-distance bills when they called each other from their college dorms. "She would tell me her problems, I would tell her mine."

Another, more constant, factor is the gradual process of the girl's learning to be sensitive to her relationships. Thus, the feminization of sisters tempers their overt rivalry and expression of anger, just as it does with their women friends and colleagues. As sisters gain insight into what such personal injuries as yelling, blaming, and teasing can cause, they hold back.

Harriet Lerner, who has written extensively on women and anger, believes that this cushioning of anger is not necessarily a bad thing, nor is it something that sisters should be ashamed of or concerned about. Indeed, it is often a rational, convenient, and sensitive way of handling relationships. Part of it is simply a matter of geographics, Lerner told me over the phone. "For example, my sister lives in Cambridge. If I'm going to only see her once or twice a year, I'm realistically going to be careful of what I'm going to bring up in a brief visit."

When Natalie Low and I discussed this issue at the Cambridge Hospital, I gave her the example of a sister who felt she was being "dishonest" with her younger sister because she never confronted her about her promiscuous sex life, yet it angered her terribly. "Why should she tell her?" asked Low. "The younger sister isn't stupid, she knows her sister doesn't approve. The older sister is just being considerate of her feelings." If the whole of the relationship is more important than the annoyances, says Low, then it's wise to remain considerate.

Lerner concurs that there is no virtue in expressing our anger, and that the deliberate confrontation only causes more trouble. "I think there is a big difference between anger and addressing the issues," Lerner told me. "The older I get I don't say, 'I'm really pissed off at you.' I think it's important that sisters address the issue, rather than let off steam. If the relationship between the sisters is close, daily, flexible, you might be able to handle these issues easily." But realistically, says Lerner, the issues are more loaded and more intense because sisters don't have such availability to each other.

Keeping the Issues Separate from the Anger

"I ignore issues between me and my sister. I wouldn't tell it to her face. She can get very nervous and cry more easily" (forty-seven-year-old, older sister of two).

Initially, the anger between sisters usually stems from the competitive triangular relationship with a parent. Over the years, however, we have seen how that competition is replaced or disguised with more tangible and diffuse issues, from money and life-style to the way a sister compulsively keeps house, whatever the issue may be, it looms large within the sister-to-sister relationship.

What *do* sisters typically do with their criticism and their angst? How is it expressed? Each family has its own style of response as well as its own style of communications. As one woman describes what happens whenever she meets with her sister to discuss the family estate: "My sister can get very controlling, and I will sulk." Such a reaction she says is "over forty years old." When they were little, they did the same thing when they argued over a toy or who got to sit in the front seat of the car with their father; one sister bossed while the other sulked in silence.

134

Generally, we can describe the way sisters handle the issues between them in five ways: *distancing, skirting, sarcasm, commiseration,* and *resolve.* Note that any of the first four methods can interact with another. For example, the three sisters at the beginning of this chapter both distance themselves and commiserate with each other and their mother; they also skirt the issues when together and rely on sarcasm to get them through their vacations.

Distance Makes for Healthy and Unhealthy Hearts

Women who *distance* themselves from their sisters are usually avoiding the uncomfortable honesty of their rivalry and feelings. At times this is considered an *ambivalent* stage, when sisters can't take a strong stand either way so they keep apart, call infrequently, or simply stay in their separate worlds. We will see in Chapter 9 how those worlds invariably come together when there is a crisis or a change in life-style.

There is both a healthy and unhealthy side to distancing. Unhealthy in that it gains one little. Seeing your sister once a year or talking to her only at Christmas robs both of you of a potentially sympathetic and enriching relationship. The longer you distance and delay resolving your differences, the more difficult will be the recovery. Many women told me that this is also what they do when their friendships with women become too troubled or loaded. Rather than discuss the problems or end the friendship, they simply "pull back" from seeing each other without explanation.

The healthy side to distancing is that it may be the only course available at the time. We all distance at one time or other, in our marriages and with our children. It's as if we need breathing space to figure out where we are heading; it's a time to relieve ourselves of the emotional pressures of intimacy. Women who have more than one sister are fortu-

135

nate because they can distance with one sister and still remain close to another, so at the time of distancing there is little sense of loss—until guilt or reality hits. One woman described "a heavy feeling" after vacationing three full days with her older sister. "We had a wonderful time, but in a few days it hit me that I hadn't even telephoned my younger sister in over three months. Her marriage is a mess, but she never wants to talk about it. She probably thinks I'm going to tell her to leave the guy. She's right."

Skirting, the Art of Female Diplomacy

A woman in her early thirties has a younger sister to whom she loaned a considerable amount of money several years ago. Her sister has yet even to start to pay back the debt. When they are in touch, which is several times a month, both she and her sister deliberately *skirt* the issue of the loan. "It's not worth the bother," points out the older sister, who prefers to talk to her sister about her love of music rather than her budget. To her, the skirting is harmless since she doesn't really need the money now, and it apparently keeps her relationship with her sister comfortable. She knows it will turn into a problem when the skirting becomes uncomfortable for one or both of them, but for now she's willing to play the game. Another woman insightfully points out that she settles the tension with her sister by "going shopping" the minute they meet. "We both love to shop and it keeps us distracted and busy. She knows it and I know it . . . it's no problem."

Sarcasm

Aggie can't tolerate her sister Liz's advantages in life. She resents the fact that her sister doesn't work nine to five the way she does, and that Liz's husband makes more money

136

than her husband. None of this comes out in the open; instead, Aggie is a master at sarcasm, which hits Liz harder than any physical blow or angry words. When Liz was telling Aggie how concerned she was about her college-age son's work in the inner city, where the crime rate was high, Aggie cracked that "it's only a problem for kids who have led an easy life . . . welcome to the real world." Hurt and stunned, Liz didn't say anything more to Aggie about her son. But she did vow to herself for the hundredth time, "Don't tell Aggie anything about our life-style."

Paula Marantz Cohen, thirty-eight, is a literary critic with an interest in family and family structure, particularly during the nineteenth century, the Victorian sister era of Austen and the Brontës. Part of Cohen's work focuses on the role of the *sarcastic voice* between sisters. "It's a way of blunting rivalry, placing or distancing oneself from everything," Cohen explained to me. "Jane Austen and her sister Cassandra did it and I hear the sarcastic voice that I use with my own younger sister. Sarcasm takes advantage of the rivalry and parodies it. The sister converts the rivalry and it is so obvious. She publicizes it."

Cassandra, who dutifully read her sister's manuscripts before publication, at one time had the uncomfortable task of requesting from her sister a *second* copy of *First Impressions* (the original title of *Pride and Prejudice*). She was supposed to have read it much earlier, and apparently had "lost" her original copy. As expected, Jane sent a second copy of the original manuscript with a sarcastic note: "I do not wonder at your wanting to read 'First Impressions' again, so seldom as you have gone through it, and so long ago."[3]

After that terse observation, I doubt if Cassandra had little choice but to read every single word the second time around. When I suggested to Cohen that the Austen sarcasm was fine but could also be dubbed passive–aggressive behavior, she didn't agree (though other critics do). We did agree, however, that the Victorian climate was ripe for sarcastic banter. The Austens, like many Victorian sisters, necessarily lived together and functioned together well into their adult years; it was not unusual for Victorian women to share a household when one was married and the other remained single. This arrangement provided both an economic means of housekeeping and a sympathetic ear for the married sister. "Because of this closeness everything was grist for the Austens," notes Cohen. "Jane and Cassandra were very uncomfortable with sentimentality. I think I'm that way with my sister. We are much more comfortable with satire than sentiment. We feel that sentimentality takes refuge in false agreement."

Commiseration, a Natural Evil

Most of us, at one time or another, have turned to *commiseration*, talking about one sister with another sister, or our mother, or our friends, or our family. "Commiserating is totally human nature," Lerner told me. "It's like a law of physics, it's what we do." According to Lerner, it is as if we "are wired for triangles"; when the anxiety between two people can no longer be contained, a third party is involved. It can be a temporary phase, where you call one sister and complain about the other. She may listen and suggest that you go back and talk things over with the offensive sister. Or, notes Lerner, it can be more rigid and unuseful, if the sister you call joins in on the blaming—or you continually call each other to rake your other sister over the coals, without any change in your communication.

Harmless commiserating can relieve tension and reassure the sister who is feeling uncertain. Like gossip, commiseration creates an affinity with the person in whom you are confiding. It sets up a bond that provides some temporary security.

"We all talk about each other when one isn't there, of course we do!" exclaimed sixty-four-year-old Rosemary, the second youngest of the four musical sisters (Chapter 4). "And it's all done with love. I had to laugh at Stella; Esther had sent her some flowered sheets and Stella can't stand anything but white sheets. Each of them told me her own interpretation of the gift. What makes the difference is that I know we all love each other."

Sociolinguist Deborah Tannen points out that girls tend to gossip because of their inclination to "criticize peers who try to stand out or appear better than others."[4] I would add that for girls in grade school and high school, the desire or need to gossip often facilitates the need to commiserate about or criticize their sisters. It was not uncommon for women in the survey to recall how they would complain about their sisters to their closest friends. Or, how they "couldn't believe" how their wonderful friends could have such "horrible" sisters.

As adults, the danger from commiseration comes when we continually talk behind the sister's back without bringing it to a resolve, face-to-face. This, Lerner agrees, is useless and destructive, just as when we continually commiserate with our women friends. Commiseration is a hard habit to break for sisters who do not see each other frequently or who harbor an ambivalent relationship, or for those who are in a situation they feel is beyond their control.

Elsie, thirty-one, "talks and worries" about her middle sister Chrissy, twenty-nine, with her sister Eileen, twenty-six. "Chrissy has always been the least ambitious, she's never explored herself or her abilities. So I'll say to Eileen, 'God, what is wrong with Chrissy? She doesn't like to travel, she stays in that little town.' It bothers me because she just remarried and I think she did it just for financial security. I just think that is a shame. I just think she would be happier in the long run if she tried to find a life for herself, this seemed like the easy way out."

When Elsie talks this out with Eileen, they invariably conclude that there is nothing they can do about Chrissy's way of life.

"Besides," adds Elsie, "I don't have a five-year-old like Chrissy does. I don't know what it's like."

"Mom, I Don't Want to Hear About It"

There is no commiseration more potentially destructive than that between sisters and mothers. Again, it is only natural and bound to happen in any family; the problems are when sisters become so accustomed to being their mother's sounding boards (or vice versa), or when sisters communicate only through their mothers. A sister may understandably discuss with the mother her concern about her younger sister's health; or a mother may make a remark that she is tired of her sister's arguing. The danger to watch for is when there is already such distortion in the family communication that the mother and sisters use the information as a way of targeting one against the other.

Sisters in the survey who were also mothers often said they commiserated more about and with their daughters when they were feeling particularly insecure in their lives, such as during a divorce, poor health, or a job crisis. When a mother is angry or upset with her daughter, instead of speaking directly to her about the problem, she may complain to another daughter, or put it in a leading guise, such as "I'm worried about your sister, she has been keeping awfully late hours lately."

Jenna has four sisters and one brother. Her parents are divorced and she, at twenty-eight, is the deemed "peacemaker," a role difficult to play when her mother, distraught from her divorce, is continually manipulating her children.

"Mom did a nice job targeting us against each other. She still does depending on what goes on in her life. She targets one and talks behind her back. I figured this out early. When my younger sister Meg was getting a divorce and getting along real well with my father, Mom would call me or some of us and say, 'I can't believe this!' and then she would draw us into what Meg was doing. Or she would be in a room and completely ignore Meg."

Mother–daughter commiserations can be harmless if the receiver of the complaint doesn't overreact or remains neutral. "Amanda's only fault," says twenty-nine-year-old Carolyn about her younger sister, "is that she is flighty as all get out . . . a complete airhead. She has a million irons in the fire all the time and she's always twenty minutes late, she can never find her car keys. Mom is hyperorganized, she knows where everything is. Sometimes I will be on the phone with Mom and she will say, 'Your sister is driving me crazy.' I'm then in the position of the counselor, saying, 'Well, it's just a different style. Go with it.' I don't take it seriously. But I know that's because I'm not living near them. Given enough time spent with my sister, I would start feeling the same way."

Carolyn's commiseration with her mother is rather harmless because she has been able to keep a neutral position. Also, she and her sister have always been able to talk to each other and separately to their mother, so their lines of communication are rarely snagged. The situation would be quite different if Carolyn and Amanda were highly competitive for their mother's attention, or if their mother was jealous of one or both of her daughters. The risk would be that the mother would use her information as a way of targeting the sisters against each other, or that the daughter would rise to the occasion and feed the fire of complaints in order to gain favor with the mother.

"I love my mother, I just have to learn to get on top of her tricks." So says a forty-one-year old woman who has a reasonably comfortable relationship with her younger sister, but whose mother has always been manipulative by using her "aches and pains" as a way to express her angst about one of her children. For example, if the youngest invites her mother to come and visit, the mother will call the oldest daughter and say, "Your sister wants me to come and stay with the children, and I've been having those dizzy spells." This is not only a cue for the oldest to call the youngest and make her sensitive to Mom's needs, it's a subtle way of commiserating by putting the sisters in a compromising position.

"I'm very protective of what I tell my mother," explains a forty-year-old woman whose sister is ten years older. "My mother now doesn't cope well. Anything I say [about my sister] can be convoluted and come back to hit me. Mother was never a problem solver, everything became a tempest in a teapot. Nothing was ever handled factually. So I listen a lot if she is talking about my sister. I am an observer. I don't say anything."

To a great extent, this woman's silence is a sensitive resolve. Her mother is aging and not about to change her habits, and she doesn't take the information she receives about her sister to heart or as grist for the mill. Commiseration can be harmless, if you keep a neutral position, or if, as Rosemary mentioned earlier, it is done with love.

Talking About Our Feelings: How Far Can We Go?

"My family doesn't show emotion, when my mother died we never talked about it, we never talk about our feelings" (thirty-one-year-old, oldest of three sisters).

"[For years] my sister kept up a facade on the phone. . . . I poured out my soul about my marriage and what I got in return was this rigid, socialized, pat crap. So it was not an intimate exchange" (fifty-eight-year-old talking about her early relationship with her younger sister during her divorce).

"My sister and I are best friends, we would do anything for each other, but I'm not sure we are as intimate as I am with my women friends" (forty-one-year-old with thirty-nine-year-old sister).

"I tell my sister everything. There is nothing we don't know about each other" (thirty-eight-year-old with a forty-one-year-old sister who "never fought").

A common assumption I have heard from those outside the survey (from men and women alike) is that sisters will *reveal all* to each other. "If two sisters are soulmates, they must reveal their innermost feelings and secrets," remarked a woman who has no sisters. She, like many women without sisters, believes that sisters are safe in knowing they can tell all and it will not go any further. Such an assumption, however, was not fully supported by my interviews. More often, I heard an ambivalence or a contradiction as to whether they could open up to each other and talk about their worries, their concerns, whether it be about their marriage, their children, or their goals in life.

A woman may want to reveal herself to her sister, but the opportunity is not always appealing or feasible. She opens up to her sister only when the emotional climate is right, that is, when there is already some degree of safety and intimacy. When she needs to talk, she has to trust her sister not to repeat her intimacy to mother or father or another sibling. Above all, she has to have some sense of self-esteem in order to reveal her vulnerabilities.

Sisters are more likely to reveal their problems if the degree of competition between them is currently manageable, latent, or minimal. In my survey women with more than one sister spoke of revealing things to their younger sister but not their most immediate sister, with whom they competed.

If most or some of these factors aren't present, women are more likely to reveal their deepest feelings and concerns to their women friends rather than to their sisters. Several women in the survey elected to have "chosen sisters," women who were their idealized sisters, to whom they could tell anything without fear of judgment. This is the same idealistic relationship that sisterless women have with their close friends.

This doesn't mean the sister-to-sister relationship isn't valuable, or that it takes second place to the friendships women have with other women. Rather, it shows how our sisters serve as prototypes for what we want to gain or avoid in our relationships with other women. It also demonstrates how powerful the sister-to-sister dynamic is: right or wrong, a woman holds back with her sister because she may fear her sister's rejection, her judgment, or, worse, her lack of sympathy when she needs it most.

Another reason for the ambivalence about talking to sisters is strictly geographical or circumstantial. If your women friends live next door, work with you, or are just a local call away, it seems more convenient and likely to lean on their shoulders—whereas calling a sister long-distance, and finding the privacy and the time to tell her about your broken love affair or your problems on the job, is much more of a hassle.

"When I need support I call my friends first, they are here in this city," said a thirty-year-old who is single, living in Washington, D.C., with two younger sisters living in California. "But if I found out I had a terminal illness, I would go straight back to California where my sisters are."

"I really want to reveal more of my feelings to my sister, but I'm afraid what will happen," said a friend of mine who was preparing to go on vacation with her older sister. "Actually, I don't know how to go about it." I found that many women in their forties and fifties feel this way as they enter a period of change or reconciliation with their sisters. I particularly feel this way with my youngest sister, Janet. Because we are so far apart in years, distant in miles, and a bit proud with what we can and cannot handle in life, we don't totally open up to each other. I have hope that our reserve will dissipate with age, and more frequent visits.

Sisters on a Seesaw: Unbalanced Intimacy

Unbalanced intimacy is another phenomenon in the sister-to-sister dynamic. One sister reaches out and tells all, the other holds back, playing the role of the strong one, or the counselor. This works to a point, until the sister who is more open realizes that she looks like she's the only one who has problems. The same dynamic holds true with our women friends; once the imbalance of power and intimacy is

145

obvious it becomes hierarchical and spoils the relationship. If you find that you are telling a friend all your problems and she never confides in you, she becomes the stronger one, the listener, the adviser. At some point, however, unless you force the issue or ask for her to open up, the friendship will weaken with the imbalanced dependency. Sisters are perhaps more tolerant of unbalanced intimacy than women friends because it is part of their role-making in the family. We come to accept the fact that one sister is a listener, another is a complainer, and another is known for "tackling" her problems.

It helps to understand the reason for the differences between how you and your sister share intimacy. Joan (see Chapter 4) explained that she is the one who goes to her older sister (the compulsively organized high school principal) when there are problems, because she is "more laid-back and analytical."

"But I am not the first one my sister would call if she had problems; and I'm not sure she would call anyone," says Joan. "Though I'm noticing that she is calling me a little more frequently." This imbalance in their intimacy doesn't stop Joan from talking to her sister because she has an understanding of her sister's compulsive personality. "She is like a machine, she doesn't want to be shown as human or vulnerable. She is like the rabbit beating the drum in the Energizer ads."

If the telephone companies did a study of communication trends, they would probably discover that calls between sisters are a major contributor to their business. Women told me that it didn't matter how little money they had, their long-distance calls to their sisters, domestic or international, were carried on as if they were chatting across the kitchen table. There is indeed a comfortable and comforting language among sisters. We don't have to explain ourselves or even finish our sentences, because so much is understood. It is ironic that with all this common language and feeling, and the laughter we share, we are unable to express our feelings or our anger fully. But for the very reasons that we are drawn to each other in conversation, we don't want to "tell all." Sisters, ambivalent and loving, either cherish their relationship or sense that it should be cherished. That reason alone is a good one for holding back the words that would hurt one another.

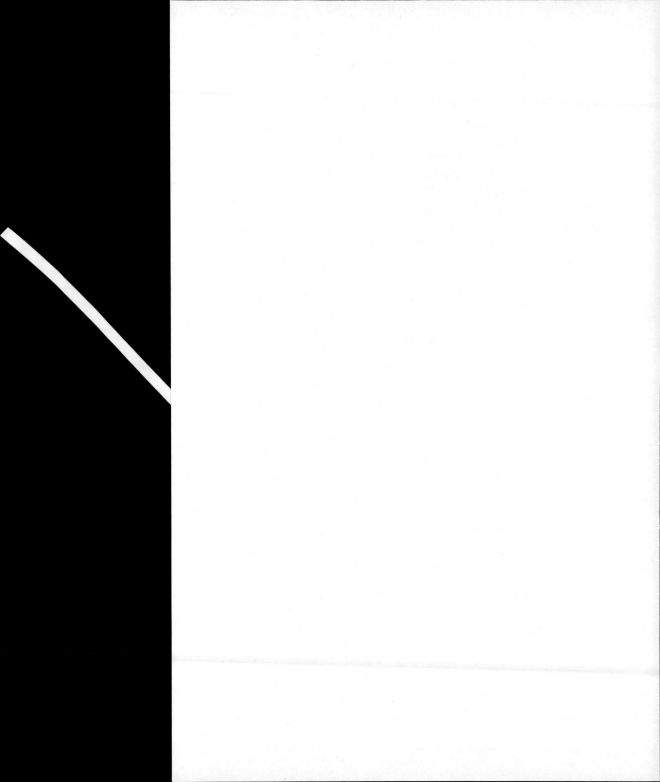

7

▽

Smothering Love

WOMEN WITH SISTERS are often asked, "Are you close?" I wonder if when we women ask the question, it is out of a need to reassure ourselves that our own ragged relationship with our sisters is "normal." Whenever I ask the question, I notice how many women hesitate or pause before they answer. It is as if they aren't sure they know what closeness means or what degree of closeness they may claim. Often women qualify their answers.

"We're not particularly close now, but we were a few years ago."

"We are close when we need each other."

"I consider us close, others might not."

Most of us long to bond with our sisters, especially those of us who have periods of ambivalence and emptiness in our biological sisterhood. Somehow we know the relationship could be better and trust to the stars that eventually there will be some magical, magnetic draw to one another. There are sisters, however, who do more than bond; they share an exclusive closeness that wraps them in a possessive state that leaves the outside world behind. This chapter is not about the kind of bonding where sisters come together in empathy and acceptance of one other (we will examine that in the last two chapters). Rather, it is about sisters who find it difficult or painfully impossible to separate, whose love and devotion goes beyond expectation. It is also about sisters who are possessed by wanting to achieve this inseparable connection, and those who are willing to let it go.

The origins of such seamless devotion are typically traced to our early childhood years, well before there is a spoken language between the siblings. Psychologists Stephen Bank and Michael Kahn note that when the parents are emotionally absent, it is highly likely that "the fusing process will become prolonged if the siblings are of the same sex and close in age."[1] Fused or fusion is a term to describe both an internal and external concept in which one family member does not differentiate between thought and feeling, or between herself and another family member. In traditional psychology this phenomenon is called *nondifferentiation,* and would be seen as a problem with separation–individuation in which the person remains dependent on the love object. Fusion or nondifferentiation is not bonding, it is the disguised, unhealthy version of too much togetherness, where a sibling loses herself in another sibling. Psychiatrist and author Michael Nichols refers to fusion as "emotional stuck-togetherness," and describes fused family individuals as those who "react emotionally to the dictates of family members, arguing or agreeing by ingrained instinct rather than thoughtful reflection."[2]

One of the most explored sister relationships is that between Vanessa Bell and Virginia Woolf. Their exclusive love is a classic example of the fused relationship born out of a need to replace the love and attention of distracted parents. Their mother, a generous woman who diligently cared for her seven children from two marriages, and also nursed the poor and sick in London clinics, couldn't give the individual and intimate time that her two daughters needed desperately. When their mother died from exhaustion at the age of forty-nine, Vanessa assumed responsibility for her siblings, especially Virginia, who didn't recover from her mother's death until well into her adult years.

Before and after their mother's death, the two sisters were with each other every waking minute, in the crammed nursery with their other siblings, during their schooling at home, and even into the night hours, when little Virginia didn't want to fall asleep until Vanessa did. They had their arguments, like any siblings who share such tight quarters, but their fights were brief and soon overcome by an obsessive love that bred jealousy. Biographer Jane Dunn tells us: "As a girl Virginia had a habit of fingering a necklace of Vanessa's and with each bead naming someone who occupied a place in her sister's affections. Such adoration bestowed its own power."[3]

There was more to the power than love, there was also a matter of covert and intense competition. From an early age, both sisters were keenly aware of one or the other's prowess in the arts. "I can not remember a time when Virginia did not mean to be a writer, and I a painter,"[4] wrote Vanessa in her memoirs. Tirelessly, the two girls monitored with both pride and envy the other's growing talent; despite their awareness of their competition, they were cautious in expressing it, particularly Vanessa, who always felt in Virginia's shadow. Undoubtedly, Virginia was the more articulate, intelligent, and generally successful of the two (in the early 1900s, a career in writing was more acceptable and held more promise than a career in painting, particularly for women). Though Vanessa was eventually enriched and happy raising her own family, her self-deprecation and uncertainty about her work in comparison to her sister's was to remain with her through her entire adult life. As for Virginia, from her earliest years she had a "subtle, absurd" way of retaliating when she felt her sister's talent was superior. "When someone had remarked that Vanessa had a harder time practising her art because she had to stand all day at her easel," writes Dunn, "Virginia promptly ordered a tall desk to be made for herself at which she could stand to write."[5]

Interestingly, the competition served to feed into the insatiable need they had for each other, and their work ultimately inspired the other's creations. But Vanessa and Virginia's fusion was destructive, and it doggedly stymied their social and emotional growth. As adults, the two talented sisters attracted other writers, artists, and critics, but no one, not even their husbands or children, were considered as important as their own relationship. What looked like sweet love and loyalty between these two remarkable women turned into an emotional prison.

"Always Loyal to My Sister": Jesse and Gwen

Jesse was five years old when her mother died of a stroke. "In one month I would have been six," Jesse says solemnly, somehow suggesting that her reaching the age of reason was important in the whole scheme of things. At the time, her sister Gwen, thirteen months older, was two grades ahead in school and already a parentified child. A year before their mother's death, their parents had divorced after a stormy and destructive marriage heavily affected by their father's alcoholism. But Jesse, now eighteen, remembers her early years only in terms of comfort and good times.

"I remember snatches of my mother, very pleasant memories. She was nice, she was a nurse. I always remember her helping people out. She worked in a home near my nursery

152

school. I would see her doing that . . . helping people. I worshiped both my parents. While my parents were still together we lived in a big house, a nice neighborhood, just like on TV, where all the kids played in the street. Gwen and I had bedrooms that were right next to each other. We played games and watched TV, mostly we played along pretty well. There were the usual fights. Gwen was the stronger one. One time I wanted to color or use something of hers, she lashed out and scratched me across the face . . . left me with a scar."

Immediately after their mother's death the two girls lived with their father, who was still drinking. "I couldn't comprehend what was going on with my father," says Jesse, "but I know Gwen was aware of it. When Mom was alive she would call the house from work and ask Gwen if Dad was drinking, and I would think, well of course he was drinking . . . you know, water. We were both young, but it became an issue for me when I was nine and Dad was really getting into problems."

When their father went into rehabilitation, the two sisters were sent to live on a farm with a "loving and generous" aunt and uncle, and things began to normalize somewhat; unfortunately, within a few years their beloved aunt died, and they were left alone with their uncle, who unbeknownst to the family was in the first stages of Alzheimer's. Again, the two sisters were thrown into a nightmarish bond.

"Our uncle used to hear noises in the night, voices in his head, and he thought it was the radio. He would bang on our bedroom door and yell at us until it was time to go to school. We just knew we had to take care of each other. We would try to spend the night at our other relatives' houses. But they would want us to leave, so we just had each other.

"That was our real bonding time. Gwen and I both consider ourselves very strong because of everything we've been through. But I think Gwen is the stronger one, she is more reluctant to talk about it. When Mom first died, Gwen made up stories and wouldn't tell people what really happened. After that she was my mother figure, she was the only one with me my whole life, so she feels she has to be strong for me. We talk about it sometimes. We will look back on the past."

Four years ago the two sisters were reunited with their father, who had completed his rehabilitation and was working full-time. Gradually, they stabilized their life as best they could. At first it wasn't easy for the sisters to make friends at a new and strange school, and their fusion didn't necessarily help them. "We both didn't know anybody," says Jesse. "We spent the whole first year exclusively together, ate lunch together, everything. We didn't go out for friendships. The next year we started branching out . . . our friends weren't so much in common this time. I liked meeting other people, but it was kind of hard, because I think I made better friends faster than she did and I felt bad that she wasn't doing that yet. People describe her as shy and she doesn't like that description. She is very nice and friendly."

Despite her caring very deeply for her sister, Jesse is very open about how she competes with her academically. "I always feel I have to perform up to her, and it's difficult to follow her. She had straight A's and very high SATs. Sometimes I think Dad thinks she is better than me. I try to do well. I'm doing better in high school than she did. She's also good in athletics, and I'm completely unathletic. She never flaunts it though. She'll say, 'I can't believe I got an A.' I've heard people say that she is prettier, but I think we both have things going for us."

For a while, Jesse and Gwen tried therapy to work through the pain of their childhood, but again they looked to each other for their responses. "It didn't really work," says Jesse.

"Gwen won't talk, and if she doesn't talk, then I feel bad talking. It turns out to be a big waste of money for everyone."

What is helping the most is that the girls are getting older and separating in school. Gwen is now away in college, and Jesse is involved with her boyfriend, and making plans to go to college nine hundred miles away from her sister. "With Gwen gone it wasn't as bad as I thought it was going to be. I have my own friends here," says Jesse. "We had been slowly growing apart anyway. When she first left we kept in good touch and talked for hours. . . . I'm confident we will always be close. I'm usually very close to all my friends' mothers, especially my boyfriend's mother, she doesn't have any daughters. She will buy me things and want to talk to me. Gwen doesn't have that. She had one friend at the farm, whose family she kept up with."

Despite the growth apart, the sisters' relationship is still enmeshed during vacations and in the summer when everyone is back in the house. We met during spring break when Gwen had been home for several days, so the issue was fresh with Jesse. "I don't think Gwen competes with me, except for my attention. She doesn't like it when I spend a whole lot of time with my boyfriend, she expects me to be there. I keep it to myself and do what she wants.

"She is my sister, I owe her loyalty. Sometimes I get angry about it. I wish she would get a boyfriend of her own, so I wouldn't feel I owe her all this, because of all we've been through."

Whether the cause of fusion is an emotionally distant parent, divorce, death of a parent, or the distraction of a chronically ill sibling, the void and the emotional climate are enough for two siblings to seek each other out for reassurance and identity. Until recently, the fusion between Jesse and Gwen has helped them manage their life of chaos. But now Jesse senses that she and her sister will gain more from learning to live separate lives. She "owes" Gwen loyalty, but she also wants to have her own life being with her boyfriend and pursuing her education.

"I Like Being with My Sister Alone": Wendy and Ruth

Wendy considers herself "very lucky" to have an older sister like Ruth, and she describes their relationship as "very normal." And yet there is a sense of longing, a pall that affects the voice of this twenty-four-year-old. Wendy and Ruth's parents divorced when the girls were young. The broken marriage and the father's abandonment is never talked about, so that the father is a lost and demonic figure from the past. According to Wendy, her mother, an only child, is a "smart, independent woman, always doing something . . . she doesn't cling." When Wendy was ten and Ruth was eleven, their mother married a man who had an eight-year-old son, thus giving her daughters a stepbrother whom they have just gotten to "really know" during their college years. But even with her warm relationship with her stepbrother (she endearingly calls him "brother"), Wendy's sense of family revolves around Ruth, particularly now as she struggles with her post-college goals.

Several years ago Wendy deliberately transferred to attend an East Coast university where Ruth was studying. Now Ruth has moved to the Midwest to do her graduate work, and Wendy, who is working as an administrative assistant at her university, is grappling with career choices and a general sense of abandonment. A week before we talked, Wendy had been so upset and "homesick" for Ruth, that Ruth bought her a plane ticket to come and visit her.

"I'm planning on going as soon as I can get off work. We

have no other relatives in the world, except each other," explains Wendy, absently leaving out her mother. "When we were growing up we were so close, we played together at home, but Ruth never wanted to play with me when her friends were around. We are night and day. She's very intelligent, always known what she wanted. She wanted to be an anthropologist and now she is. She's very shy and quiet. It's hard for her to meet people, talk to new people, a lot more serious than I am.

"Of course we fought when we were young. And nobody can believe we are sisters. I have blond hair, blue eyes, she has brown hair, dark eyes. She claims that I was the favorite with my mother, I don't know why. A touch of jealousy . . . we are both jealous of what each other has, her sense of direction, she's gotten what she's wanted. She is so different from me and yet she thinks the same way I do. When I'm upset I can call her and she knows what to say or what I should do; she doesn't push me, she is better to talk to than my friends. We are much closer than we were when we were younger.

"We never got along with each other's friends. In school she was into the sorority thing, very self-conscious. But I can now talk to my sister, she won't break confidences. I don't even have to say 'don't tell.' "

There is definitely love and support between Wendy and Ruth, but there are times when the fusion sacrifices Wendy's separate identity and prevents her from fully socializing outside her family. "When I'm with my sister and stepbrother, I don't feel as good about myself. They are both so successful, getting their Ph.D's. And I don't have any idea where I'm going. I feel really stupid around them, even though I know I'm not. I don't feel that way with my friends.

"My sister visited a few months ago and she was so uncomfortable around my friends, I like being with her alone. I can talk to her, but not to my friends. All of us in our family are pretty closed up. She's my sister."

The High Cost of Devotion/A Broken Engagement: Toni's Family

Not all enmeshed relationships have to be a result of divorce or absent parenting, or the death of a parent. According to Michael Kahn and Karen Gail Lewis, "Intense relationships [between siblings] can also occur when the parent or parents want their children to have a close relationship. Projecting their own needs onto the children, parents can form an idealized version of closeness which the children live out."[6]

Toni's parents were "always available." When things would go wrong between the eight children (four boys and four girls), her mother and father would discuss it privately between themselves and then one of them would speak to the offending child. Sometimes, but not always, there were spankings. But spankings were seen as acceptable discipline, not abuse. Only the youngest, Daniel, was exempt from spankings. No one questioned the parents' "ways and wisdom," and in retrospect they all consider the parenting they received a valuable experience.

Toni is twenty-seven, single, working in research in broadcast news. Her sister Sandra, thirty-two, is a doctor; Judy, thirty, is a pharmaceutical representative; and Willetta, twenty-eight, is a homemaker with two small children. The brothers, all college graduates and professionals, range in age from twenty-two to thirty-three. All of the siblings live near their family home, except for one brother who is married and lives abroad, where his grandmother resides.

Toni describes her parents' tight discipline as "caring": "When Sandra and I were allowed to spend the night at a friend's house, my parents would call before breakfast and say, 'It's time to come home.' They just couldn't imagine us away from home," says Toni, smiling.

It's hard for Toni to criticize a dad who was always there helping with his sons' and daughters' paper routes or picking up his daughters after their night jobs at the mall. As for her mother, she was always encouraging her children to pursue the opportunities she didn't have. Consequently, Toni and her siblings were known and admired in their suburban community as members of the honor society, musically talented, and artistic children. It was a proud day for all when Toni and her mother received their bachelor degrees from the same university together.

Now the mother and father have surprised everyone by selling the family home and moving away from their adult children to live in Europe, where the father is working in a government position. The mother makes six-week visits home once a year, during which she brings a heavy load of luggage and travels between her children's homes. Toni sees this as a crucial time to stay loyal to her family, and finds herself clinging to her sisters and to their past. Though they had fought as children, especially she and Willetta ("We shared the same room, went to the same schools, saw each other every day, and she was so smart, so smart, all the teachers knew her, and then here came Toni behind her"), their inclination to stay close was well established long before the parents' departure.

"When we were younger we barely used to hug a lot. Now that we are getting older we are hugging more. My parents have been gone for two and a half years and will be gone another two and a half years. My sisters and I have been reminiscing about the past. Also, my parents over there are becoming closer. They are sort of different than they were when they were here. That's why we are doing what we are

159

doing . . . we have to look out for each other. We all take care of one another."

Toni talks to her sisters religiously every day, shares clothes, meals, and baby-sits, and generally absorbs as much of their lives as she can. When a sister needed a blouse, Toni went out and bought it for her. If Toni can't get her hair to look the way she wants, she can go over to Judy's and "put on a pouty face and say, 'Would you please comb my hair?' " She knows that Judy loves to comb her hair. At Thanksgiving time Sandra gave a dinner "for all the single siblings." When one of the brothers gave a Christmas party for a needy family, his sisters pitched in to make all the arrangements. Things aren't always so compatible. The old competition and quarrels still seethe between sets of siblings, and yet this conflict can coexist with the fusion. Currently, Toni is upset because Sandra refuses to deal with Willetta "about a personal problem." And Toni is the self-made mediator in a subtle rivalry going on between Willetta and their thirty-one-year-old brother, Brian, who has disapproved of Willetta's marriage from the very beginning. "They compete over the size of their houses, and other things like that . . . they are trying to work on it, but it's still a big thing that looms. . . . I want to keep everyone together, so I help make dinner arrangements and do what I can."

With all this mediating, and caretaking, however, it still isn't satisfying to Toni, who is discovering the frustrating and inevitable way in which siblings hold back from total intimacy.

"The ideal would be if we could really talk the way we want to talk. We always wind up holding back, sometimes we are afraid to step on each other's toes. Sandra is thirty-two and hasn't had any boyfriends because she is so withdrawn and shy. It drives me crazy. She is intelligent, pretty, but she is shy and you try to bring her out. If I weren't afraid to step on her toes, I would say something.

160

"With Willetta we talk sort of, but she will ask me why I broke up with my boyfriend and I will say, 'None of your business.' We go back and forth like that. She's had some strange dealings with her husband where he disappeared for a few days and Willetta wouldn't tell me what it was all about, she denied there was a problem. Told me, 'None of your business.' This is Willetta, she is so independent. She wants to let everyone know that she can make it. She wants you to know, but she always pulls back.

"I was supposed to get married last June, my boyfriend and I are still close, but one of our problems was that I was spending so much time with my family and not enough with him. He has one brother and his parents are divorced." There's a long pause; finally, she continues in a strong voice. "When I worked at a shoe store, and I worked all the way through college, if someone were to call me at work and say that something was wrong with my family—I'm gone. My family always comes first, and I let anyone know that.

"But that wasn't my boyfriend's viewpoint. He's sort of a 'me first' person, and I'm not, and I've never been. If anyone in the family needs something, I'm there to do it." Then she laughs at herself. "I try to cut down on this. You can overdo it.

"I have more family than friends," explains Toni. "I have women friends at work, but usually if I have a problem with them, I shy away from them. The family takes up a lot of my time, less now than they used to."

Toni has recently been thinking about moving to the West Coast, where she hears she has a better chance for promotion in her field. "My sister doesn't like the idea. I talk about California, it's so far away. Willetta always challenges me, 'So you are going to go out there without a job.' Judy is fine, Sandra doesn't like the idea at all."

*　　*　　*

With no exception, all of the women described in this chapter as being tightly enmeshed with their sisters were empathetic, sensitive, nurturing women. There was little or none of the anger or bitterness I so often heard in the more differentiated sisterhoods. These emotionally bound sisters, like Toni, exuded such open kindliness and love for their families that it was difficult to acknowledge and identify their situation as problematic. And yet the unhealthy component of their togetherness lay in the small clues—the offhanded mention of having few friends, the reluctance to vacation separately, the desperation for more frequent letters or phone calls.

Ironically, there are sisters who long to be enmeshed in their sisters' lives. They feel as if they are the outsider looking in, banging on the window with no one paying any attention. Their obsessive desire for involvement may be ungratified, but it is a form of enmeshment.

"Tea and Sympathy": Beth, Annabelle, and Sherry

When Beth welcomed me into her kitchen where she fixed us a pot of tea, she turned and pointed to the refrigerator door, remarking, "That's where my husband left me a note saying he was leaving me. We had been married seventeen years." With that cliffhanger, Beth led me upstairs to a tiny, charming room that she had recently decorated. We sat, almost knee to knee—she in a rocking chair, I on a small couch, facing a wall lined with bookshelves and family photos. Beth insisted on putting a shawl on my lap and legs because she thought the room was "chilly" (it was). So there I sat with my herbal tea, being tucked in by this fifty-seven-year-old woman whom I had met only ten minutes earlier.

Beth grew up in a small southern agricultural town where her family had originally settled in the early 1700s; "We lived in a house across the street from the Baptist church and also across the street from my grandparents, who were members of that church," says Beth in a soft southern drawl. "Everyone in town would say to me, 'Remember your name.' We have deep, deep roots, in more ways than I would like to think. Those roots keep tripping me up, and I keep trying to pull them up ... after the divorce, it was an extraordinary experience to change my name back to my maiden name."

Beth and all three of her siblings were born in their parents' small house. With each birth, she remembers being "taken away," so she was never witness to the sacred event, but she warmly recalls how much she loved her younger siblings. "When they were toddlers they were so blond, cute, and fun," she says, showing me a photo of pudgy towheads squinting into the sun and standing in stubbly grass. As Beth puts it: Her brother Paul "came" when Beth was four, Annabelle "arrived" when Beth was nine, and Sherry "completed the family" when Beth was eleven.

"We were very poor. My father traveled through the Southeast driving a produce truck. He was often gone seven days at a time. My mother worked in a factory doing piecework, eight hours a day for many years. My parents are both English and Irish. I don't think it was a particularly good marriage. There was no spontaneity, no joy, no creativity. For years I have blamed them for so many things; now I realize they did the best they could do. We all went to college, and we all worked our way through. Poverty was such an issue. It took all their energy to pull themselves up and the church had such a hold on them. Morality was dictated by what people in the community thought. There was a whole thing, looking back I can understand it, of duty, responsibility, straightness. There wasn't a know-how about being warm, nurturing, or being supportive of people, you just kept moving."

As a young teen Beth became the serious surrogate mother to her giggling younger siblings, and the chief "housekeeper" for her mother. Stressed, and overworked, her mother often had fits of anger with her children. "She would push or haul off and hit us especially at night when she was alone without my father." The mother's anger was routine and short-lived, but she never allowed her children to vent their feelings. "I couldn't show my emotions. Once in the sixth grade I was angry about something and said the word 'darn.' I had to wash my mouth out with soap. I can still taste that soap."

Several years ago when Beth's mother was dying, she "gratified" her by sincerely apologizing for not giving her oldest daughter a childhood. The apology could not, however, undo Beth's sense of isolation from her sisters and brother. That became even more of an issue after her husband left her and she needed more of her sisters' understanding and support than they have been able to give. In the past few years the sisters have shared family beach vacations where Beth has noticed their different styles of communicating and responses.

"They can laugh quicker than I do. My sisters can laugh about the times, and the summers that they had spent together when I was already gone. Plus they have children and I don't. So there is a kinship there. I feel a little left out, they can't help that. I have felt competitive with Sherry. She was always my mother's favorite; she has a vulnerability about her so my mama always came running when she thought she needed her. My sister Annabelle had her babies all by herself, Mama never sent her anything. Annabelle is much more independent."

Getting up from her rocker, Beth brought me a handwritten letter she had recently received from her sister Sherry. The first page was filled with shaky six-inch letters, exclaiming, "What's going on . . ." Near the middle and end of the letter the writing is smaller and more legible. Apparently, Sherry wrote the letter at work, and didn't have much time to go into details, but she wanted to invite Beth to visit for Easter. "She doesn't have time to write because she doesn't have time for relationships," says Beth with an edge in her voice. "I feel bad about this, but I'm not going to get that relationship from her. My other sister doesn't have time for a relationship because she lives in France. I don't dislike them, I just don't have what I need from them." Beth reads from the letter again, picking out pieces that show how busy her sister is with children, dogs, family. The invitation to visit isn't received warmly by Beth. According to her sister's letter, the house will be filled with other guests; Beth knows there will be little or no time for the sisters to be alone.

"For so long, especially after my husband left, I didn't know what I felt," says Beth. "Now that I am feeling emotions, I feel better about myself if I express it." But Beth admits that she has "to watch herself" with her many women friends because she tends to "jump in" and be the surrogate mother again, the silent nurturer—"I need to find my voice." Interestingly, several of her friends are younger women, the ages of her sisters, who, Beth says, give her a sense of what she "lost" in her sisters' lives. She also notes that she rarely expresses her anger to her friends, though she's "working on it."

"The only anger I feel toward my sisters is that they don't understand, that kind of thing. Maybe I am angry to know that they don't have time for me, that I'm not first in their life."

I ask if they are first in her life.

165

There is a long pause as Beth looks around the room at all her family memorabilia. "They could be. But I have made a point not to make them that way because I don't get it back. It's kind of like keeping the brakes on a little bit."

Beth didn't convince me that her brakes were on. When I asked if there was anything she wanted to add, her answer confirmed her attachment.

"When I was taking care of them, when they were younger, I felt I did not represent myself well and I worry about them. I didn't laugh with them, or read with them, or have fun with them, I was so caught up in the extension of Mama. If she didn't like what they were saying or doing or being, she would come and talk it through with me. And then I would feel caught in the middle. I don't even see things that they see as funny. It all seems so sad to me. So I have this love–hate thing about it, or push–pull."

When Beth walked me to the door, she asked me if I had noticed the cobwebs upstairs in the room where we had talked. Before I could think of an answer, she laughed and said that there was a time when the cobwebs would greatly upset her. She is finally learning that she doesn't have to keep the perfect house as she did with her mother. "My life started," she said, "when I left home."

At some time or other, says Michael Nichols, "we are all vulnerable to the state of fusion, especially during highly anxious times."[7] It is also possible to come out of the state of fusion and achieve differentiation. We aren't totally stuck. We have the means to break loose and define ourselves, as we will see in the next story about Frances and Dorothy.

166

"We Could Never Live Together": Frances and Dorothy

The younger of the two sisters, Frances, read my mind at the start of the interview. "People always comment on how Dorothy and I look alike, especially as we get older. Even when we were younger, sometimes they would ask if we might be twins." Three years apart, Dorothy, seventy, and Frances, sixty-seven, are identical in their slight build, light weight, and general attractive appearance. I sat by myself on a full-size sofa, while they sat close together across from me on a small love seat. Each sister was neatly dressed in surprisingly young clothes with short skirts and handsome jewelry. The only clue as to who was younger was in their personalities. Frances is more emotional and has a much faster way of talking; Dorothy is more controlled and speaks cautiously and deliberately, though she knows how to laugh. At one point during the interview when Frances began to cry about their bond, Dorothy teased her little sister. "You had better find a tissue if you're going to do that."

Dorothy and Frances didn't start out close. Frances had a twin brother, Albert, who was her constant playmate when they were little growing up in the southern countryside in North Carolina. With few neighbors and no other children around, Dorothy often felt "left out" of the twins' fun, especially as she took on the distant role of "big sister." According to Frances, who speaks proudly of her sister, "Dorothy was a responsible and very reliable child, a typical big sister, but I never thought of her as the surrogate mother or 'the boss.' " When Dorothy was thirteen and Frances was ten, their father died, and their lives and roles changed drastically. "Mother really turned to Dorothy for her support," says Frances. "Undoubtedly, the death had more of an impact on Dorothy, she was much more aware of what was going on. I didn't realize that my parents were separated a year before he died, but Dorothy did. My mother had said at the time, well, we are going to move away because of better schools, and I accepted that completely. When my father died we stayed away another year and then we came back to this small town in Kentucky where my mother was born and grew up and where her sister lived. My mother was the youngest in the family and her mother was killed when she was seven years old in a home accident. My mother never spoke of it. She always did that, she erased everything that was bad."

Dorothy recalls it somewhat differently.

"I wasn't her full support. Mother had her older sister. I guess I mostly remember the financial struggle which was going on in the mid-1930s, everyone else was struggling. There was no employment for the men in town, people were suffering reverses. Our parents had been separated for at least a year and there had been problems before that. These days Father would have been called an alcoholic. Partly as a result, he could not support us. He had a good mining business, then came the Depression. Mother had a high school education. She never worked, and there was nothing for her to do in that small town."

"Well, she had too much pride to join the WPA," interjects Frances.

Dorothy agrees. "The only thing she ever did was work in the lunch program so that we could get a free meal. We didn't qualify because we were above the [low] weight requirements, but we had no income. So Mother managed the school lunchroom without pay for a year. Mother had a small pension from a brother in the service, which lasted six months after I got my first job." Dorothy's voice becomes tight and high for the first time in the interview.

"My mother's goal was for us to get educated, so that we could get a job somewhere and support her."

168

What was your mother like? I ask. "First, she was beautiful," says Dorothy. "That is her picture right there," pointing to a portrait on the table. Beautiful, yes, unquestionably, but apparently also a manipulative and dependent woman, who fretted over "what the neighbors might think" in a town of five hundred, where she instructed her children that there were "certain people" they could not play with. "She demanded obedience without having to explain herself, which is what most parents did in those days," says Dorothy. "If we wanted to challenge what the neighbors thought, we didn't dare say it, she had a way of putting you on the defensive. I suppose you would say I'm a repressed child. But I think we had a lot of freedom in many respects. I was allowed to ride the train by myself. We handled money, bought groceries.

"Mother had a dual personality, in many ways she was strong. I remember once saying to her, 'I have a headache,' and she said, 'Children don't have headaches.' Well, I have never had a headache, and I still don't have headaches."

Dorothy finished high school in three years and then moved to Raleigh, where she went to business school and worked until she got a job offer to work in the War Department in Washington, D.C. In 1943, Albert joined the navy, and Frances and her mother moved to Washington to live with Dorothy. The sisters were then in their early twenties and their mother was forty-six; both Frances and Dorothy worked, but their mother, who was strong and healthy but unwilling to take direction from anybody, made it very clear to her daughters: "Well, I've taken care of you. Now you can take care of me."

"This is a very southern expectation," says Dorothy matter-of-factly, "her sister did it, the women did it. They took care of things, not the men."

"We came from a generation," says Frances, "where I took care of my mother not as a duty, it was just expected.

Looking back on it, if we had been willing to make the financial sacrifices, Mother would have been happier in Raleigh, but I wasn't willing to support her in a separate place from where I was living. So as a result I don't know if my mother lived with me or I lived with my mother." She laughs weakly.

Their mother did all the cooking and cleaning in the apartment, and kept active with her church group and a small circle of friends who played cards. Meanwhile, the two sisters worked and limply tried to maintain a social and dating life outside their mother's watchful eyes.

"I never felt comfortable bringing someone home, she would end up fixing the dinner for my date," says Frances, with Dorothy nodding her head in agreement. "Even when I had the girls in to play bridge, she would fix the dinner."

"She was definitely, always *The Boss,*" says Dorothy, cryptically.

After "some very rough times" their mother eventually came around to letting go and accepting her daughters' choice of husbands—Frances married at thirty-six, Dorothy married at forty-four. For the next ten years there were pleasant family gatherings, though no one could drink alcohol in front of their mother without causing tension or a scene. Then in 1975, stricken with ministrokes, she entered a retirement home. Six years later she moved to the nursing center where she died in 1984. During that entire time, a total of nine years, Frances and Dorothy alternately visited her every single day, without fail.

"The biggest problem was that she wouldn't take her medication and the nurses couldn't force her to take it," reasons Dorothy. Every Sunday afternoon the two sisters would get on the phone and work up a schedule for the week. Frances had moved to a home on the Chesapeake Bay, but she managed the commute with an apartment in town. The sisters admit that when their mother was in the nursing home those last three years, the nurses gave her the medication, but they went every day anyway.

"Before Mother got sick, we were always there for her dutifully," says Frances. "I don't think we became close emotionally until we had this responsibility for her when she needed care."

"When I think back, we probably went too much," deadpans Dorothy. They both laugh about "keeping the nurses on their toes."

Dorothy and Frances's fusion was also seeded in their early years with a father they could never depend on for emotional support, or even to come home in the evenings. "I always knew my mother would be there for me," says Dorothy, explaining her lifelong loyalty. Seven years after their mother's death, each sister still checks in on the other daily, if only to leave a message on her answering machine ("Where *are* you?"), and they see each other once a week, "sometimes not for at least two weeks."

With all this togetherness, however, they have deliberately and steadily managed to keep their separate identities just as they did in their earliest childhood, when Frances played with her twin brother and Dorothy remained "outside." According to Frances, "I consider Dorothy my best friend because we enjoy doing things together. But then we both enjoy doing a lot of things with other people."

"We have some good mutual women friends, but we've always had separate friends, which is good for both of us," says Dorothy.

After Dorothy's husband died, she became actively involved in church work and took a paid job with a nonprofit social service. She and her sister both travel abroad at least once a year with each other or with friends.

"We know there are certain things we cannot do," says Frances.

"We know we cannot live together," laughs Dorothy.

"We can't share the same kitchen," explains Frances. "She is Miss Perfectionist. I am Miss Slobbo. I don't hang things up right away. She likes everything very neat." There is a pause. "I think in our later years we would like to live in the same vicinity, though, don't you think so?"

"Oh, yes," says Dorothy, catching her sister's tearful eye.

All of the women described in this chapter had the potential to change their situation, as Frances and Dorothy did. If and when Toni moves to the West Coast, her sisters may protest, but she will have the time and energy to devote to friendships and dating. Jesse and Gwen are already differentiating from each other as they attend separate colleges and leave their father to lead his own life. Wendy is sensitive enough to realize she shouldn't be feeling so incompetent with her sister. Beth may be sad, but she is putting all her energy into changing her ways in her friendships and by accepting her sisters' busy lives with their own families. The possibility of finding her own identity is within reach for each and every one of these women. What is encouraging is the knowledge that they will thrive once that freedom is realized.

8

$\triangledown$

Twin Sisters

MOST OF US WOULD ASSUME that there is a certain degree of fusion with twin sisters. We generally don't think of twin togetherness as a dysfunctional or troublesome phenomenon. Fascinated, we believe that twins are meant to be matched identically, from dressing alike to thinking alike. As a young girl, you may have fantasized having a twin, someone who was a true reflection of yourself and not the mismatch you had with your own sister.

The story of togetherness is quite different, however, from the twins' point of view. I interviewed five women from five separate sets of twins (four are represented in this chapter, one is in Chapter 10). While this selection disproportionately represents the general population where twins are only one percent of births, their stories serve to underline what we learned in earlier chapters about the origins of our differences and how highly critical we are of our sisters. Notice how important it is for these sisters to be accepted for who they are *individually*. In her work on siblings, Monica McGoldrick points to the numerous studies on twins that indicate that identical twin sisters are less likely to be as competitive as identical twin brothers. "It would seem that women, being raised to think of life relationally, are more comfortable with the idea of a twin who shares their thoughts and feelings."[1] But McGoldrick acknowledges that there are times when twins "are not as fused as others expect them to be, or even as they may expect themselves to be. . . . Nevertheless, the remarkable aspect of 'telepathic bonding' is a special and undeniable feature of twin relationships."[2]

Twin sisters are unquestionably linked to each other emotionally, some would even say spiritually, and yet the twins I met with adamantly insisted on, or yearned for, their own space and their own voice. One twin told me sarcastically that whenever her childhood friends would "gush" over her being a twin, she would fantasize that she "had a triplet somewhere out there." Someone who would be far away from all this fuss and represent the singularity she longed for. The twin testimony here is a poignant lesson to the rest of us who impatiently want our sisters to conform to our own reflections, and yet long for their approval. Ironically, this desire for individuality or independence doesn't preclude these twins from being highly critical and judgmental of one another. We have discussed how impatient single sisters are with one another's idiosyncrasies; it is as if each twin's impatience with the other is dramatically compounded because of their unique circumstance. They *want* to be separate selves, but they are so mirrored in their image that they find fault with any act or image that doesn't meet their expectation.

"Are You You, or Are You Your Sister?": *Theresa and Tanya, and Dawn*

Twenty-five-year-old Tanya's first strong memory of what it meant to be her sister Theresa's twin was when they were in separate first grades and Theresa got invited to a classmate's

174

birthday party and Tanya didn't. "Now that I look back on it I realize there wasn't any reason for me to have been invited. The boy didn't even know me," recalls Tanya, smiling broadly. "But I cried, I thought it was so awful, it was so upsetting."

Though they rarely dressed alike, Tanya and Theresa are unmistakably sighted as twins. One time in high school, someone patted Tanya on the back and said harshly, "Are you you, or are you your sister?"

"I looked at this person and wanted to say, 'Who do you think I am?' That made me very mad. I'm *Tanya*."

Identical in appearance, voice, and mannerisms, Tanya and Theresa are fair-skinned and attractive, with long, uncontrollably curly blond hair. They are both "amazed and annoyed" by the fact that they gesture identically with their right hands when they talk, they both eat with their hands in front of their mouths, and they have the very same voice and inflections.

"Whenever I meet somebody who knows Theresa and not me, the voice is the first thing they notice," says Tanya, the youngest by three minutes. "But when I hear Theresa's voice, I still hear her voice, not mine . . . so that's weird."

Not when you think about how determined these two have always been to be on their own. It was simply accepted that these two sisters, who were rarely disciplined by the parents, would fight. They hated being dubbed as "the twins." They even resented the fact that their parents gave them both names that began with a "*T*."

"We shared a room, we always did," says Tanya glumly, adding that their younger sister, Dawn, who is now twenty, was blessed because she always had a room of her own. "Theresa and I always used to fight about everything in the room. Obviously we wanted our own space and the fact that we had to share a room was so hard . . . you had to carve

175

some space out of the twelve-by-fourteen room, two beds, two dressers. I was much neater so I would get mad when she'd have things on my half of the room. We would draw these imaginary lines down the middle. She has a quick temper, we both do, but I always think hers is quicker than mine. I am more verbal. In high school we fought constantly about clothes, or whatever . . . but never boys, we had different taste there.

"We were never very twinny, we never liked doing things together," insists Tanya. "People always labeled us. She was always the more athletic one, I was the more academic one. I had better grades, but I was actually better in sports more than she."

When the twins went off to separate colleges, they were surprised at how the separation affected them. "I missed Theresa more than anybody else in the family," admits Tanya. "I remember crying at the end of September. It was so odd because I don't think of us as being particularly close. It was the first time that we had ever been apart for any length of time and in a completely different environment."

Despite the sadness, there was a promising side to the separation for both girls. "It was very interesting to just be me and not have anybody know my sister," says Tanya thoughtfully. "Nobody ever called me the wrong name. When we got together during holidays and breaks we fought less, I think we were happy to see each other. At school we wrote to each other *a lot*; we didn't have money for calling."

Their newfound bonding was challenged just after graduation, when Theresa announced her engagement to a young musician. The family held back from telling her how they disapproved of the match, but finally, one day, with Dawn sitting between the twins in their old bedroom, Tanya "blurted out" how she felt about the impending marriage.

176

"We had it out for almost an hour, Dawn was our mediator, telling each of us what we were trying to say. Even though she is so little, she was very helpful. And then it was fine. Our family doesn't talk about a lot of things usually. Whatever I said that day, I really hurt her a lot. I was supposed to be her maid of honor, but after that fight she said, 'No, you're not.' Later, she reinstated me." But the reconsideration didn't make things too much better. "Her wedding was really casual. I felt sort of demoted," says Tanya stubbornly. "I ended up being maid of honor, which meant nothing else than standing next to her. I think I had a tissue to hand her, and the ring on my finger. I know she'll be my matron of honor, that's never a question."

After looking again at the wedding pictures she had brought, I asked her why she felt "demoted." It certainly appeared to be a full-fledged wedding ceremony with the sisters in lovely gowns and carrying bouquets. Tanya didn't answer my question directly, but her tone told me that she wanted more intimacy and peace with her sister.

"Well, in some ways that fight sort of relieved us because we could talk about it. But in other ways it told her exactly how I felt and that sort of hurt, I think. About a week after that we arranged a shower for her. I wrote her a real nice card. I told her things, I don't remember what it was exactly, but like, 'I was worried about you, that's why we had the fight.' I saw her with all these women around, reading the card, welling up. She never said anything, but I know that touched her and after that it was okay. That meant more to me than being her maid . . . you know," says Tanya, beginning to lose her own control. "In the past our fights would be over in a matter of minutes or a few hours. Someone would say something neutral, like 'Hand me the pen,' then we knew it was over. But this time it was a week, and that's a long time to allow each other to cool off. It was my job obviously to make amends. After that we went back to being our regular selves around each other."

With Theresa married, Tanya, who lives at home with her parents, decided to remake their bedroom as her own. "I got rid of Theresa's bed, her desk, and I redid the whole thing, wallpaper, curtains. It's my room, not a thing in there is hers, I was so thrilled. I had told my sister I was going to do this, and she had been out of the house for a while so she said to go ahead. But when she saw it she felt really kicked out. One night when she was visiting she had to sleep on a cot," whispers Tanya devilishly. But this leads her to a more serious thought. "I think the only thing Theresa is jealous of is not the new bedroom but that I have money in the bank. And I'm jealous of how she is out of the house; I'm trying to do that."

I was curious if Tanya's friends are like Theresa in personality. Her answer was that of a young adult who still carries childhood remnants of open competition. But it was also an insightful, honest answer, one that countless mature sisters may have once felt but forgotten in time.

"No, I think of Theresa as being very stubborn, strong-willed ... not critical, but she likes things her way. My friends are much more relaxed. But I think I'm different around my friends than I am with my sister, that's how I interpret it. Around my sister I want things my way too. With friends I will compromise."

Conditional Love with Tears

Twins exemplify how sisters often send the mixed and confused three-part message: "Let me be myself, love me, but don't upset me." Jasmine "can't remember" all the ages of her nine siblings, they range somewhere between thirty and sixty, she tells me without offering any of their names. Jasmine also doesn't want to tell her own age, but says it is "somewhere in the middle forties." Raised in a picturesque northern coastal village in Jamaica, Jasmine now lives in Washington's inner city and each day she works two jobs, as a domestic, and as a hospital housekeeper. Jasmine has a twin sister, Lillian, who lives in the South. At first Jasmine had little or no interest in telling her story, but her indifference painfully told how much her being a twin affects her very deeply.

"Being a twin is not special to me. I've seen other twins, they move together closely." Jasmine spoke bitterly, without looking at me and without using Lillian's name. "After we left school we went our separate ways. I'm always interested in her, but she never tries to reach me. I'm the older one, that's why I care and call more than she does."

Once that was said, it took Jasmine a considerable amount of time to gain confidence and continue talking. There were long silences, shifting of feet, one- or two-word answers or a mere shake of the head to my questions. When I was just at the point of leaving her, she began to talk. "My sister next in line looks just like me. Lillian is fairer and heavier." (Jasmine is dark and stocky, she moves deliberately, carrying an invisible weight.) "I'm more moody than Lillian is. I'm much more serious from childhood growing up. I don't talk much if I don't have to. I have friends I talk to, but I don't socialize. When we were children Lillian talked more. We took care of our small brothers and sisters. Mother didn't work. Father was always there for us until he passed away. He was a carpenter. We are very dedicated Christian people. We were raised in a strict Baptist household."

When their father died, Jasmine told me, their mother

moved to the States, where her children all soon followed—now everyone is scattered between Canada and Florida, but the siblings try to visit or call as often as they can. Every year their mother visited each and every one of her daughters, spending equal time in their homes. Three years ago the joyful rituals ended when her mother suddenly died. Now Jasmine says she "feels very alone," and there is "nothing to plan for." Jasmine has a family of her own to distract her, three daughters and a son, as well as several grandchildren, but with her mother's death and her alienation from her twin, her sense of isolation prevails.

"My mother doesn't get along with Lillian as much," says Jasmine stubbornly, as if her mother were still alive and the battle for favoritism goes on. "I don't think Lillian is the same type of person. My mother is quiet, she doesn't like company, just like myself. She doesn't like a lot of men, she likes one, my father, and when he died she said she would never remarry. I never heard them fuss or fight."

Jasmine and Lillian as children were "always fighting" no matter how hard her parents tried to instill peace. "I was much brighter in school . . . for that reason Lillian didn't like that. She would catch a lizard and tie its tail to coconut straw and then chase me with the lizard. I was so frightened." But the fear makes Jasmine laugh. Amused, she tells how her siblings all know her fear of lizards, so when they gather for special occasions, they put plastic lizards in her shoe or in the bed and wait to see her run and scream.

Lillian, however, is not part of this adult game. Abandoning her harsh words and the game of lizards, Lillian "now never fights" with Jasmine, and she "never visits." It is the worst tease possible for Jasmine. "Yes, I would like to be close. I call her up and ask her, why don't you come? *I* visit *her*. She always says she's working, she doesn't have any money. It could be. I haven't seen her in three years.

Sometimes I really get depressed being alone. I am so used to a big family. Right now to me, it doesn't matter being a twin or being single, because I'm always on my own."

When I'm leaving Jasmine she warmly tells me that her daughter also has twins—little boys. "She dresses them alike and they fight too, just like we did," she says, smiling. "My mother never lived to see the twins. She always would say to my children, 'Which one of you is going to give your mother twins?" There is little doubt about her purpose in telling this. One time, Jasmine and Lillian were considered a gift to their mother, and Jasmine wishes she could restore that feeling.

The Role of Parents and Twins

Twins, like "single" siblings, have their separate personalities and roles within the family. Their differences, however, are more dramatically obvious because of the expectation that twins are "alike." Yet we see that the same myths that affect single siblings, affect twins. Health is always a factor, particularly surrounding the birth, which is a monumental event for parents of twins. If one twin is heavier at birth, she will usually be considered the "stronger" one, even if her twin puts on equal weight in the later years. Also, the twin born "first," even if by only two minutes, is often deemed the more independent. (Though this was contradicted by one twin who followed her sister by ten minutes and still insists that is the reason why she is stubborn with a mind of her own.)

A mother of twins tells me that one of her daughters is "the voice" for the other daughter. The one twin is very quiet, but she knows her sister will represent her in tight spots, even with her teachers and friends. All of the twins I interviewed spoke of deliberately choosing and excelling in separate subjects and interests in school. Only one set of twins felt they were equally equipped in athletic ability; the others claimed that one twin was more athletic and the other, more academic.

Parental favoritism affects twins just as it does single siblings. Parents see themselves or the people they always wanted to be, divided in two. How easy to dub one daughter the "go-getter," and the other daughter, "the stargazer." I did note, however, that among the sets of twins with whom I met, the less involved the parents were, the more intense was the twin relationship. This could be a healthy or an unhealthy intensity. Jasmine, for example, loved her mother dearly, but clearly she couldn't receive all the attention from her that she needed and wanted in her childhood. Though her mother never left home, she was enormously busy and distracted caring for her nine children, making their clothes, cooking, cleaning, and generally organizing her days and nights in order to maintain a well-disciplined household. This left little or no time for sitting Jasmine on her lap and telling her, and only her, her favorite story; or when Jasmine was on the brink of puberty, taking her aside and asking her what has been troubling her. Instead, Jasmine grew up looking to her twin for companionship, or to her sister following her. But the two sisters couldn't possibly give Jasmine as full and unconditional a love as she needed from the mother. In time, Jasmine filled part of that need (or diffused it) by being a mother to her younger siblings.

Tanya told me that she "never noticed" if her parents had a favorite, but that her mother "tries to be fair," and her father is a "traditional male who doesn't really talk about things." It may not have been just living in the same bedroom that inspired all the arguments between Tanya and Theresa; part of it may have been due to the noninvolvement of the parents, particularly the father. "Theresa and I didn't get a lot of praise," says Tanya, "but then again we weren't getting a lot of criticism. If we got a B in a course, that was 'good,' if it was a C, that was 'all right too.' My dad did come to the swim meets and take home movies, but it was for him, he loved coming home and working on the movies. He likes that, he did it for us, too, but it was always much more for him. I guess it was just the little feedback we got from him. I wouldn't picture him as a dad, he wasn't around kids. He doesn't have friends. He's very happy on his own."

"Mama Gave Me My Strength": Beba and Boletta, and Elsie

Beba is proud of the fact that her father was considered a "reckless Swede, a black sheep" who left his immigrant family of musicians and made his way across the country, where he got into the construction business and made his fortune during World War II through government contracting. He met and fell instantly in love with Beba's mother, the oldest daughter of a wealthy Swedish family which was ruled by a tiny but austere matriarch who was honored and feared by the Swedish community both in the Midwest and on the West Coast.

"My own mother was just the opposite from Father," says Beba, speaking with perfect diction. We were meeting in a large lecture room within her workplace, where she directs a medical program for the aged. As we talked there were several interruptions from her colleagues asking her questions, and with an air of importance Beba also let me know that if her "beeper went off," she would have to leave immediately to attend the emergency.

"My mother was raised to be very conservative and very socially correct," continued Beba. "Everyone thought it was the worst match in the world with my father riding his motorcycle around, and my mother so conscious of social propriety." But the marriage lasted fifty-seven years. Beba and Boletta were born in 1932, and four years later their youngest daughter, Elsie, arrived.

"Father was not thrilled that we were not sons," says Beba matter-of-factly. "He was in the building trade and having sons was important to him. But he was always sort of a proud father that he had three daughters, and having twins made him *really* proud, it established him in the Swedish community, which was his big social life."

The mother's reaction to her daughters was far less equivocal than the father's. Enraptured with the power of her own mother (she telephoned her every single day throughout her lifetime), Beba's mother turned all her strength and attentions on Beba, who reminded her of herself. "I was always the strongest of the three," Beba says spiritedly. "Mother always felt that I would be the one that got ahead, so she really decided my life for me."

With no apology, Beba sums up her twin's lesser role: "Boletta was the weakling, the one who had rheumatic fever, who broke all the bones, who never could go out and play. To me she was an embarrassment when I was little because she was always so weak. It was like having a shadow around, it was awful. I hope I treated her right. I took care of her whenever something was wrong with her, so I guess that was all right. When she got her first period she was hiding behind this tree, so frightened. I had to walk her home and take care of her."

At first, Boletta was also a poor student, while Beba excelled. But during Boletta's bout with rheumatic fever she had a tutor who raised her confidence and her grades, which continued to stay high "straight through college." Beba is proud of her sister, but she can't tell the story without adding that she, too, got A's in her graduate studies. Nor can she resist repeatedly pointing out her expertise and accomplishments in her field of nursing. Scholarly and professional prowess appear to be everything to this woman, though apparently it wasn't to her twin, who wasn't as involved with their mother.

When I asked her what her sister does, she replied swiftly with frank self-centeredness, "I talked her into nursing." There was a pause. "And then I ditched her. I didn't nurse for twenty-five years and then I went back into nursing and took my degree work all over again. So *I* talked her into it, because she never knew what she wanted to do. She always had her head in a book. Her world was and still is books, even though she is married and has raised three children of her own and has two adopted children."

Boletta and Beba met and married their husbands on the West Coast, and after a few years the two couples, who were good friends, decided to continue their careers back east, where they have remained ever since. The twins' mother considered their move east as an unforgivable slap in the face, always referring to it as "an abandonment." In retaliation, especially directed toward Beba, the mother now poured all her attentions on Elsie, who, long starved for her mother's approval, gladly took Beba's hallowed place.

But Beba says she was "happy and ready" to break loose because she no longer had to worry about her husband's and mother's growing list of disagreements, and she could concentrate on having a family. Both twins eventually had three children of their own. In fact, as they love to recount in great detail, their first babies were boys, due and born on the very same day. Boletta "beat" Beba by delivering her son just a few hours earlier. Their second births also had the same due date, but Boletta miscarried at five months, and according to Beba, she talked Boletta into trying again right away.

Years later, she says she also talked Boletta into adopting two babies who were premature and struggling for life in the hospital where Boletta was working. Beba had been a foster parent to two teenagers at one time, and she felt it would be a rewarding experience for her sister. Unfortunately, Boletta's adopted children had a problematic childhood and adolescence, and only recently were diagnosed as schizophrenic. Beba somberly admits that her advice to her sister to adopt "may not have been good."

The power this woman gives herself over her twin and others undoubtedly derives from her relationship to her mother. It is a disconcerting, thrilling, downright narcissistic empowerment, and yet she mixes it with a genuine love and concern for her twin. When she related the following story about Boletta's brush with death, she focused on how she saved her sister. All other players, including Boletta's husband, fade into the background.

Several years ago, Boletta was leading an active, physically strenuous life, but was suddenly bedridden with a debilitating arthritic condition that was dangerously weakening all her joints. The prognosis was alarming: Doctors told her she would be crippled and confined to a wheelchair within three months.

"Boletta sent her husband and kids away. She said she was going to talk to me. When she called, I said, 'Well, what are you doing?' And she said, 'Well, I'm lying in bed and I'm depressed, but I can't move, the prognosis is bad . . . I think I'm going to commit suicide.' And I said, 'Oh, no, you're not,' and I talked her out of it. She had told me that she had seen this kind of joint degeneration in her patients and she was ready to commit suicide, but she *needed to talk to me*. I'm not a psychologist, but I knew I needed to act. So I called her husband and said, what are you *doing* leaving her alone? He did come back, talked to her for several days, and within a few months she was well. When we celebrated our parents' fiftieth wedding anniversary, that gave me another chance to talk to her."

Eight years later, and within two years of each other, both parents died. The father suffered a long bout with Alzheimer's ("I'm a specialist on Alzheimer's, I give support groups and lectures on the topic," says Beba when describing her emotional witness to her father's growing dementia). The mother suffered a cerebral hemorrhage, and was dead in three days, attended by only Elsie and Boletta: Elsie claims to this day that she couldn't reach Beba.

"Hey! I sleep in my house, I'm at work where I can be reached, my children were home," says Beba, raising her arms in exasperation. Finally Boletta's husband alerted her that the mother was dying. Power was handed back to Beba, however, when she called the hospital early one morning and was the one who first learned of the mother's death. "I was doing a death-and-dying seminar. . . . I didn't have a chance to get out before she died. After I talked to the hospital, I had the opportunity of calling my sisters and tell them of the death . . . I was able to chat with them, so I became a part of that."

Chat with them! I exclaimed.

"Yes, it was awful," Beba allows, her voice getting softer. "But people do things for different reasons. Elsie had a need to do that. She had a period of time where she really tried to be Boletta's best friend. I don't have a need for that. I deal with death and dying in my job and I know that families do crazy things. I don't appreciate it at all. She's always been very competitive, so I have to be real sensitive to that."

It was understood that there would be no memorial service as stipulated by the mother. Feeling the need for solace, Beba decided to join her husband in Spain, where he was working. When she got to Spain, she learned that Elsie had gone ahead and had a memorial service. It was a devastating blow from a younger sister who never before had such power. Sure of her twin sister's love and devotion, Beba concentrates on her history with Elsie. "She is so busy at trying to compete that she doesn't understand that it's not necessary, so she does odd things that I don't appreciate. It's really a very fine relationship, but I get upset sometimes, like now with the estate being settled so slowly by Elsie, who is the executor. I get annoyed with her because I think that she's trying to prove something."

While she talks about the delayed settlement and her sister's "simple decisions," Beba's forehead turns a bright crimson. "I could easily do the job because it is easy for me to think." When she recently offered to relieve Elsie of her executor duties, Beba acknowledges that "it nearly killed Elsie.

"I get very mad at her, but thank goodness there are a lot of miles between us so she doesn't see any of it."

Minutes earlier Beba had said that she and her twin were "very sensitive" to Elsie, noting that she and Boletta decided to name Boletta's second child after Elsie (Beba had named her only daughter after her twin). As we parted Beba told me, "Sisters are a real job when you are trying to keep things smooth, it's like marriage."

Since 1979, more than one hundred sets of reared-apart twins and triplets, identical and fraternal, have been studied by a team of social and medical scientists at the University of Minnesota. Based on the dramatic evidence of similarities in personalities and behavior of twins reared apart since birth, the twin study maintains that genetics play a decisive role in our development. But the study also concludes that the genetic factor does not preclude or detract from the importance of parenting and education, and other early external interventions. For example, according to the study, if the trait of leadership is defined as genetically based, we can also acknowledge that when parents, teachers, and friends consistently react to this particular trait in a child, the child's role as "a leader" is thus maintained.[3]

The Minnesota premise supports what has been demonstrated in this book, which is that we are products of many external factors, from parental favoritism to birth order but are also products of one another's innate personalities. Beba undoubtedly had the trait of strength and leadership to which her mother responded. Boletta was more reticent, not as stimulating to her mother. The most victimized in this arrangement was perhaps Elsie, who had to wait so long for her mother's acceptance.

Twins Gaining Strength from Each Other

Gloria and Lucy look out from the picture taken in 1925 when they were "four going on five." Precious identical twins with round dark eyes and bobbed black hair, they are dressed alike in white pinafores made by their mother, and look very smart in white lace knee-highs and black leather single-strap shoes. Despite their best party appearance as they pose in front of the hollyhocks in their backyard garden, the twins have an audacious air, with Gloria's arm around Lucy's shoulder. They look as if they were sharing a naughty deed.

"Look at our bangs." Gloria laughs, showing the picture again. "We needed a haircut, so we each cut each other's bangs just before the picture was taken. We chopped them. There was nothing Mother could do about it."

189

The twins' parents were a warm and generous couple who enjoyed such tricks from their little girls. First cousins from a large Jewish family, they had married and settled in a small New Jersey town where neighbors were often cousins as well and everyone knew everyone's business. The twins' mother was a full-time homemaker always available to her children, and their father was a builder who "adored" his family. Gloria remembers that there "seemed to be no favorites" among her and her twin, and her two other sisters (one is four years older and the other four years younger).

"On Saturdays our father would assign us our chores by wrapping a white handkerchief in his hand. One end of the handkerchief was knotted, and the knot was hidden in the palm of his hand. Whoever chose the knotted end was spared the cleaning. Often it was our baby sister who was spared, but no one minded, we all adored her."

Despite all this love in the family, the twins grew to be "shy and nervous" girls. When they were very young, their parents noted they were always "daydreaming" or not looking at them when spoken to; the only way their mother could get their attention was to tap their arms lightly before she spoke. By the time they entered school they had learned to play with the children in their neighborhood, but they were still so nervous about talking to other children that they would each have to carry a white handkerchief for their sweaty palms. When they entered school, many of the children were fascinated by these shy, wide-eyed identical twins, but they made fun of them for talking with an unusual accent.

No one understood the source of the girls' growing nervousness until the third grade, when a teacher kept them after school and deliberately asked them a question with a book in front of his face. There was no response from either Gloria or Lucy, who were considered excellent students. When he put the book down, he asked them sternly, "What did I say?" "You didn't say anything," the twins answered sadly, twisting their handkerchiefs. They were frightened, what were they doing wrong? Again, with the book in front of his face, the teacher asked a question. Again, no response from either twin. This time when he put the book down, he sternly and accusingly asked if they "read lips."

"We didn't know what he meant, we had never heard of this, so we laughed," recalls Gloria. "We ran home to tell our mother."

It was only after that episode that the twins were examined carefully and finally diagnosed as deaf. They had "naturally learned to lip-read." The deafness remained undetected for as long as it did because they lived in an era when pediatric care was minimal, and because the twins had a natural ability to discern words from moving lips.

Gloria and Lucy drew closer together when they faced lessons in hearing schools with "mean teachers" who refused to hold still and stand in front of the room so that the deaf twins would be able to read their lips. When Gloria once asked her teacher to "hold still up front," the teacher retorted in front of all the students, "If you can't understand, you don't belong here."

By high school the twins were wearing their first hearing aids—two heavy batteries strapped to the legs with a long cord strung up through their clothes. Gloria remembers vividly how embarrassed they were to be so "hitched up." Boys would pull on the cords during gym period, and the teasing was sometimes so intolerable that she and Lucy would take the bulky equipment off and hide it in brown paper bags.

Despite all this embarrassment, the twins never felt any sense of hopelessness. They had each other and the love of their family. Equally significant, says Gloria, they were "athletically matched," a feat that gave them strength the rest of their lives. Everyone knew that the twins could skate, play ball, run, and beat anyone who challenged them. In softball, their favorite sport first learned on the dirt lots in the neighborhood, Gloria was always the pitcher, Lucy the catcher. Whenever teams had to be selected, they were chosen first— every child's dream.

Just before graduation from high school, the girls met a married cousin who was deaf and who told them about Gallaudet College in Washington, D.C. "We were thrilled," says Gloria, "but he told us that we first had to learn to use sign language before we could apply. He introduced us to a man teaching night school in sign. Before going to the first class, we looked it up in the *Book of Knowledge* and tried to memorize all the signs. When we went to the class it was all old people, who had a ball watching these two kids being taught. We were *so* embarrassed with things like . . . the sign for 'please' is rubbing the chest . . . it made us laugh and our hands were dripping."

But together they passed the course. After high school, the twins first had to attend a residential state school for the deaf, where they could take preliminary courses before qualifying for Gallaudet. It was the first time they had been in a school for the nonhearing. "We blossomed, we were top bananas," says Gloria, beaming. "We were twins, a novelty, and we graduated from a hearing high school." In a year Gloria passed the entrance exam and in 1939 entered Gallaudet as one of 150 students. Lucy was third on the waiting list, so she continued at the state school for a year before joining Gloria. "It wasn't hard being without Lucy," says Gloria, anticipating my question. "We both needed the challenge and separation. But every award I got at Gallaudet, Lucy got the next year. We competed, but it was not in a vicious way. When we fenced together we could never take the sport seriously, and we would get so hysterical laughing."

The twins also fought, as young sisters do, especially over the hand-me-downs from their older sister, sent to school by their mother. But their fights never lasted long, says Gloria; they were having too much fun. "We both lost our shyness at Gallaudet." They also gained a tremendous amount of respect for and a sense of dedication to the deaf community. Both women married deaf men, and both sets of husbands and wives are strong advocates for national services for the hearing-impaired. Gloria and Lucy were unable to have children; Gloria adopted two hearing children, one of whom is mildly retarded; Lucy was unable to adopt—thus defining one of the few differences between them and that imposed by state adoption regulations.

Gloria enjoys telling all the "spooky" twin stories. When Gloria was at Gallaudet and Lucy in New Jersey, their "identical" letters crossed in the mail, each saying she had just read *Gone with the Wind* and each quoting her favorite passage—the very same passage. And then there were the many times, when Gloria lived in Michigan and Lucy lived in Illinois, that they exchanged and surprised each other with the very same Christmas presents: the pewter pitchers, bags from France, portraits in leather frames. They also always got sick with the same illness, just as they had during childhood. When Gloria learned that she had to have hip surgery, Lucy called to say she was having hip surgery.

Then, five years ago, things began to go differently for Lucy. While her husband was in the hospital recovering from a mild heart attack, Lucy felt chest pains and called the paramedics herself on her TYY system (the phone communications for the hearing-disabled). For five days she was hospitalized for a mild heart attack. Before she returned home she took a stress test, which she told her sister over the TYY "was very difficult." Two days later, while at home with her husband and a nurse, and just settling down to watch the evening news, Lucy collapsed and died of a massive heart attack.

Gloria feels bad that she wasn't there, but she was recovering from her hip surgery. She did manage to speak at Lucy's funeral, however, and it has left her with a tremendous sense of pride and closure. "It was attended by seven hundred people, Lucy's former students, their parents, her colleagues. She was a strong advocate for TTYs and had much to do with their being freely available in the state of Illinois. There are also scholarships named after Lucy. When I stepped up to the podium, I could see the astonished look on everyone's faces. It was as if Lucy were up there looking at them, we look so alike. I relieved their grief. I told them right away that Lucy was so polite, even the day she was born she said, 'You go first.'"

Gloria can talk about Lucy without crying; she is so proud of her sister and continues the volunteer work they shared in Florida, where both sisters worked four months of the year with hearing-impaired senior citizens. "We are both people-persons, activists," she notes. "Both of us needed to be needed."

Gloria is now seventy; I tell her she looks sixty. "But I feel forty-five," she laughs. She is a petite, handsome woman, strong from her years of playing sports. Her youthful look also stems from a constant smile and apparent pleasure she gets from talking with people. She is so totally aware of how her struggle with deafness was aided by being a twin. When she and Lucy "blossomed" after high school, they did it together and then were able to go their separate ways, and come together when they needed or wanted to.

"My only grief is that I had not been with Lucy more. We

were just getting ready to go back to Florida, and we were going to write a book about twins and our experience. But it never happened.

"I thought of doing it myself, but it wouldn't be the same," says Gloria, smiling.

Gloria and Lucy's story is unique, but I include it because it shows how sisters can support each other during challenging, difficult times without losing their love and joy of life. I never knew Lucy, but from what Gloria has told me, I am convinced Lucy enjoyed people and teaching as much as her sister does. I was also impressed with how they could healthily compete with each other. Gloria enjoyed telling me how Lucy followed her a year behind in college but won the very same prizes and citations. She was also very proud of the work she and Lucy did for the hearing-impaired. My guess is that Gloria will eventually write the book about deaf twins, because once she has recovered from the loss of her sister, she will go back to being the autonomous twin.

The following chapter on the death of a sister was inspired by Gloria's story of Lucy's funeral. Also, when I interviewed young Tanya, I asked her what she would do if her twin were to die before her, and she responded immediately, as if she knew the question well. "That would be the hardest thing. I can't imagine anything worse happening." In fact, says Tanya, her voice getting thick, "If I think about her being in an accident or something, I think I would really lose it. With anybody else, I would be strong and try to get through it. But I think with her . . . it just would be too awful. I know she has the very same feelings. We've talked about this, not a lot. But if our deaths were to be premature, not in our eighties . . . not that it would be easy anytime. I don't even like to think about it."

Most women don't like to think about the death of a sister. Good or bad, sisters are inextricably connected, so that one sister's death is threatening to the other's survival. The very thought of a sister's death may also be a reminder of how much needs to be reconciled and understood; the welling of tears tells how much caring does exist.

9

▽

In Her Memory:
The Death of a Sister

A TEN-YEAR-OLD GIRL developed a reaction to her teenage sister's sudden death that was frightening to witness, but all too revealing of her anguish. Without warning, she would tightly grab hold of an object, such as a doorknob or the end of a table, or a bed, and firmly plant her feet on the floor, making an intense singular motion with her whole body, as if she were grounding herself. Refusing psychotherapy, the girl suffered this way for nearly two years until, with her mother's example of strength and hope, she was able to begin her life anew, without her sister. "I took her out of school and we lived in Italy for a year," said her mother. "I wanted to show her that we could both survive."

It is a dramatic and unusual example, and yet this young sister's attempt to "ground herself" proclaims the devastation a woman feels, at any age, when she loses her sister.

The taunts and jeers of childhood still ring in our ears:
"Drop dead, stupid!"
"You could have killed me!"
"Bang! Bang! You're dead!"
"I wish you were never born."

Except for traces of guilt from our childhood games and death wishes, the last thing we want is for our sisters to die. Grown women openly worry over the fact that their sisters smoke, work too hard, eat fatty foods, or neglect to have their mammograms. At least ten of the sisters in the survey remarked to me how deeply concerned they were about the fact that their sisters smoked. "My sister won't let me bring it up," said one woman in her late forties, whose older sister has been smoking since she was in her teens, and now has bronchial problems. "For her birthday, I am thinking of giving her sessions with a hypnotist, like I did for my mother-in-law. But I don't know if she will accept it."

"I don't want to think about it," said many a woman when I asked if they ever thought of their sister's death. "It would kill me," declared a twenty-year-old woman who claimed to be disengaged from her younger sister. "It's too horrible to contemplate," said a woman in her thirties with two sisters. "I put it in the same category as the death of my children. Sisters aren't supposed to die."

Most of us expect our parents to die before we do and therefore grateful there is some emotional preparation for, or acceptance of, their death. But when a sister dies, it is typically a frightening and threatening experience carried with you long after her demise. No matter how different you are, you shared a life and so, in turn, you share the death. I agree that a sister's death *is* uncomfortable to think about, and yet the subject cannot be ignored because it so clearly demonstrates the emotional and feminine connection between biological sisters.

Doctors tell us that women whose sisters have died of cancer carry a tremendous anxiety, almost a premonition that they, too, will die of cancer. It is a justifiable anxiety, given the hereditary pattern of cancer; but the same premonition or dread may exist if the sister died of pneumonia, or committed suicide, or was in a fatal car crash. If it happened to her, it could happen to me, the sisterlike mind whispers.

I met with eight women whose sisters had died, and numerous stories of other surviving sisters were told to me. Most of these surviving sisters were fully aware of their premonition of death, the fear that they would die the same way. But they were also aware, particularly after the first year of mourning, how to control their anxiety—through better health care, diet, exercise, and the distraction of work and family. Judith Viorst had a sister who died of breast cancer during the time Viorst was writing her book on separation and loss, *Necessary Losses*. Viorst told me that she handles her anxiety with four breast checkups a year, one of which is a mammogram. "I don't think about it the rest of the time," says Viorst. "I have absolutely no power over whether I get breast cancer, but I can fight it with early detection."

Another woman went into crazed, manic activity *during* her sister's last months of life. In addition to being with her sister every day at the hospital, she built a dollhouse from scratch for her young daughter, finished her doctorate, worked part-time teaching, and sewed a quilt for her best friend. After her sister's death, a family friend, a psychiatrist, told her that she now had permission "to slow down and live her life."

A woman gains control over her sister's death by focusing on the enduring connection, the happier times that live through her own memory. The woman who built the dollhouse keeps many framed pictures in her home that show her sister in happier times, long before her terminal illness struck, looking beautiful, laughing with her children. She tells me that it's been ten years since her sister's death, but she and her family especially remember her sister each and every gathering, because "that is what she would want." And when Yom Kippur comes and she is remembered within the tradition of their faith, says her sister, "we are still teary-eyed."

My Sister's Halo—Fifty Years Later

Jane, a British woman, now in her early seventies, tells me about her sister Helen's death some fifty years ago, when she and her sister were on the brink of womanhood. In a forthright, apologetic manner, Jane insists that hers is "not a significant story," and that she doesn't like "to moan about the past." She boasts very properly, "I think we British are brought up fairly tough, which I imagine comes from our surviving the war years."

Jane's sister didn't die in an air raid, but rather from the insidious killer that links itself with war and catastrophe: tuberculosis. When describing her sister's illness, Jane maintained her aplomb and her poise seemed flawless, yet throughout our talk, she always described her sister as "three *and a half*" years older than she, with emphasis on the "half," as if the six months were crucial to the distance between them.

"I loved my sister, adored her. She really was lovely, very much the older sister," a hint that Helen was revered for her seniority from the time of nursery days. Later she mentions her father's long absences because of his career in the navy, and her parents' disappointment that she, Jane, wasn't a boy—"I was supposed to be named John."

"Helen had lots of friends, and I suppose I was just the little sister. If she had lived longer, we certainly would have gotten close. We didn't quarrel, but one looks back on people who died with sort of a halo around their heads, doesn't one? Because she was so very much loved, she must have been a very sweet person, I know that, I remember that now. She also had a quick sarcasm that she used on me, but I don't remember being jealous of her or anything like that, I just thought she was the best thing since sliced bread."

Living in a house set back, away from the neighbors, young Jane would deeply feel the isolation when her older sister went off to day school, especially after her brother was born when Jane was nine and her mother was so distracted with the care of the much-wanted son. Fortunately, Jane was an imaginative child, with a stubborn sense of positivism. "I can remember sitting in the apple trees, or dressing up in Mother's clothes in front of the mirror. In the afternoons I would sit for hours in the hedgerow waiting for Helen to come back from school," recalls Jane. "It was her school that separated us so much."

She is referring to the boarding school in northern England where Helen went when she was thirteen, leaving Jane resigned to the fact that she would see her sister only on holidays and in summertime. Four years later, just before Jane was finally due to enter boarding school herself, her parents were notified that Helen had taken seriously ill with a bout of pleurisy, a not uncommon problem because of England's damp, cold winters and poorly heated schools. Helen soon recovered, but her parents were never told (they learned at her funeral from a classmate) that four weeks later she had had a relapse that was so serious, the students were asked to pray for her in chapel. Apparently the relapse left a patch on her lung that lay in wait for a deadly infection.

That summer of 1936, the family headed for the south coast, where they and a bevy of young friends spent idyllic days, sailing, fishing, and playing Monopoly, the new game of the season, a panacea for the hard economic times. Then

201

oblivious of the world's mounting problems, Jane now shudders to think that all five of the young boys in their party were later killed in the war. "The only consolation is that my sister never knew that, because she died in 1937, before the war."

Their personal bomb fell in the midst of this blissful summer when a cousin joined the family for a two-week visit. "She was blond with very, very red cheeks, which should have warned one. We later learned she had tuberculosis, and that patch on Helen's lung which my parents didn't even know about was there ready to receive it. Over a period of a year Helen started this horrible cough."

Later that winter Jane returned from the boarding school she now attended to join her sister and be with their family for the holidays. With the memory of that night, Jane softens her voice, and speaks slower. "The whole scene was *La Bohème*-ish. We lived way in the country where we had oil lamps and candles. It was late, very cold, and Helen was waiting up for us. She was in her white dressing gown and she came to the door with a candle in her hand, coughing, coughing, coughing. I remember then thinking, this is quite awful . . . but I was quite young, there was *nothing* I could do."

A few months later Helen took critically ill as she excitedly prepared to go to a dance with a boyfriend on a naval vessel. Her parents summoned the "biggest specialist," who diagnosed the tuberculosis in both lungs and immediately put her in London's Brompton Hospital. "It was an old, rather gloomy, dismal place," Jane says peevishly, still frustrated that her sister was a victim of the times and system. "When I would visit her she would say to me, 'I'm being treated like a number, I've got to get out of here.' That really was how they referred to her, you see, not as a person; she was 'number six' for her treatments where they would collapse her lungs. And her room looked out on a sort of lift shaft, so there was no light. She had six months of that dreadful gloom. My father had been told by the specialists that there wasn't much hope, but he didn't tell my mother, which now I think is simply terrible."

At this point Jane's toughness wears down, and her voice cracks at the thought of her mother's suffering. "My mother was not emotionally prepared to lose her beloved first child. She fought tooth and nail to get her out of this old hospital and take her to Switzerland, where the air would be good for her. My father and the doctor gave in, knowing that she was going to die. Mother and the nurses were dressing her for the trip when Helen collapsed, and a few hours later she was dead. She just couldn't take it, you see, and what was worse, no one told my mother it was that serious.

"I was at boarding school when the headmistress, a very tough, unfeeling woman, summoned me into her office and told me, in not very nice terms, that my sister had died. The next day my parents collected me, we went to the funeral, and within three days I was back in school with no real comfort. I remember going to the loo and crying and crying. After days of this, my friends reported my condition to the headmistress, and she told them, 'Oh, leave her alone, she'll get over it.'

"I had weeks of this crying alone, but you know, somehow it didn't affect one in the end. I cried it out, I think. I think it's better to cry it out, don't you?" Jane finishes her story neatly, stacking the figures from her family history with a sad assuredness, "So there she went. I was sixteen, and she was nineteen and a half. She died in 1937, this is fifty-three years later."

But I ask if her parents had treated her differently after the death.

"Ah, well . . . that was something else. My mother went into the deepest mourning I've ever known. She was living then in a large house of a friend, and my father went abroad, keeping a stiff upper lip, I suppose. Mother had a room set aside for her where she placed a little antique silver vase and filled it with flowers every day. She would hang the vase in the room, and pray in there, mourn in there. Nobody else was in the room with her."

Her parents' way of mourning, concedes Jane, "totally, totally, shut me out." But with her self-appointment as protector of her parents, she adds, "I have to say that my mother and father were lovely people, they just couldn't help themselves. The one big resentment I have was that Helen went before we could become friends." Jane apparently knows that it was more than friendship that was lost. In mock despair, she grimaces. "Those twelve years that I looked after my parents, I would think, 'Oh, Helen, if you were only alive you could have shared some of this.' "

Ordinarily, Jane doesn't dwell on her sister's death, or on the repercussions it caused in her life. The memory of her sister lives energetically in Jane's only daughter, whose middle name is Helen. "I did that deliberately. I'm always seeing my sister in my daughter. It's incredible. They have the same sense of sarcasm, very bright, quick wit. Even the same voice and posture.

"I don't look for sympathy, for any of this," concludes Jane, brightly. "It's been fifty-three years. And I've talked a lot of rubbish." Just minutes earlier, however, she had quietly observed, "Helen's death *must* have affected me for years. Even *La Bohème*, I can't see that performance without . . . I remember the first time I saw it after she died, I was a mess for days afterwards. The music, the whole story, and the scene always conjures up my sister coming to the door in her dressing gown, with the candle, coughing, coughing."

The Bleak Side of Death—Guilt

Jane's brusque mention of how she was too young to realize the seriousness of her sister's illness, or to do anything about Helen's care when she lay in her bed pleading to leave the hospital, is disturbingly honest. Many sisters feel guilty about a sister's death. Part of the guilt stems from the anger that once played out between little sisters when they fought over a toy, a dress, or their place at the table next to Daddy. But much of the guilt stems from the frustration women feel about not having done their *best* to provide the right medical advice or protective care for their sisters. After all, weren't we raised to be sensitive to one another's needs, caring and considerate? Our self-made role as little mothers, or fairy godmothers who take care of all hurts, automatically sets us up for guilt when death of a loved one inevitably strikes. Surviving sisters weep that they didn't warn their sisters that extra hundredth time not to sit in the sun, or smoke that cigarette, or drive without a seat belt.

Cassandra Austen reveals her particular guilt in a heavy tome she wrote shortly after her sister, Jane, died in her arms. First, Cassandra declares her love for her sister, "I *have* lost a treasure ... she was the sun of my life, the gilder of every pleasure, the soother of every sorrow." Then she admits her fault as she scrupulously sees it: "I am conscious that my affection for her made me sometimes unjust to and negligent of others." And thus, she declares, she has received her punishment, "& I can acknowledge, more than as a general principle, the justice of the hand which has struck this blow."[1]

A more contemporary source of guilt, and an uncomfortable twist in this argument, comes from assisting in a sister's death. A doctor tells me that when one of her patients, a

205

forty-five-year-old woman with ovarian cancer, was sent home to die, her sister and her college-age daughter made the monumental, wrenching decision to end her suffering and provoke her death by administering barbiturates. This was done without the doctor's permission or inclusion, nor did the husband participate, though he was supportive of their intent. Such instances will undoubtedly be less rare, unless the laws are drastically changed. But mercy killing, euthanasia, or whatever you may wish to call it, unquestionably will be the ultimate occasion of guilt and love for the surviving sister who becomes involved in her sister's caretaking.

Caring Too Much Means Slow Healing: Kelly and Peg

Walter Toman contends that it is hardest for the youngest sibling to lose an oldest sibling, rather than the other way around, simply because the youngest has rarely been without the oldest. He also points out that it is typically difficult for the youngest surviving sibling to make new relationships (especially as a teenager or adult), because of the fear of again losing someone significant.[2] There is an indisputable element of reverence in the youngest's eyes as she keeps her sister "with her halo" as her ideal. If that vision goes, who is she to trust or turn to? The aftermath of a sister's death is further complicated if the sisters have been infused or dependent on each other from childhood for whatever the family reasons. With the oldest gone, the surviving sister feels a deep anger and isolation that may last for years.

Kelly vividly remembers sitting on her sister Peg's hospital bed, watching the historic moonwalk on television. "One giant step for mankind, one leap backward for two sisters," quips Kelly dryly. "Peg had had a mastectomy that was horribly disfiguring, and she had a lot of pain in her right arm. They weren't as careful as they are today. The whole time, though, she didn't want any of us to worry."

For the next five years Kelly and Peg talked every morning on the phone for more than an hour, twirling and twisting long phone cords, as they routinely did their household chores. In the afternoon, when their children were home from school or up from their naps, one sister would visit the other for more conversation and support. Sitting at the kitchen table or on the porch, they talked about everyday things, but they also talked about the cancer and their fear of losing each other. There was nothing they couldn't share, says Kelly, it had always been that way. But the question remains why the two sisters needed each other so strongly, and ultimately was it good for them, individually.

"As a child, I was distant with my mother, closer to my sister," explains Kelly, now forty-eight. "We were each other's confidantes. When Peg married at nineteen, I was ten years old. I never liked her husband. I cried from the moment I got up to the altar, until after the reception. I was in the bathroom crying my heart out, when my brother-in-law came in and shook me to get me to stop."

Kelly watched her sister closely during the first years of a difficult marriage. Confused and frightened, she soon pieced together the fact that Peg wasn't a virgin when she married and that this angered her husband, a religious man with strong beliefs, who physically abused her when she was pregnant with their second child. "I woke up in the middle of the night and Peg was home. Here she was, pregnant, spotting, with broken ribs, and a black eye. My parents didn't want to tell me what had happened. But there she was on the couch in the living room, battered. Later, my brother-in-law knew that I knew." No one else wanted to point the finger at the perpetrator, however. Peg's parents felt that this was "very unusual behavior for their son-in-law." And the parish priest they called in to console their daughter advised her to forgive her husband and never mention it again.

With a child's reasoning, Kelly decided "then and there that I had to be a virgin when I got married." But with wisdom that lasted into adulthood, she kept her distance from her hot-tempered brother-in-law.

In time, Kelly married a man Peg admired and felt comfortable with, because he was kind, not threatening like her own husband, whom she had grown to hate but was emotionally unable to leave. Kelly was always the "stronger" sister, the more aggressive, take-charge type who worked part-time with her husband in their accounting business. Peg, the reserved, subservient sister, was a full-time homemaker with a penchant for home-decorating crafts that she was always making for her family and friends. Their contrasting personalities didn't annoy them, says Kelly, but instead it enriched their relationship. And there were many things they shared, such as the love of their children and family rituals, and the lure of nature. The two sisters especially enjoyed when they could get away and spend a weekend at a small lake cottage where the pace and demands of their suburban life were forgotten. When the cancer hit the final time, they had just come from bicycling on back roads in the countryside, where they had gathered basketfuls of black-eyed Susans and clover. Peg complained to Kelly that the cycling was unusually hard, and that her knees hurt. Checking with her doctor the following week, she learned that the cancer had spread to the bone. Four years later after a wretched ordeal with debilitating treatments, Peg died.

"It's natural to lose a parent, but not a sibling," says Kelly, still aggravated about the humiliating circumstance of her sister's death, her disfiguration and suffering. "I miss her when I want to share something. I go to the cemetery . . . damn, it makes me angry still. No one goes to the cemetery except me. The longer someone is dead, the harder it is to go. She loved daisies, I bring those."

Estrangement Outlives the Dead

We know that sisters do hate each other, and that there are estrangements that last beyond a lifetime into the next generation. Death doesn't always resolve the differences between sisters. But just as the estrangement was passionately *involved* in a lifetime, so too does it *thrive* after death. The irony of connection is seen when one sister dies and the other continues to do nothing but complain over the way the funeral was managed, or who benefits most from the estate, or who was always the favorite, the privileged child. Such negative reactions may be more common among elderly sisters who are themselves in failing health, depressed, and feeling abandoned. Their anger at their dead sisters is more current, an acting-out of their fears of being alone, and their dread of their own death.

A Sense of Peace

There are always exceptions to how a family responds to death. One of the most poignant is when a sibling dies after a lifetime of mental handicap or mental illness. Two of the women I interviewed grew up with sisters who were mentally impeded; one had a retarded sister, the other a schizophrenic sister. Both had been brought up in homes that managed as best they could until the sisters were committed to an institution in their mid-teenage years. In the first family, the retarded sister had been doted on by the mother, dismissing her other daughters' needs as "selfish." In the second family, the parents were supportive of their children but heavily burdened by their schizophrenic daughter, who was hallucinating and hearing voices from an early age—a decidedly frightening phenomenon for the younger children to witness. Both women died of pneumonia in their early thirties; at the time of the deaths, the retarded woman was out of the mental institution working as a household maid to an elderly man to whom she was devoted; the schizophrenic woman was in the same sanitarium she had been in for fifteen years. I tell the stories together, though they have no personal connection, because the reaction of the surviving sisters was identical. That is, there was a tremendous sense of relief and open joy that their sisters had "found peace." Another notable similarity: long before their sisters' deaths, the oldest surviving sister in each family decided to enter a medical profession. Neither of these women drew a connection between their sister's handicap and their choice of career. When I suggested this, they were thoughtful. "It just happened," said the woman with the schizophrenic sister. "I've always wanted to be a doctor. But I do agree, it is a way of staying in touch."

The turning point in any grief, for parents, children, spouses, or siblings, is when we make the decision either to move forward and get on with life, or to stay as we were, caught in the grip of the deceased's life.[3] Some women move on with a crusade in their sister's name. I learned through a mutual friend of a woman in the Northeast whose sister died of breast cancer nine years ago, and who now directs a foundation that offers health care to the city's poor. She was very interested in being interviewed for this book but she canceled her first two appointments because of a busy schedule. On the last cancellation I changed my mind about making the trip, but she called me back to apologize, and insisted that we meet, saying, "It's so important to me." I got to her city on a cloudy, cold fall afternoon, and we met in her enormous, attractive office overlooking a gray skyline. Minutes into the interview I learned that her late sister was a half sister—a family configuration not included in my survey. I was embarrassed that I had neglected to ask that question when we first set up the interviews; and she had apparently failed to mention it to me or her friends because she has never considered her sister anything but a full-blooded sibling. I didn't inform her of the misunderstanding because her earnest manner and story were spellbinding, and I felt that what she had to say was legitimate for all sisters.

Yes, she is still angry with how her sister didn't get a second opinion until too late. Yes, she is still furious that her sister who was so beautiful had to go through such a horrible, disfiguring, humiliating experience (the same words Kelly used about her sister's fight with cancer). Yes, she will always be proud of how her sister fought up to the very last minute and didn't reach that stage of acceptance so widely esteemed by scholars of death.

But life goes on, she said gamely. She has left her career in teaching urban planning to directing a major nonprofit health foundation that offers, among many things, mammography exams to the indigent women in the city. With her arm sweeping the city outside, she said, "I'm putting all my energy into it."

She is also energizing her relationship with her youngest sister, who wasn't as involved in her sister's medical treatment, but who felt the loss just as deeply (indeed, they were full-blooded sisters). Though they live hundreds of miles apart, the two surviving sisters make a point to visit regularly, share vacations with their children, and talk on the

211

phone every week. "We don't worry about it, or work hard on it, it comes naturally, and we love being with each other.

"I'm not going to make that mistake again. There were years when I didn't see much of my older sister, and now I've lost her."

The Final Call for Intimacy

In Ingmar Bergman's disturbing, magnificent film *Cries and Whispers*, two sisters, Maria and Karin, come to the bedside of their dying sister Agnes. With their ambivalent, cruel thoughts and deceiving gestures they touch each other's faces and hands without offering a trusting love. In so doing, they act as their mother once did with them, and they leave us empty.[4]

I met with Betty, an eighty-five-year-old woman who revealed a story similar to that of Bergman's sisters, but without the masochism or narcissism. She, too, had a mother who provided a home for her, but never or rarely held her tightly, touched her face, kissed her warmly or shared a joke. A middle child, she and her older sister, Nan, and three brothers grew up in a flat over their parents' store in a small town. Hers was the only Jewish family in a Catholic neighborhood, and Betty carries fond memories of playing tag and "colors" with neighborhood children across the street in the park. Her memories of home life, however, hold little warmth or fondness.

"We did what our parents said, and that was it," says Betty. "My parents had to work very hard, and so did we." Her older sister, Nan, was a particularly obedient, serious child and her parents' favorite, but even she received a reserved affection and strict discipline. Betty can't forget, though, how Nan got "all the attention" from their father, who often brought her jewelry and made her beautiful clothes. But it was Betty, the so-called forgotten daughter, who managed to go to dances and have girlfriends into her room for sodas when her parents were downstairs working. As a young teen, Betty and six girlfriends formed a club called WAJIS, an acronym for the first letter of the first names of their boyfriends. With their "uniforms" of white blouses, knickers, and knee-socks, she and her friends had wonderful times, especially in the summer when they would picnic and gossip until it was late and time to come home.

It hadn't occurred to Betty until recently that her social life must have been hard on Nan. The two sisters shared a small bedroom and a three-quarters bed. Many a night, Betty would come home after one of the Jewish dances, or after skating on the lake with friends, and her sister would be feigning sleep after being home all night with her parents.

Betty contends that she and her sister were "never close," but later, she describes two surprise birthday parties planned for her by Nan, one when she was twelve, the other for her "Sweet Sixteen" birthday.

"Wasn't that proof that she cared for you?" I ask. Betty looks astounded. Yes, it was nice, but no, she shakes her head, she wanted the kind of proof offered by a hand, a kiss on the cheek, the words "I love you." Deprived of that physical and emotional "touching" from her mother, Betty longed for it from her sister, whom she admired and thought would take her mother's place.

Betty, who had started dating in her teens, married young, while Nan, who didn't date, continued to work for their father in a demanding and restrictive routine managing the store. By the time Nan did marry, she was too old to have a child and unable to adopt. Betty, meanwhile, had one child, a daughter whom she loved passionately. "I vowed I would never treat my daughter the way I was treated and it has paid off. She is a wonderful, thoughtful girl who loves me. When she was younger, I used to hug her and kiss her. I refused to bring her up the way I was brought up."

Nan also admired and loved Betty's daughter. Through her the two sisters developed and maintained a friendship, boosted by the fact that their husbands, who both owned clothing stores in nearby cities, "got on" so beautifully. For twenty-some years Betty and Nan made the hour-long car trip between their homes several times a month, to visit, go out to dinner, or look after their elderly parents. All that time, according to Betty, there was never the "touch" of intimacy. The only breakthrough came when Nan told Betty that she was always "jealous" of her having friends and dates when they were growing up.

As a married woman with no children, Nan continued to be the favorite of their elderly mother, whom she took into her home when their father died. Haplessly, Betty worked hard at gaining her mother's favor. Every Thursday she would drive to her sister's city and relieve Nan of the mother's care by taking her wherever she wanted to go or doing what errands were necessary. And each Thursday night she would return exhausted, and disappointed that her mother never reached out except to criticize that she wasn't doing things right or as well as Nan. Betty's husband would always ask, "Why do you go?" "She's my mother," Betty would insist, "and you have to be respectful."

"If you want to know how cold my mother really was," says Betty, "she told me on her deathbed, 'I want you to get away from me.'

"I wasn't hurt," Betty says cavalierly. "I *did* get away from her. My youngest brother was in the room and he heard her say it, he was her darling. I just let it roll off my back . . . but you *don't* say that to a child, 'get away from me.' "

214

A few years ago, Nan, by then a widow, was diagnosed with pancreatic cancer. In the three months of her painful illness she had full-time nursing care in her home, but she also had Betty, who lived at the house and wouldn't leave her side except to fetch whatever Nan or the nurses needed.

"Why don't you go home and take care of yourself?" Nan told her sister one day, realizing she had lost weight and was exhausted. "You look terrible."

"Thanks," joked Betty, "I'm here to take care of you."

Shortly before Nan died, she told Betty that she loved her.

"It was what I always wanted to hear," says Betty with tears welling, and twisting her hands. "But why did she wait so long to tell me? It's not so hard to say."

Betty did not continue to make close friendships in her adult years, as she had with the women in the WAJIS club. Perhaps most of her energy was focused on her sister, mother, and her own child. "I always say you have a lot of acquaintances, but few friends." There was always that search for intimacy, which few of her adult friends were able to give her sufficiently. Now widowed and living in a retirement center, Betty, who is physically fit and bright, tells me she has no intimate friends, and wishes she had at least one. But she does mention that last year her daughter gave her a wonderful birthday party at the retirement center (an attractive facility for "healthy" senior residents), to which "lots of people came." When I chide her that she can't be all that unknown or lonely, she smiles. She knows she has the potential for making friendships, she says while walking me outside. Some of the women she is acquainted with are seated on benches, chatting while waiting for a bus; they look up and greet us amicably. It's all too clear to Betty that she has to take the risk and reach for friends who may or may not give her a hug or a tender touch of the hand.

The Strength of Survival

Christina Rossetti, the nineteenth-century poet, wrote in her diary a surprisingly hope-filled tribute to Maria, her "irreplaceable sister and friend,"[5] with whom she was virtually affixed throughout her lifetime. While at her sister's funeral "the November day brightened, and the sun (I vividly remember) made a miniature rainbow in my eyelashes. I have often thought of that rainbow since."[6]

Even the most tragic sister stories have their miniature rainbows. I don't think it's blind optimism that paints the bright picture after death, but rather the resilience of women. I was particularly touched by Melanie, a twenty-three-year-old woman who had a two-month-old baby girl named after her sister Julie, who had died two years earlier. It was the baby her sister never saw, a baby such as Julie always wanted herself. But Melanie wasn't crying or morose the day we talked. She was comfortably telling me how her baby was "stubborn and strong" like her sister. "When my sister was just two and a half months old, she got so mad because she wanted to sit up, so she just did. My daughter is the same way. She's determined to hold your finger and pull. If I look at my daughter a certain way, I even see a likeness to my sister. I know I look like my sister, so it may be that simple, but I'm hoping she *is* like my sister . . . Julie was very independent, a go-getter."

When Julie was twelve, she suffered from kidney and lung disease and couldn't seem to stay well or gain weight. A popular girl, she didn't let her failing health keep her from her friends or school activities, but the challenge came when she was seventeen and was diagnosed as having a rare blood disease that usually doesn't strike children. After a brief remission, Julie became seriously ill, and tragically, one of

216

the drugs she was taking "caused" leukemia. When they informed her of the leukemia, Julie, who had been completely unaware of her impending death, cried for a day and then determinedly told the nurses, "Okay, I'll just fill out my adoption papers now."

"Julie was quite serious, she had always wanted to have children and she was planning for the future," explains Melanie. Two weeks later Julie died in a coma. For months she had fought the blood disease, participating in all decisions, including whether or not to have brain surgery or chemotherapy. In the end, Julie fought so violently that when they started to put a mask on her (to administer a drug), she cried out her mother's name in desperation. It was the last thing the mother heard as she was led by the nurses and taken out of the room away from Julie—something she has always regretted, feeling she had let her daughter down. But at least Melanie was able to remain at her sister's side until the very end. "I cried," said Melanie, "but I felt I had to keep my emotions up for my mother." Julie was only nineteen when she died, Melanie was twenty-one, and newly married.

How does a woman survive such a loss? Melanie did it by naming her new baby daughter after her sister, and by every day talking to her mother, who lives hundreds of miles away. She admits, however, that she is having trouble making new friends in the town where she and her husband recently moved. And she knows that her mother is clinging to her, but for now she can't let go. "We need each other."

Most important, Melanie recognizes that she did what she could for Julie, making her last days as comfortable as possible. "At the hospital I read her the books she loved when we were kids. I read *Eloise,* her favorite, and *The Little Engine That Could,* just because of what it had to say. I would tell her all the latest with her favorite soap operas. And I also kept in touch with all her friends for her . . . I still do." They had fought when they were little, observed Melanie earlier, but they were also close, sharing the same friends and "always going everywhere together."

The first night after Julie died, Melanie slept in a room with a friend because she was terrified of her nightmares from the past week, in which Julie appeared without her hair, bloated and hemorrhaging, just as she looked in the hospital. "I somehow thought she was going to come back looking like she did when she died and be mad at me. Or come back and laugh at me for being scared."

Now the nightmares are gone, says Melanie, and they've been replaced by frequent "happier dreams" where "Julie is always alive."

"The dreams are very realistic, Julie is always doing things with me. It's as if we are taking up right where we left off."

Though we don't like to consider the death of a sister, we can learn from these stories how sensitive and deep the sisters' union is. As in one woman's emotional tribute to her forty-nine-year-old sister who had died of ovarian cancer just a year ago:

"I think of her every day, I ask her for help and I know she has been there. I feel very connected to her. I feel she has left me with a great deal. I have this sense of being an extremely fortunate person, I felt that way all my life because of her, and I still feel that. When I said good-bye to her on that Tuesday, she died that Friday. I told her that I loved her and she told me I was beautiful and she loved me too. Everyone thought I was the strong one, but I knew she was. She was more beautiful than ever. Her body was enlarged from the treatments, but she wore baggy clothes. She was radiant. She had conquered pain, she had the power to do that with her mind."

10

▽

"I Need Your Help"

PROFESSIONAL PHOTOGRAPHER Birgitta Ralston, who is sister-less and a magnificent pictorial chronicler of sisters, ob-serves that "Some sisters have ongoing arguments, but even that seems better than the silence of being alone in your generation."[1] Ralston makes the familiar assumption that in times of stress or need, sisters turn to each other for support. It is not a naive assumption. As most of us already know and as the stories in the book demonstrate, sisters *do* come to the rescue in times of need. They listen, or give needed advice, or simply embrace each other with no words spoken, but they usually make themselves available to their frightened or ailing sisters when they can because it is within the expecta-tions of the gender and the relationship. Unfortunately, crisis or change may also challenge or threaten the sister relationship, particularly when the stress centers on the care of one or both parents.

When Crisis Hits

All but a few of the stories told to me were marked by some major change or crisis that in turn affected the sisterly bond. Crisis, the very "stuff" of life, can be avoided by very few of us in a lifetime. Whether it be a husband's abandonment, the death of a child, a parent's failing health, a job loss, or one's own poor health, it is a *crisis* that jars our familiar, safe world and shakes the very foundations of our existence. Many women told me that if a crisis were to hit their lives, they knew they could depend on their sisters, but they thought or imagined that they would first call on their women friends. It was interesting to note, however, that the women who did report a crisis, such as learning they had cancer, were the ones who called on their sisters first. Perhaps the explanation is that when a woman is actually, and not theoretically, faced with a life-threatening situation, she returns to her family of origin for empathy, compassion, and a sharing of strength. A sixty-five-year-old woman with three sisters who have supported each other through everything from alcoholism to bone cancer, observes wisely, "In times of crisis . . . women need to mother themselves, you can do that through your sisters."

"You are all I have," has been said by many a woman to her sister in a time of need, even though she is rich with support from friends, husband, and children. One theory as to why we turn to our sisters was given by a woman whose older sister's teenager was hospitalized for drug abuse. Her sister had been leaning heavily on her for weeks, a marked change in their relationship that in the past had always been rather cavalier. "Right now my sister sees the strong part of herself in me," reasons this woman, "and she needs to call on that strong part in order to get through this."

*   *   *

Dr. Anne Moore is a New York oncologist specializing in breast cancer. For years she has witnessed firsthand the "amazing support of sisters" during times of hope and despair in the diagnosis and treatment of cancer. Moore emphasizes that she has nothing but respect and admiration for the sister who comes to her ailing sister's side, but she also points out that the support may add another dimension or complication to the illness. In the typical case where the sister is so attentive that she accompanies her sister through all the appointments, goes through the radiation or chemotherapy treatments with her, or practically feels every stitch the surgeon puts in, there can be a bonding that is burdensome to the patient, who is already and needlessly steeped in guilt for having cancer, for not caring for her body, or for upsetting her husband and children.

"It adds another worry to the patient," says Moore. "The worry that her sister is being so affected by her own cancer. Patients often say, 'I feel bad dragging my sister along, I can see how worried she is.'"

Out of concern for her ailing sister, the healthy sister often insists on second, third, and fourth opinions, miracle diets, a trip away, anything to ward off the threat of death. Second opinions are always respected, says Moore, but it is difficult for the sister with cancer to feel that she has to answer to her sister's expectations of a cure, and to her sister's natural anger and denial that all this is taking place. The sister with cancer ends up "carrying her beloved sister and her anxiety," says Moore, "and it is an added burden."

Moore knows and is relieved that there are innumerable, unrecorded times when sisters support each other without adding to the burden. In the hospital, sisters bring makeup, music, and laughter, and provide endless trips in the wheelchair up and down the corridors. They read to their sisters, talk to them, rub their sore limbs, buy them wigs, nap with them, cry with them, and listen, listen. One woman told me that she broke hospital rules and dressed her sister up, marched her out of the hospital to take her to the finest restaurant in Chicago. By the time they came out of the restaurant everyone was staring at her because her IV was "wrapped around her knees."

Turning to sisters for support is not a universal or automatic reflex to tragedy. Much has to do with each sister's stage of development, or her place in the family order. Several women said they have always felt guilty for not being able to give the support that was needed during their childhood, adolescence, or young adult years, when their concern for their sisters' problems was ambivalent or they simply weren't equipped to handle major problems that should appropriately be dealt with by parents and professionals. Watching a sister waste away or collapse with an eating disorder is a terrifying thing to a teenage or school-age girl. She feels not only powerless, but frightened that she may have contributed to the illness with her constant quarrels, or that she, too, may have such tendencies to abuse her body.

The youngest sister of three says she felt "useless" in supporting her oldest sister during her battle with cancer because her middle sister, who had always been the "take-charge" one, was "running the whole show. I felt completely left out."

A forty-one-year-old woman who today is extremely supportive of her sister during her recent struggle with Lyme disease, still finds it hard to relinquish her guilt over her teenage years when she was unable to help her sister through a depression and separation anxiety.

"Around the time I went to college and my sister was at home, things got really bad . . . my sister became borderline suicidal. I tried to be supportive, but I couldn't help her. She wanted me to be supportive, and she didn't reject my attempts; I just couldn't help her the way she wanted."

Adulthood, too, has its drawbacks in our expectations of support from sisters whom we make into the perfect mommies. Some women complained about how their sisters weren't able to spend time with them during a crisis, because they were "too wrapped up" in their own jobs and families. The very fact that this feeling of abandonment is a complaint, however, indicates how important the sister relationship and support system is. As repeatedly pointed out throughout this book, each family is different in its responses and we are products of our families. But generally, most of us assume that our sisters would respond if we should personally need them. And our histories prove that this is usually so.

Sister Support Is Universal

There are numerous studies that show how cultures differ in their family and sibling support, though no study focuses on sisters. This book cannot possibly address the cultural issue because it doesn't have the appropriate sample; but I will note that in all of the cultures represented in this book—American, European, Middle Eastern, Hispanic, and black—the women all testified to biological sisterhood support, but they may have *expressed* it differently, or experienced it in different degrees. Whether they spoke of it passionately or stoically, the support was there.

Ramona is twenty-two years older than her sister, Tina. To some, that age span diminishes the very possibility of bonding, but Ramona has always counted on being there for Tina and expects that love to be returned. This is not a surrogate

BETWEEN SISTERS

mother–child relationship, as one might imagine. Ramona's mother took loving and full care of Tina, just as she once did with Ramona and her three brothers when they lived on a small vegetable farm in Mexico. But Ramona remembers how she used to "instruct" her mother that Tina should always be "dressed nice and clean," and it was Ramona who sent her sister beautiful handmade clothing when she moved to the States. Every summer Tina would visit her older sister, who soon married and had three children of her own. One night Tina, then twenty, saw her brother-in-law, drunk and furious, kick Ramona in the stomach. From that moment on the sisters became each other's stalwart protectors and constant support systems.

"My husband is now mad to Tina because she go and call the police," says Ramona proudly. "He won't talk to her. But I tell her, 'Tina, don't worry. He's a crazy person.' So now if I want to go to Mexico and see my family, I do what I want and he don't bother me." According to Ramona's faith and culture, divorce is out of the question, but gradually she is building her defenses and a life of her own with her baby sister standing by. "He don't drink . . . he stay at home. He doesn't speak to Tina. We don't care, we think of him as a little pillow on the sofa."

Tina has now moved permanently to the same city where Ramona lives, and they both work as housekeepers and share jobs on the weekends. Ramona claims to "take care" of Tina by watching over her social life, a job she presents as an act of love, not control, which Tina welcomes and appreciates. "Ramona wants me to enjoy life," she says smiling warmly at her sister.

"I don't want Tina to live the life I lived," says Ramona with no show of martyrdom. "I am not unhappy now. I like to do my hair pretty and see all my women friends. I say the same thing to my daughter: 'Take care of yourself. If a man

224

is not nice to you, send him back home.' I was with my husband nine years, he was very nice before we got married, we grew up in the same town. But it was very, very terrible after we married. I don't want that to happen to Tina."

Giving a Free Rein to Love and Support: Mattie and Tess

Support for a sister may ultimately mean stepping back and letting her make her own decisions. In Ramona and Tina's tight-knit family that may not be as likely as in an urban American family where sisters by choice are often separated by career, friends, and family duties. Also, in the past ten or fifteen years with the rise of twelve-step programs, our society has been putting a greater emphasis on the need to "let go with love," that is, don't try to control other people's lives. Where do sisters draw that line between support and control? For many the moment comes when the support is recognized as detrimental to growth, or when the crisis is so overwhelming the supporting sister no longer has the energy to cope. It is then that the stricken sister may gratefully find her reserved strength.

Ever since Mattie can remember, her life has been filled with needy people. Growing up during the Depression in a small town in the Southwest, she and her twin sister, Tess, watched their parents unflinchingly assist countless needy families who were without jobs or unable to sell their crops. "We lived in a teacherage because my father was the school principal and my mother was a teacher," says Mattie in her soft drawl. "The house wasn't very large, but my memory is of our kitchen with a trestle-like table and many, many people eating around it from morning through night. We had a nursemaid while mother taught and usually a grandmother was there. The first thing they did in the morning was put on an enormous pot of pinto beans, it was sort of

225

a filler for whatever they were serving. It sounds like grim times, but it wasn't for the children. It was very busy."

Mattie talks about the times when she and her twin, Tess, and their cousins who lived with them, were allowed to play all day in the surrounding canyons, where they would walk on the railroad trestles or climb up and behind the immense red-colored rocks. Nobody ever worried about them, says Mattie, the grown-ups knew the children would come home "when they were hungry." Then without warning tragedy instigated by the Depression hit the family. Mattie's father drove to Arizona to pick up a townsman and his family who were stranded without money or jobs. On the way home late at night, his car was hit by a train, just thirty miles from home, killing everyone in the car. "From then on our world changed and my mother worried about us," says Mattie. "My sister Tess and I were eight."

A year later the anxiety peaked again when Mattie was bedridden for eighteen months with rheumatic fever. "My mother and aunt thought I wouldn't survive, so they made Tess my caretaker once I was back in school. They told her to not let me run, and to watch me if I got pale. Tess tells me that several times she went to school crying because she thought that when she came back home I might be dead. She has always felt very protective toward me."

Given this history, it is amazing that Tess, as an adult, supported her twin sister's wish to be on her own and take risks in times of crisis. It happened when, after twenty-three years of marriage, Mattie gained enough courage to leave her alcoholic husband. It was a monumental decision for Mattie, who typically holds back from expressing her anger and tries hard to appease people who offend her. Though Tess was at first frantic about her sister, who had no money and two children to support, she finally gave in to Mattie's idea that she wanted to leave her husband and pursue a career elsewhere. Before her divorce, Mattie had been active in state politics and had held a small local office. Her plans were to become a lobbyist and work for some sort of non-profit organization. That was fourteen years ago. Today, each twin has successfully carved out a separate career and life-style. Mattie heads a major research organization, and Tess is a published novelist. Their concern for each other shows in the fact that they "never miss" their Saturday morning ritual of talking long-distance "for at least an hour." Mattie's personal problems continue as her grown children react to their parents' long and difficult marriage. Mattie tells me that Tess's advice isn't always what she wants to hear, but her opinions are minimal, says Mattie, and "well-meaning." Stepping back is not easy for these two who have been virtually inseparable.

"I was raised in the same crib with Tess. We always slept in the same bed until we were married. After my divorce it took me a long time to be able to sleep . . . I was so used to hearing someone's breathing," laughs Mattie without smiling. "My sister is very generous, good, and funny, she is a realist. I have many women friends, but it's not the same. My sister is a great comfort to me."

Last summer the two sisters ventured on a white-river raft trip on the Shenandoah. "Tess was always considered the athletic sister," says Mattie, "so it was interesting that I was the one that wanted to do this. It was supposed to be a tame ride, but the river was up and Tess fell in the first few minutes of the trip. The guides got her back in the raft immediately, but it frightened her a lot. Now she is begging me not to do that trip anymore like I have planned. But I was so touched by her that day. Everytime we would go through the rapids she would turn around and say, 'Are you all right?' and I would say, 'Are you all right?' And then, here I was saying, 'Now Tess, just stay in the bottom of the raft.' "

Mom and Dad Make a Difference

The whole picture of sisterly support and concern changes, or is at risk, when the crisis centers on the parents. Learning that your mother has Alzheimer's creates a markedly different dynamic between you and your sister(s) than learning that your husband is leaving you, or that your child is a manic-depressive, or that you have cancer. In the first instance, you and your sister have to collaborate to figure out the best care for your mother; whereas in the other two instances, your sister is called upon to respond to you and only you.

Ideally, when the crisis involves a parent, you intend to share the responsibility equally. But what if you live in the same city as your ailing mother, and your sister holds a full-time job five hundred miles away? Or what if your brother is contributing only money, but not time? Right away you are in a loaded, difficult situation that depends heavily on full cooperation and open communication, a tall order for most family members. Your decisions are further complicated by how you have always perceived each other in relation to your mother. If the sister at home feels she has always been the responsible one since childhood, and she perceives her sister as the privileged one, and her brother as the provider not the nurturer, the chances of the mother's care going smoothly are quite remote.

Nell, fifty, apologizes for how angry she feels every time her fifty-seven-year-old sister, Billy, visits their ailing ninety-year-old mother once or twice a year for a week. "Billy and her husband do a lot of things, they hang her drapes, wash her windows, repair a chair. Then Billy will say things like, 'I think you should take her to the doctor,' or, 'I think she should have her ears checked,' and I get very resentful. Fine, why don't you come here and do that, I'm thinking. *I'm* the one who comes to see her every week. *I'm* the one who makes sure she has food in her refrigerator, and I've got a full-time job as well. And then I think well that's really not fair, Billy lives away, I live here. I do resent that, but I know it's something in me. Billy does as much as she can, believe me, for someone living out of town."

These two women have a long history of cool separateness, even though Billy has lately tried to come closer to Nell, there has been little feeling of sharing, which they have always attributed to the distance in age and the contrast in their personalities. More powerful than age is the fact that Nell has always felt that her mother favored Billy, who was a more serious and studious child than Nell. Unfortunately, Nell has not been able to discuss with Billy her resentment over the mother's care. It isn't Nell's style to say how she feels, or to "get angry" with her sister. Nell boasts that she is working on an alternative plan of hiring regular help for handling her mother's laundry and shopping. The money spent is well worth it, she says. As for asking Billy to share the cost—that's apparently not even a consideration, because Nell sees herself as "better off" than her sister. There is actually an enormous amount of caring from the younger sister to the oldest—it is expressed not through words or embraces, but through financial considerations.

Another pair of sisters testified that there has never been any marked differences between them and their father, so the level of support during his nursing home care has been more comfortable and equitable, even though geographical distance is still a factor. The sister who lives away is responsible for all the legal- and paperwork. She also preschedules visits home several times a year, when she can visit her father daily, thus giving the other sister planned blocks of time when she can count on a respite.

229

We can prepare for our parents' health crises if the doors of communication are open between siblings. Several sisters mentioned that they have "worked out" or at least discussed the way they would share the care of their parents once their health fails. Two sisters whose parents are in their early seventies told me that they have mutually decided that if and when it's necessary, the older sister would care for the mother because of the "intensely difficult" relationship the mother has with the youngest. The younger sister, in turn, would handle her father, an "aloof" man who has always shown that she is his favorite.

Two distinct lessons emerge from these stories:

** When the crisis or change involves the parents, such as their failing health or death, the sisters' support system is complicated and affected by any unresolved history of jealousy or competition in the relationship with the parent.

** When the crisis or change involves *principally* the sister, such as her bout with a threatening illness, divorce, or the death of her husband or child, it is highly likely and assumed that the other sister or sisters will offer immediate and empathetic support.

For many sisters, these two lessons have been realized within one passage of time.

The Forgotten Bond Before the Quarrel: Rosalyn and Adeline

Rosalyn, with great calmness and objectivity, relates her story of a devastating quarrel she had with her sister Adeline two years after their parents' tragic death in a car crash. According to Rosalyn, it was a "frightening ordeal," with Adeline throwing dishes and hysterically crying at her sister. Up until the quarrel, the two sisters, both in their fifties, had been openly supportive of each other during their oppressive mourning. But under all that show of initial support was the lingering issue of Adeline's unspoken jealousy over Rosalyn's success in her career and her marriage.

"Our parents' death magnified our differences," observes Rosalyn in the professional, matter-of-fact tone I imagine she uses with her clients in her law practice. "Even as a teen, I was protective and Adeline was intimidated and jealous. I was more assertive and competitive in school, she was shy. Her dream was to marry and have children, 'the white picket fence' and all, she even used those words. I was more focused on my career. We both eventually married, but she divorced and has no children."

Since the quarrel, the two sisters only relate to each other through humorous birthday cards and "funny notes," mainly from Rosalyn. Both sisters were badly shaken by the words that spewed between them a year ago, and Rosalyn, at least, regrets that now they can only "connect through humor."

"I wonder if it would have been different if the crisis didn't involve your parents," I say.

"What do you mean?" Rosalyn says cautiously.

"Well, I have found that sisters who are deeply estranged still run to each other's side when one is stricken with a threatening personal situation, like cancer, divorce, or loss of a child."

Then in a soft and shaky voice, far different from the strong voice she used to talk about her parents' death and the quarrel, Rosalyn tells me how a year after the car crash and a year before the "outburst," Adeline had a "major cancer scare."

"I flew to Georgia and took her to the same hospital where our parents had died," says Rosalyn, crying for the first time during the interview. "I'm sorry, I didn't realize that this was so hard . . . I brought her back home to her place and she was okay. It was her birthday and I always make a big deal out of birthdays. We had a wonderful time. . . . I guess I love her very much . . . and I worry about her."

The Sting of Love: Linda

Linda was locked in a vicious, complicated battle with her younger sister over their mother's failing health. As we sat on her back porch looking out at clusters of colorful flowers, I kept thinking how this idyllic setting didn't fit the family nightmare Linda was describing in staggering detail. Though I taped the interview and took notes, it was nearly impossible to make sense of all the complicated tales and accusations, from stealing a dead uncle's silver, to rewriting the mother's will umpteen times, from stonewalling visits in the mother's home, to threatening letters between sisters and the mother. The crowning blow apparently was that Linda's oldest sister vehemently denies that the mother is mentally incapacitated and insists she doesn't need medical care.

At the start of our conversation, a bee flew into Linda's face and landed on the floor a few feet from our chairs. Rising slowly, Linda crept toward the bee and then quickly stepped on it, killing it. Returning to her chair, she remarked offhandedly, "That bee is my sister."

The hatred was there, but so was the ambivalence. Later, Linda misspoke: She meant to say "the best thing is." Instead, she said, "The worst thing is, if my mother dies I can cut off my relationship with my sister. My sister will have nothing to come back to me on." When she tried to correct herself, I took a gamble and asked, "Would you come to your sister's support if she was very ill or dying?"

"If you hit me at the right time, and she needed a kidney, I can't decide if I would give her one," she said with a glint in

232

her eye. "Isn't that terrible?" Then, after a long pause, Linda said resignedly, "I think I would, because I think my dad would want me to do it."

Linda had observed earlier that "all the goodness in my life comes from my father and the evil comes from my mother." Neither she nor her sister had ever been close to their mother, a woman who used to leave her young children unattended in a playpen while she went into town for hours to see friends or go shopping. Now both sisters are embroiled in an obsessive pitch for their dying mother's attention. As long as their battle involves their mother, they seem to be getting nowhere. And yet, in memory of her dead father, whom she loved dearly, Linda can imagine or even consider some sort of reconciliation with her sister if she should sorely need her.

The Imbalance of the Support System

It would be interesting for future evaluation to demonstrate whether sisters are more likely to support each other than are brothers, or brother–sister combinations. Sisters are *linked* emotionally, whereas brothers are more equipped with autonomy, so that when a change or crisis in their life occurs, such as a job loss or health scare, brothers may comfortably prefer to deliver a message of strength rather than need for support.

Some women told me their husbands don't even inform their brothers of major incidents in their lives, often citing the reason as there being "no point to it" when the brother lives so far away. I think the deciding factor is how flexible and empathic to each other the brothers have always been. I have presented this question many times to men and it never fails to create an emotional debate. One woman who sat on

233

my right at a dinner party became very upset because she felt that my theory implied her husband was "insensitive to his brother's needs." She went into great detail about how supportive and "nurturing" he has always been to his brother and how they keep in constant touch, something she hasn't been able to do with her own family. She also told me that her husband's mother had died when he was very young so he has always felt "responsible for his younger brother." As I say, each family is different, so we shouldn't make generalizations about the different styles among our sisters and brothers, but in this case it is noteworthy that the nurturing son was taking on the role of the nurturing mother, the woman.

Does Support Mean Intimacy?

We have examined how sisters are stereotyped as intimate but that, indeed, they often fear intimacy because it touches on the competition and vulnerability between them. This holds true even in time of crisis, but fortunately it doesn't have to weaken the strength of the support.

Connie was thirty-seven when she discovered that her husband had broken off a two-year affair with a woman with whom he was still deeply in love. At first her anger energized her and Connie found herself the most assertive and capable she had ever felt in her imbalanced relationship with her husband. Ironically, it was he who insisted that he wanted to stay in the marriage, even though he was depressed and confused. Frightened by his ambivalence and her dread of "breaking up the family," Connie nose-dived into a constant state of anxiety, afraid to even collect her child at the nursery school or venture to the grocery store. Her women friends were supportive, her therapist was a "godsend," but what she now recalls most was the support of her younger sister Marie.

"I never thought that Marie even cared about me," says Connie in retrospect. "Marie is only three years younger, but she leads a life totally different from mine. At the time of my crisis, she was divorced, with no kids, and dating a whole bunch of different guys. Before she came to be with me I couldn't help but think, 'what does she know about infidelity, or even about my fear of leaving the marriage?' "

But Marie and Connie went out each day for a week giving Connie the incentive to fight the growing agoraphobia. "One afternoon we took the children to the park and Marie and I sat on a blanket while they played. We sat there saying very little . . . finally she just let me talk and she didn't argue with me . . . I had expected her lectures on how I should leave him. Instead she told me that some day I could look back at this and laugh because I would have had my own affair. At first I was incensed that she would say such a thing, but it has proved to be true. And when I think about it, it didn't matter what she said, I was just so touched by the fact that she was there for me."

Intimacy doesn't have to be demonstrated with in-depth revelations of fears of death, or pending doom; it can be whatever the family is comfortable with in their expression of togetherness and strength. Two years ago when I was visiting my mother, her older sister Ellie was hospitalized and in a coma because of a sudden imbalance in her electrolytes. Mother and I hurried to the hospital, an hour's drive away. We were allowed into the intensive care unit to see Ellie for "just five minutes." A tiny woman, Ellie looked like a young child curled up under the blanket. My mother smoothed Ellie's hair and rubbed the top of her hand. "It's me, Ellie, it's Franny, I'm here," she said, over and over, while

I paced the room and looked away. Just as we were leaving, Ellie woke and started to cry, recognizing "Franny." My mother, who has never liked display of emotion, would have no part of it. "No crying, Ellie," she said lovingly but firmly. "You're going to be all right, your family is coming. I'm here." I hid my tears from Mother as well. Would another friend of Ellie's have allowed her to cry? It didn't matter. My mother spoke the lesson from her family of origin—"Don't cry." It was her uncanny signature of intimacy and support wrapped in one.

"What's a Six-Letter Word for Affection?" Adele and Evelyn

"I cannot say that my sister Evelyn is my 'best friend,' " says Adele, fifty-three. "We are close, not intimate. We don't exchange feelings, we never did. But neither did my family. I realize that I'm more intimate with my women friends. I exchange more personal feelings with my friends. But my sister will always be there."

Adele and Evelyn have had to depend on each other since they were born. Both their parents were deaf, but the two sisters had no hearing disabilities, which imposed on them, at an early age, the role of caretakers of their parents and themselves as well. Both girls could use sign language before they learned to speak. As the oldest, however, Evelyn carried most of the burden of interpreting for her parents. Neither sister had an intimate relationship with either parent, not necessarily because of the deafness (intimacy is possible through sign and body language), but because their mother had never known affection in her own family.

"My mother was the baby in a very large family," explains Adele. "She was only four when they discovered she was deaf and they sent her away to a special boarding school. She only saw her mother in the summer and her mother didn't know

236

how to communicate with her." As for their father, he was a formidable figure who suffered from paranoia when the girls were teenagers, an awkward, frightening time when they could "never approach him or talk to him." But Adele keeps "the softer memories" of her father when she was much younger—when he would hold her hand as they walked on the street, play Chinese checkers with her on summer evenings, or teach her how to make a tie on her pajama strings.

By the time she was eighteen, Evelyn married her high school sweetheart and gladly took off. "Then I became the one that had to be responsible," says Adele. "I ended up being the interpreter and my sign skills got better. I learned more than Evelyn ever had. It became a career for me. I went to college, Evelyn didn't. I went off to France for half a year, and I became more adventuresome. Evelyn had taken her risks early, but not anymore."

Their father died when the girls were in their twenties, leaving their mother "alone" with her older sister, Mabel, who could hear and finger-spell. "My mother was taking care of Aunt Mabel financially and practically, while Mabel was her hearing link," explained Adele. "Aunt Mabel was sixteen years older than my mother. They didn't like each other when they were growing up and they didn't like each other when they were living together, but they each needed the other." That arrangement worked for several years until Mabel died, and their mother's care became a full-time co-operative effort between Evelyn and Adele, who by then had families of their own. They visited their mother "religiously" once a week for ten years. "We worked it out that we should visit Mother together because it created less strain in the relationship," says Adele. One day the sisters discovered tiny cockroaches swimming in their mother's cereal, which their mother couldn't see. After that alarming incident, they took their mother into their homes, six months with Evelyn, six months with Adele. That arrangement went on for several years until the mother was in a car accident with Evelyn (she had refused to wear her seat belt) and had to be put in a nursing home. For the next three years, the two sisters each had to spend every other day with their mother in order to provide hearing interpretation with the nursing staff. All that time Adele was working part-time and managing her family of two children, and Evelyn was caring for her family of four children. Just a year ago, their mother died peacefully in her sleep as Adele was placing her mother's clean clothes in her dresser drawer. "We shared washing her clothes," Adele adds, as if it helps with the closure.

The amazing thing is that during all those years of cooperation and support with their immense load of responsibilities, Adele and Evelyn never shared intimacies. Adele claims that her sister is "too uncomfortable" with the fact that Adele sees a therapist. "We talk daily," says Adele. "We know a lot about each other's lives and the surface kinds of problems with kids and husbands, but it's pretty much at a fact level. When I told her some personal things that I have thought about, about my husband and myself . . ." says Adele, lamely fighting her tears. "I can feel it welling up already, let's change the subject. When I finally told Evelyn some of it, she was so-o-o stiff that I decided this isn't what she can take. So I just avoid that."

There was one crisis that Adele couldn't avoid. Ten years ago (when they were immersed in their mother's care), Adele went for a routine checkup and learned she had a cancerous tumor on her inner thigh. "I called my sister right away and told her everything. I was given a forty percent chance to live for no more than four years. Before I went to the hospital I stopped at a card shop and picked out a card with two funny little creatures on the front; the sentiment was 'thank you for listening.' One creature was crying, the other was listening. I sent it to my sister. I don't think that anything over the years touched her so much. Later on, after it was all over, she mentioned the card and I could see that I had really touched her. That was probably when she was the most close."

Adele has found through therapy that she repeats with her husband the fear of intimacy that she has with her sister, and that she has to work hard at keeping emotion and communication lines open with her children. Adele also believes strongly that her cancer was a product of her not bringing out the stress. "Even though I'm outgoing, I don't deal with the real intimacy problems with my husband. I'm a believer that your body tells you about your mental health.

"I've talked with other women about their relationship with their sisters, and when I hear what they share and do, I think, isn't that interesting. It's not envy, but sometimes it's surprising to me." But she and Evelyn have their own ritual of love and support that some may find "very strange," says Adele.

"We get the Sunday paper and do the crossword puzzle on the phone together. We each do it separately and then we compare notes, and we always get stuck at the same place. People think this is nuts, but it's the most comforting thing. It's something that we both enjoy. It's light, and it's fun. And it's safe."

Pick and Choose Your Support Sister

There is an obvious advantage to having more than one sister in times of crisis—you get multiple support, and you can take your pick of the kind or *flavor* of support, from serious to good-humored. There is no shame in this privilege, but it does come with its risks. Marty is the oldest of four sisters, whose ages range from thirty-two to forty-four. All are four years apart, and all are married, with children, and live in different states. "I'm closest to Sissy, my sister third in line—she is the most fun of all, the most relaxed," says Marty, who is admittedly the more reserved sister. "If I weren't as inhibited from what I consider being the first child, the good daughter told what to do . . . if I could be like any of them, I would be like Sissy. She takes life seriously at times, but she really knows how to have a good time."

This upbeat view of life is important for Marty because much tragedy has recently threatened her own family life. Her only daughter, a beautiful, intelligent twenty-one-year-old, was diagnosed as having Hodgkin's disease, which is now in remission; and Marty's husband has been hospitalized several times for manic-depression, complicated by his being allergic to the most effective medication. Marty has had to curtail her plans for returning to college, and is now working full-time in a sales job because her husband has not been able to work.

When Marty's husband was first hospitalized, Sissy came to be with her sister. The second time, when his condition was far worse, Sissy came again. That time Delia, the second sister, dubbed as "the complainer," was deeply offended because she hadn't been called to help, even though she lives closer to Marty than Sissy. (The youngest sister didn't mind that she wasn't called on because she was newly married and managing two toddlers.) "But Delia wasn't the kind of help I needed," explained Marty. "I needed someone to tell me about the good things, not the bad things."

The word "crisis" is derived from the Greek *krisis*, meaning "turning point." Crisis does not have to create a void, it can be the trauma or loss that causes incentive to change. When crisis comes into our lives, our instinct is to survive and be in touch with someone from whom we can draw strength. Our sisters are our most natural support system during our own personal crisis. But when the crisis involves our parents, such as their failing health or death, the sisters' support system can be complicated by unresolved differences and an imbalance of responsibilities. Adele and Evelyn showed us how two sisters can support each other through childhood, a mother's care, and their own illness without sharing their deepest fears and intimacies. Doing their crossword puzzles on Sunday mornings is their way of staying in touch. Adele may envy her women friends who are more intimate with their sisters, but she understands Evelyn's history of reserve, and she accepts her sister for who she is and values what closeness they do have.

11

▽

Celebrating Change Together

Up to now we have focused on crisis and the tragedies that affect the relationship between sisters. We need also to recognize how the inevitable, noncatastrophic changes in life bring sisters closer together, or threaten those who have a fragile bond. Change denotes the passages of life, from childhood to adolescence, from adulthood to midlife and, finally, to our elderly years. We have no rituals or holidays to celebrate the sibling relationship, but we do have the ceremonies or marked events within our life cycle that typically bring sisters in touch, especially marriage and the birth of children.

Something Old, Something Blue, and My Sister as Maid of Honor

The younger women I interviewed invariably brought up the issue of choosing a sister as their maid of honor or being a sister's maid of honor. One bride-to-be fretted about how her mother was insisting that her sister stand up with her even though they "weren't close," and how she had other friends whom she would rather consider. "But I feel so bad because I know that if she weren't my sister she wouldn't be my maid of honor." A woman in her early thirties says that she and her sister "always fought," until they were in college, when they became confidantes who good-naturedly "butted into each other's business." "My sister *demanded* that she wanted to be my maid of honor even though I had a friend in college who wanted to be," she says, laughing. "I don't care though, I wanted my sister to be it."

Whether maid of honor or not, sisters are invariably affected by one of them taking a hand in marriage; they may bond or separate depending on each other's needs at the time. Proximity helps with married sisters, but it is such a rare treat in this country—most of the women I interviewed lived away from their sisters, some an entire country or even two continents away. Contact and support is thus attempted or maintained through phone calls, letters, and yearly visits. Several noted that it helped immensely to know that their husbands got on well with their sisters' husbands, so that they could count on sharing a vacation or holiday together. "It takes real work to keep up the relationship with my sister," remarks a thirty-four-year-old woman who works full-time and spends much time traveling. She and her older sister, who also works, try to call each other at least once a month, but like many young sisters, married and working, there are times when the months slip by and then there is just "too much catching up to do."

And Baby Makes Three . . .

Once a sister has her first child, the pregnancy and birth often impact the sister(s) not giving birth. It is all part of the symbiotic union, the gender identity that we share, and the emotional appeal of holding and loving a baby. One sister has her first child, the other sister "feels pressure" to have a child even though she's been perfectly happy with just her career. Or one sister has her first baby and the other sister is so happy for her, she is inspired to have a child "within the year." Who is to be the godmother? Shall we name the baby after my sister? Will my sister help when the baby arrives? A teenage girl gives up her summer vacation to help her sister with the new baby. A forty-year-old woman sends her younger sister a package of beautifully preserved, hand-knit hand-me-down baby clothes for her first baby. A single sister frets that her married sister should "wait longer" before she returns to work: "It's too soon after the birth . . . she needs her rest, the baby needs her." And over and over again, I heard the story of the married sister who took her sister in when she was pregnant out of wedlock.

When a woman begins her family, she serves as a prototype or as an inspiration to her sister; but she also needs the sister's acknowledgment, her approval, her *support* and love. Whether she gets it depends on the existing relationship between the sisters, and the different stages each is in. A thirty-eight-year-old woman recounts how she became closer to her older sister when her initial efforts to have a full-term pregnancy failed and her sister who already had three children was empathic. The younger sister now has one child, and no regrets or envy. "We hadn't been close in college, but when I was going through the infertility we became very close. I'm happy for her that she has more children; I'm really fond of them. My sister was waiting to be enthusiastic during my pregnancy, I always thought that was very kind and polite of her."

Come and Visit My Empty Nest

Another predictable change in the course of life is when children leave the nest and sisters find that they can spend more time together. It is a welcome and precious change to most of the women who brought it up. As we will see in the final chapter, this is an enriching time for sisters to go off to the beach, the family home, the spa, or to the movies when there are no children to lug along or worry about. These past two years I've made quite a few trips to Milwaukee, where my sister Ruth and I invariably share a meal at John's Sandwich Shop, a neighborhood restaurant where businessmen eat hot oatmeal and senior citizens take the first pick of counter seats. Ruth and I sit at one of the two window tables that get the sun (a wise choice when it's ten below zero outside), and we talk and talk and eat the fatty foods of our childhood without wondering where our grown children are or what time we have to be home.

Senior years can be rewarding for sisters if their health is good and they have some sense of adventure. Two sisters in their seventies told me in great detail how together with their husbands they travel to Europe in the spring, take their summer vacation at adjacent lake cottages, and spend winters in Florida. "We've never been to Alaska," said the oldest, "that's our next trip."

Unfortunately, countless sisters find that they are traveling only between hospitals and nursing homes, or that they can't see their sisters at all because of failing health. "I want to enjoy my sister now, while I still can," observes a sixty-seven-year-old woman whose younger sister's husband has recently died. "We all know that these are our final years."

*   *   *

Sisters have their private rituals that don't need to be marked by a passage of time or event. These are the precious comforting moments that come without deliberation and serve to keep the relationship alive and thriving. The rituals may begin very young. A mother tells me how her two young daughters often reach out from their twin beds and hold hands before they drift to sleep. In another family, the five-year-old goes to bed each night with her door open, and an hour later when her sister comes to bed she always checks on her before going into her own bedroom across the hall.

Two sisters in their sixties always have their hair done on the same day at the same salon. Once they are coifed and looking "very special," they go for lunch and do some shopping.

A sister with four children "expects" her unmarried sister to come for dinner on Sunday "at the very least, once a month." The single sister always brings the wine and dessert and when dinner is over, everyone leaves the table except the two sisters, who sit and talk as the evening slips away.

There are the widowed sisters who go to church together, and work at the parish thrift shop on Tuesdays. And in Dublin there are five sisters who do their grocery shopping together on Wednesdays and then go for coffee at the neighborhood pub. On Saturday afternoons, without fail, the one single sister "opens her home" for visits from the four married sisters.

In my survey I heard of sisters who diet together, and sing together. There are the sisters who live nine hundred miles away and have the same dreams at night. And many women told me how their daughters have the same mannerisms or voice of their sisters, so they feel as if they are in their sisters' company. One delightful story came from a woman who

247

went on a ski trip in Vermont with her sister when they were in their twenties. They both ended up in the hospital, she with pneumonia, her sister with a broken leg. Within a day she developed sympathetic pains in her leg and her sister developed sympathetic pains in her chest. "The nurses called us 'the sick sisters from Maryland.' "

Change and the Definition of Self

Self-identity is inherent in our discussion of change and rituals. I consistently found that women were more open to understanding and accepting their sisters during and following periods of emotional growth, often instigated by crisis and change. Most of us *reestablish* our identity with the celebration of marriage, the birth of a child, or when that same child moves out of the nest. And few of us can experience the loss of a parent or the threat of breast cancer without reexamining our goals, our purpose, our very being. Whether it is a celebration or a tragedy, the turning point causes us to reconsider who we are. The essence of the life cycle, from infancy to our mature years, is the identity of the *self*. It is a sometimes wretched, yet all in all exhilarating, experience when we question who we are and where we are going with our lives. Erik Erikson tells us that we are "most aware of our identity when we are just about to gain it . . . or again, when we are just about to enter a crisis and feel the encroachment of identity diffusion."[1] It is also during these turning points and periods of self-examination that women often seek professional counseling, which involves an examination of the past, of the unconscious, and of one's family of origin.

Sisters in Therapy

At the start of this book I noted that the sister dynamic is not recognized in most methods of psychotherapy or in psychological literature. Many women I interviewed said, regretfully, that their therapist "ignored" or "brushed over" the significance of their relationship with their sisters. There were, however, some dramatic exceptions that gave promise to my belief that understanding the sister dynamic helps a woman in the definition of her self.

Sheila's therapist suggested that she invite her mother, who was visiting from out of town, to attend a therapy session with her. When the mother came, there was a tearful, spiteful scene in which she denied all early history of drug abuse and abandonment, and demanded that Sheila should be loving and forgiving. According to Sheila, the therapy visit was a disaster. But all was not lost; it was the beginning of another kind of reparation. Weeks later, the therapist suggested that Sheila get in touch with her sister, with whom she hadn't talked in many years. Gradually, after many phone calls and much soul-searching, Sheila and her sister have come together, but not without the daily, minute-by-minute process of self-examination and rediscovery of family identity.

Covering the Scratches with Love: Yvonne and Grace

Yvonne can remember when she was twelve and waking up in the night hearing her parents punish her seventeen-year-old sister Grace for being "ten minutes late for getting home from a date."

"I could hear my sister screaming . . . you know," shrugs Yvonne, not indifferently, but without the words to describe

249

the horror. "Physical punishment was what you call today 'abuse,' but you see, in that day and time it was simply the way, and especially the way immigrant parents dealt with young children. Just pull out the belt, the strap, whatever."

Yvonne's father came to the United States in the early thirties; a young German student, he brought with him his beautiful bride from Vienna. They lived in the small European community in New York where most of her father's family also lived, including her father's less attractive sisters, who looked on the beautiful Viennese bride as a threat. As a child, Yvonne could only blame herself for the heavy air of unhappiness that permeated their family home.

"I have a sense that my parents were *desperately* hoping for a boy. All of my father's siblings had at least one boy in the family. So I think there was some disappointment on their part, especially on my mother's part, when I was born. I also think that there was difficulty for my sister when I came along because she was no longer the only child."

Yvonne is now in her early fifties and extremely attractive. When she was young, her platinum curls and doe eyes enraged Grace to the point of abuse, the family way of coping. Rubbing her hands with the cold, senseless memory, Yvonne says quietly, "I don't know why, but I would go to school with deep scratches on my hands. . . . We fought terribly, just terribly. I would have to lie for my sister, to make sure that my parents didn't know that the bruises on my arms or the scratches on my hands were coming from her. There was such *disapproval* from Grace . . . I mean it was just awful. I can remember so vividly when I was eleven, the day my period began, I came running into the house, so excited. I said, 'Guess what? I got my period.' And my sister said in this cold voice, 'So what?' Just that way.

"My sister could control our shared emotional life. If she wanted to be kind to me, she was wonderful, and if she didn't, she turned it off like that . . . and it was that power that was so overwhelming."

When Yvonne and Grace were married and in their early twenties, their parents died within a year of each other. Not surprisingly, their deaths did not bring the two sisters together—they were simply too emotionally immature and unable to sort out all the effects of the abuse and ambivalent love. Yvonne soon divorced and remarried; Grace remained in the same marriage and had seven children—a fact that Yvonne, who has one child, finds amazing, yet she admires her sister's dedication. Over the years their relationship was passively civil. Then ten years ago while they were at a dinner and the guests were discussing family memories, Yvonne opened up and began to talk about her unhappy childhood. Grace, however, proclaimed to everyone that she "had no recollection" of the difficulties Yvonne had experienced with their mother and father. "I knew damn well she had experienced them too, but she couldn't talk about them," says Yvonne. The sisters didn't speak again for almost three years, then when they did finally meet, there was a "falling out" over something that Yvonne can't even recall now. Still thinking about the dinner when Grace had denied her own experience, Yvonne felt that her sister thought she was "making up" the family abuse.

"We didn't use words . . . I just realized I didn't want to see her anymore."

Years went by, with Yvonne growing in her advertising career but unevenly growing in her marriage, where she often felt inadequate and at fault. Intelligent, successful, and capable with her clients and co-workers, she found herself tongue-tied and frustrated with her husband's constant criticism of how she handled her business and home life. A powerful businessman who prided himself in his work, her husband frequently and insensitively let Yvonne know whenever he thought her "facts were wrong." After lamely arguing with her husband, Yvonne felt as if she were "lying or crazy."

"I think those memories of my sister's disapproval carried over into my relationship with my husband, so that I felt his disapproval," explains Yvonne. "Just as I felt my mother's disapproval and transferred it over to him. So all of this is going around and around." She gestures haplessly. "I learned all that in therapy in the past eight years and I've been able to get through feeling rejected by my mother and sister. I have even said outrightly in therapy, I have married my mother and sister."

Three years ago Yvonne received a phone call from a family member that Grace's husband was going to have open-heart surgery. There was no hesitation. Yvonne called Grace, and after an awkward beginning they talked about the heart problem, and then about the fact that they hadn't seen each other for a long time. "At that point I had the courage to say to her, 'I want you to know I missed you,'" recalls Yvonne. "And she said, 'Well, if the truth be known I was going to call you.'" The following Christmas, after Grace's husband's successful recovery and Yvonne's constant support, the sisters met to "go over" the reality of their past. As they talked, Grace admitted to Yvonne that she had not been able to face their childhood before; and Yvonne gratefully accepted her sister's acknowledgment of "the pain they shared" and her apologies for her "harsh treatment" in their youth.

Today the two sisters talk on the phone every two weeks, and see each other whenever they can get away from their busy lives. When Yvonne took ill with pneumonia last year, Grace was "more than supportive"; this year they are considering a week-long holiday together—without husbands.

Yvonne has come to understand her sister and her self, by

bout celebrating birthdays. But that day Mary didn't
concerned about my neglect, so I couldn't even ap-
my guilt. It seems her morning had begun roman-
and happily: Bob, her fiancé, had given her a
ring (in addition to her engagement ring) and they
the date for the wedding.

ou stand up for me?" Mary asked, sounding like a
twenty-year-old, ready to go out and select a
I was totally unprepared for the offer, my throat
d I felt an immense sadness. How sweet of her to
w like her to find romance at forty-six.

you think?" said Mary, sensing my caution.
startled me. "I don't feel I've been a good sister
," I said, trying to sound strong and not too
c.

e lead different lives," said Mary, "but I've
u were supportive." She could always *speak*

laying all my sins of envy out on the phone
t. Besides, I haven't figured out why I feel
ing matron of honor. And damn how I hate
on." For the next fifteen minutes as we
d over the color of our dresses, the flowers,
as eased out of the heavy emotion. When I
rgot to say, "I love you," a telephone ritual
ur family. Mary said it beautifully, and I
o sign off quickly with the three magic
fate would strike either one of us.

r I flew to Arizona for Mary's wedding,
this celebration to the fullest. My hus-
re not with me, so I traveled with my
also without her family. Janet flew
sband and children and our mother.
aul, came with his wife, Chris, and

considering her mother's past. Seeing her mother as "a depressed woman who took out her anger and disappointment
in her own life," she cites the fact that she had left her entire
family and all her friends in Vienna. There is nothing that
excuses the physical abuse, says Yvonne, but at least she can
look beyond that and understand her mother's isolation and
her own need for love and approval living under the eyes of
such a judgmental family.

With the reconciliation, and the work in therapy, Yvonne
says she has "found herself" and can manage the feelings of
inadequacy with her husband by speaking up and challenging his insinuations. She is also aware of how intimate yet
forthright she is with her friends, able to express her anger
or strong points of view without fear of their rejection.

Could she or does she also do that with her sister?

"I think I could, I think we have come a tremendously
long way. But remember," she tells me pointedly, "Grace is
the only member of my family who really knows what it was
like to grow up in my household and I don't want to lose that
other perspective. So I want to do what it takes without
compromising my own feelings, or thoughts, or values, to
make sure that the relationship continues to work."

Changes and passages in life enable us to reexamine our
selves and our relationship with our sisters. If we are already
fortunate enough to have established rituals and a common
dialogue with our sisters, we are more likely to turn to them
and receive their support or reaffirmation. But no matter
how strong or weak our contact is, there is an inherent link
between sisters when change disrupts or challenges our
lives. We heard Marty's story of how she called on her happier sister, Sissy, in order to get through her crisis with her
husband's hospitalization, and how her deliberate choice
disappointed Delia, the more serious sister. Even though

Delia and Marty have "never been close," the choice awoke Marty to the fact that she wouldn't want to lose Delia's love. It struck her deepest convictions.

"I would never want to shut a door on any of my sisters. For some reason that is real important to me, never to cut off my family for some silly reason, or for any reason. You have to say you are sorry, or whatever, and open up the door right away. I don't know why, but my sisters are so important to me."

12

▽

Resolve an

FICTION WRITERS OFT
come of their storie
growth can happer
this book when I w
myself and my fa
with my sister M
the book woul
toward Mary,
worlds ahea
naively tho
work with
sister rec
book tha
rather,

Last
wor
voi
h

their then one-year-old Nels. (My brother Dick was unable to come; my late brother Bob was there in spirit.) We all gathered in the Tucson airport, most of us meeting for the first time Mary's fiancé, who seemed dazed but brave in the face of this chattering onslaught. Chirping all the way out to the parking lot, we hit the unfamiliar heat with our high-pitched energy. For the next three days we moved in small family clusters, always reconnecting over extended mealtimes. We were a family again, with our roots in the Midwest, thriving on the celebration of marriage in the unfamiliar, fascinating setting of cactus and mountains. When Mary took the limelight, I was happy for her because I was seeing her with a new and more sensitive eye, thanks to the women I had interviewed for this book. After years of fighting feelings of inferiority and rejection, I had finally realized that Mary wasn't responsible for my fear of abandonment by the men I love. She didn't solely *design* the relationship she had with my father. She didn't deliberately arouse in me the feelings that grew into a habitual distrust of younger, more intelligent women. It was *I* who was born with an intensity to be loved and to please, it was I who dutifully responded to (rather than rebelled against) circumstances far beyond my and Mary's control. When I consider our birth order, our father's alcoholism, his long absences, and his stubborn belief in the discrepant value of men and women, I realize Mary and I could have no other kind of relationship than what we did have for so long. From the time we were toddlers until our teenage years, my father separately told Mary and me that we were his "First Ladies," wooing us as if he had no wife to respect, and expecting us to care for his younger children. We were like Rachel and Leah in the Book of Genesis, sharing the same husband, a man we couldn't please. When I left home to live on the East Coast, I kept far from the family dynamics, busying myself

257

with my own children, but it devastated me to have my father, an unavailable, passionate man, remain so connected to Mary, who was closer to home and apparently was standing up to him when it came to politics or values.

There is, of course, much, much more to this story—but most of it involves family who are living and who deserve to maintain their privacy. The important point is that after the death of my father and brother, I worked hard through therapy and psychoanalysis to understand my fears of separation and abandonment, and to define myself as a valuable person. I also had to work further and independently to find out the *facts* of my childhood. I needed to encompass the entire "emotional heritage" given to me by my siblings. I went back and read, over and over, the letters Mary had written to me many years ago, detailing family history that I had put away and "forgotten" because I wasn't ready to absorb it until now. On my visits home I picked up whatever pieces and bits my relatives offered, keeping in mind that myth replaces reality, and holding on to what "felt" familiar. Finally, as I worked on the book and listened to other women talk about their ambivalent love, their envy, competition, and feelings of self-worth, I unconsciously related to their emotion; for weeks I woke fitfully from horrible, frightening dreams in which I relived the hollowness of abandonment and the unexpressed rage of jealousy in my childhood.

The dreams over, I felt a growing sense of awe and serenity as I understood my feelings toward Mary and how I so often transferred those feelings to women like her. Her impact on my life as a sister and as a woman is unquestionable, and it remains so, even though at times we may talk only when the seasons change or holidays approach. With all this work and understanding, I haven't totally lost the envy and fear of being replaced; it will be there just as sure as I can't lose my

Midwest accent. But at least these feelings don't destroy me or confuse me any longer. More important, I am tired of focusing on the "problems" of our relationship. I want to shift positions and look at my sister's and my strengths— many of which, ironically, are similar and were absorbed from our father.

A month after the wedding I ran across a small snapshot taken of the two of us when I was eight and Mary was four. With our backs to the lake, we are posing on a wide pier, squinting into the noontime sun. Identically costumed in our mother's satin slips, we nattily wear our white starched sailor hats over our pinned-up hair. With our left hands on our skinny hips, and our right hands thrust out, we pretend to be onstage, about to break into song and dance for anyone who'll listen. I loved to "play musicals," but I had forgotten how Mary would follow whatever clumsy or stylized routine I did. The photo is now pinned on my office wall within view of the computer screen. It is a constant reminder that there were good times, a sharing of make-believe and summer afternoons—and that I didn't always follow Mary.

Mary is my soulmate and my antithesis. She can be both. She left the synchroneity of our dance routine to do her own. Today, I can embrace Mary's future with nothing but the wish for her happiness. I truly love her, just as I find it so easy to love Ruth and Janet. I never thought I could say that with sincerity until now.

"Happy families are all alike; every unhappy family is unhappy in its own way."[1] Tolstoy's wisdom especially applies to the approach used in this book. I did not deliberately set out to present only the interesting, complex tales of dysfunctional families, but when I gathered the material from the interviews, it was clear that the majority of the sisters had some degree of dysfunction in their families of origin, and the minority of sisters who did not gave faith-filled but un-eventful testimony. Their stories were definitely included, but they do not stand out as much as the complex histories. If I had chosen to describe *only* the condition of the present-day relationship between the sisters, we would not have had so many disturbing stories about alcoholism, incest, abuse, abandonment, and mental and physical illness. We could easily have focused on just the sisters' frequent phone calls or how they enjoy vacations together. Because it is in the context of the family history that the current relationship is brought to light, we have seen much unhappiness, but we have also seen the resilience, energy, and courage of families. My pur-pose is not to focus on the dysfunction, or even on the re-silience, but rather on how family members—in this case, sisters—carry different perspectives of their family history, which creates tension and differences between them. I want to complete this presentation by looking at the various ways women have effectively learned to uncover and face their different roles and perspectives. For me, it came at a time in life when I was ready to risk the introspection. My sister's wedding only served to enable the understanding; a combi-nation of factors had already prepared me emotionally—my age, my need to change, and my work on this book. Other women have other incentives, be it age, the care of a parent, or just the right feeling while sharing lunch. Again, it is because they are women that sisters intuitively know and respond to the signals for understanding and reparation.

In the Cottage, Just You and Me

In the masterful film *The Whales of August*, two elderly sis-ters, Sarah (Lillian Gish) and Libby (Bette Davis), live to-gether on an island off the coast of Maine, where their days play out in their differences and memories from the past. The optimistic, sweet Sarah longs to have a picture window put in the living room of their cottage so she can watch the sea and the change of seasons, but Libby, who has lost her sight but not her bitterness, vehemently refuses, saying it's a waste of money and she holds the purse strings.

"I took care of you for fifteen years," snaps Libby, "you *owe me.*"

Sarah, who minds the cottage, cooks their meals, and lovingly cares for all her sister's toiletry needs, barely retorts, "Then we are even, fifteen for fifteen years."

Later, when the fight has subdued, Sarah says wistfully, "We are so different, you and I."

"We are strong stock, Sarah," Libby corrects her sister, "and we've precious little time to forget it."

Eventually the two come together through the sheer beauty and constancy of their surroundings. As they walk on the flower-covered cliffs above the sea, Sarah describes the sighting of the whales to Libby, who mellows as she leans on her sister's arm and happily recalls scenes from their girlhood.

Most sisters have precious little time to enjoy or appreciate what they do have. We all like to believe that we come from strong stock, strong blood, a relentless union that we cannot throw away. Women who are keenly aware of this told me how they renewed their relationship with their sisters by spending "special time" together, such as a vacation without husbands or children. My friend Lynn has a "running-away time," when she and her two sisters retreat for three or four days in a selected city far from anyone's home. Another friend, Katie, has gone to a Y camp in Colorado with her sister for the past nine years: "It's a present we have given ourselves."

Realistically, it isn't possible for all women to escape from their families for a whole week. Some can only do it by bringing along husbands and children, and carving out specific times when the sisters can be alone for evening walks on the beach, breakfast in town, whatever the escape may be. One family of sisters solves the problem by jointly hiring a set of baby-sitters for their week at the ocean. A forty-three-year-old woman reports that her first vacation with her three sisters at the beach was "a complete disaster ... it poured buckets for five solid days and nights." They got through the first two days all right, just with talking and eating. After that they all suffered from cabin fever and sister overdose.

For some women, the very thought of a vacation time together was threatening. One woman told me that she was considering it, but it was a "loaded proposition" that wasn't to be taken lightly. Her fear was that she was going to let out all her pent-up anger over the past. She knew there is always the risk of saying how you feel, and hurting each other. But she also knew the worse risk in delaying the time together and never experiencing the reconnection. The time of reconsideration and acceptance is a slow and private process. Many women spoke of how they were surprised by their sisters' responses, good and bad. The lesson seemed to be that we shouldn't anticipate the responses.

In the opening chapter you met Peg and Tess, two of three sisters who had just reconciled after some twenty years of separation. When the three sisters had met in Washington, D.C., that summer, each had been secretly concerned about how they would fill the three days they intended to be together. The problem was resolved, said Peg, when they "naturally turned to nature."

"We hadn't planned our trips. It was normal, it fell into place," Peg said excitedly. "We went everywhere with nature. Great Falls, the arboretum, we walked around and around and related how we felt about the plants, the trees." At this point Peg started to cry. "It's the way we related as children. [In Chile], we would be out in the back playing under the trees looking at the animals. So we just did it instinctively. There was no anger. I felt there was an opening up of love and peace, the beginning of something simple. We had breakfast and we talked about the chickens and the eggs we used to have."

Tess, the less emotional one, agreed cautiously with her sister. "I felt that way, but I was expecting to have flare-ups and me stepping away, and being tense. That didn't happen. It was calm."

Being with nature or in an environment that intrigues the relationship can create a calm, just as it can define the bond. My friend Punch was elated because while on vacation with her sister, Judy, she conquered her fears of snorkeling in deep, unknown waters. For Punch, the victory was symbolic of her lifelong union with her sister. (When Judy was two, her mother was pregnant and they traveled from South America to the States on an ocean liner that offered "Punch and Judy" shows for the young passengers. Young and lonely, Judy decided then and there that the new baby would be her sister and she lovingly named her "Punch.") Now, forty-odd years later, Judy led Punch through the blue waters, farther and farther from their boat and guide, pointing out the sea turtles and gauzy colorful fish. "I felt, this is all right. I'm with her," said Punch. "It was safe."

Some women can't wait for beach walks or sweet silence, they would rather plunge right in and get to the bottom of things, risking all. Emily (see Chapter 5) had a "polite, distant" relationship with her sister for some forty years. After their mother's death and Emily's divorce the sisters were thrown together, but there were still very rough edges that needed to be smoothed out. It was somehow agreed that they would meet in a motel halfway between Emily's town and Bea's town. There, for three days and two nights, the two sisters talked, ate, cried, and laughed and "never slept."

Did they fight?

"My sister and I call it 'reviewing,' " said Emily. "Bea would say things like, 'I was always jealous of your corkscrew curls, and Mother cut my hair in a short bob because it was too thick to take care of and she spent hours on your curls.'

"Or when Bea would hear Mother say to me, 'Thank God you're smart, you're not pretty,' she took that as an insult to her because she was only pretty, not smart. She lived that out in her life, she never finished school and she is just as smart as I am."

Rosemary (see Chapter 4) spent an entire month with her sister Stella in her apartment, but they made a point to have their own private times and space each day. "We had separate bedrooms, and we both did our own reading," explained Rosemary. "I would go for walks or go shopping and stay out of her way. So we didn't have this constant togetherness. We had a marvelous time. I didn't think it would work, but it did."

Many times the subject of "living together" would come up in the interviews, usually at the close. I heard the range of reactions, from how it was out of the question to how it would be fantastic. "We could never be in the same kitchen together," was said by three different sets of sisters. An eighty-five-year-old woman whose sister is no longer living reminisced about the time someone asked the two of them if they would live together since they were both widows and such good friends. "We just looked at each other and started to laugh."

There lies the beauty and essence of two sisters who have reconsidered each other. They *know* how they feel, and they allow their separate identities in their love and respect for each other. They can laugh and enjoy their differences.

Going Home Again

A woman recently learned from her elderly aunt that when she was two and her sister was six, their mother was seriously ill and the two girls had to be separated. "Because I was the youngest and most difficult to care for, I was sent to Grandmother's to live until my mother was well; my sister was allowed to stay with my mother. I was told I wet the bed, wouldn't eat, and generally clung to my poor grandmother." For years thereafter, this woman perceived her older sister as "privileged" and resented whatever good came her way. She carried this same sense of "sour grapes" with her women friends when they appeared to her to be getting a better deal in their lives with their children, jobs, and husbands. Her mother had never told her about the separation, either out of her own guilt or because she may have wanted to believe that her daughter was too young to have been affected. When her mother recovered her health and the family was reunited, the separation eventually was lost or "diminished" in the family history, but the feelings between the sisters mushroomed well into the next generation.

All the introspection in the world won't solve the problems between sisters. Some of it takes sheer detective work, where a woman returns to the scene of her youth and looks for historical data, and patterns of behavior and reactions that are repeated with her own family and friends. Visiting and *listening* to family *and how they recall* family events and moments helps us come to an understanding of our roots and of how we communicate and relate to others. One woman told me that she soon learned not to let her mother know that her intent was to gather family data. "She just wouldn't talk when she thought I was trying to get the family 'scoop.' So I would wait until we were out driving and doing errands or cleaning up the kitchen, and gradually as we talked, one memory would lead to another."

A forty-five-year-old woman taped her conversation with her seventy-eight-year-old father in which he opened up and recalled his childhood with a formidable father, a distant mother, and his three "snooty sisters." When she played the tape back to her forty-year-old sister, she was dismayed at her adamant reaction. "I don't believe any of it. Dad is making the whole thing up."

"What was I suppose to do?" the older sister asked me. "Dismiss everything Dad said? I really believed him. But I felt sorry for my sister. She was obviously too threatened by Dad acting so vulnerable."

Not all is lost. The important thing is not what the father said, or whether it was necessarily true or accurate, but rather how the two sisters reacted to his memories. The younger sister had no patience or faith in her father, a man who rarely reached out to her now or in her childhood. The older sister dutifully believed him and felt such compassion for the younger sister that she didn't argue or say anything. Both sisters were responding to the father the way they had for some forty years.

"It's important," says psychiatrist and author Dr. Edward W. Beal, "to gather the 'fact pattern,' or the factual data, but it's equally important to note how your forebears reacted and how you react to knowing about them. The reactions are often more important than the facts" (phone interview).

At the start of Chapter 2, I told you about Rebecca, who was upset because an aunt had revealed that she and her younger sister had a "lost" sister born out of her parents' wedlock. Rebecca was considering searching for this older sister, but she had no idea if the rumor was true and didn't feel comfortable confronting her terminally ill father with questions. Eventually Rebecca called me, very upset and wanting to tell her story, which sounded almost fictional but was astonishingly real. Her father had died just a few days earlier; after notification of his death, she and her husband went to his home to tend to his belongings. There she discovered a diary in which he had written on the very first page the names of his *three* daughters. The rumors were true. She had a sister she never knew. After a brief search she found her "new" sister's name, Cheryl, along with her phone number, in *three* of his journals. "He must have really cared about her," she said with open envy, "her name was everywhere." Distraught but excited, she immediately called Cheryl, thinking that she had to prepare her gently for this revelation. But Cheryl wasn't surprised, she knew all about Rebecca. Adopted as an infant, Cheryl had been told that her mother had died giving birth. Ten years before Rebecca's call, with the help of county social services she located her father and learned the truth of her birth, and that she had two other sisters. The father, still burdened with guilt, made her swear not to reveal her identity to her sisters until after he had died.

"I feel like I've been cheated all these years, like I've been deprived of something," said Rebecca. "I'm full of anger, resentment . . ." But not toward Cheryl, who Rebecca feels was only carrying out her father's wishes. Instead, she is angry with her father and mother for giving in to the shame of having an unwed pregnancy and denying her the knowledge of having a sister.

"My grandfather was always cold to me, he disliked me, now I know why. He didn't want my parents to get married.

But why should the children have to be punished for the parents' crimes?"

The three sisters met two days later in the funeral home in front of their father's casket. At first there was nervous laughter among the sisters, finally their tears and embraces came easily. Some of the elderly relatives were aghast that their meeting was carried out so openly and that Cheryl's name was in the obituary in the newspaper. Rebecca had insisted on that, she told me, she wanted no more of the secretiveness, and the shame. It had caused enough destruction.

"When we drove home from the funeral, my husband told me, 'You lost someone you weren't close to, maybe you have found your best friend.' I feel wonderful. But why couldn't I have met her at least ten years ago?"

Rebecca's is an unusual story. Our discoveries about our family histories may be far less dramatic, but just as unsettling or important. We can't expect the history and our reactions to make us immediately feel better. Because a woman may go through considerable pain and discomfort uncovering facts and feelings that have been repressed or confused for so long, it is advantageous if she can go through this process with a sympathetic therapist or pastoral counselor. But according to Dr. Beal, it takes more than just empathy to help reconnect with sisters and family. "It's a therapist's job to be sympathetic, but also realize that what we are dealing with is *anxiety,* and to get beyond that. Sympathy is good, but the patient needs to be challenged to think differently."

Remember the Good Along with the Bad

Not all memories and family myth need be sad or upsetting. Several of the women I interviewed were able to focus on their parents' strengths, and on the nurturing and inspiring times they shared with one or all the members of the family. I was impressed by how many women did this through memories of music. In some of the most dysfunctional homes, the families routinely gathered to sing or play instruments, giving the children a sense of security and hope in the most dire circumstances. It wasn't a false security, said one woman in her forties. Somehow she and her siblings knew that if the family could sing on car trips or while drying the dishes, there was still a great deal of family life to be cherished. There is also the recognition of family games and rituals that give children a sense of security and caring: rides in the country after Saturday supper, father reading the Sunday comics to the children, listing chores on the refrigerator door. Recalling these routines often puts sisters on common ground. They could approach their differences knowing that they had a positive sense of family.

Changing our attitudes and acknowledging our perspectives takes time and courage; it won't come quickly or easily with a few happy memories or by singing our favorite songs from days gone by. Harriet Lerner writes, in *Dance of Intimacy,* that when you change in a relationship, "you have to keep the *long term process* in mind, count on countermoves, move *slowly* and in a *low-key fashion.*"[2]

Some of the women in my survey came to an understanding of their sisters through an analysis of how they chose their women friends. Many said they chose the "opposite" of their

269

sisters because they couldn't possibly duplicate their relationship. Others were a little more critical and said they didn't want to have friends like their sisters because they didn't want to repeat the problems or further complicate their lives. These women often spoke of their friends as "chosen sisters" and realized that there was a need to have more intimacy and sympathy than their sisters might provide. Often such a chosen relationship is an idealized one, especially since it isn't based on any history and doesn't carry the emotional load that comes with a past.

But there were also the more loving and positive testimonies. One woman noted that she looks for women who have the sense of humor her sister has. Another admits she is attracted only to intelligent, hard-driving women, like all the women in her family. My friend Kathy's mother died when Kathy was eighteen, the oldest of four sisters. The early death, Kathy's birth order, and her contemplative personality left her with a deep sense of involvement and concern for her sisters. Interestingly, she selects her women friends in the varying reflections of her sisters. "I know because of the kinds of experiences I've had with my sisters, before and after my mother's death, that I'm very critical of the kinds of friends I have," Kathy told me. "I select my friends to take the place of my sisters who are far away."

Lifting the Load of Female Responsibility

"We are tormented by our perceptions of each other, rather than accepting our differences," Martha Gallahue told a roomful of sisters in a Sister-to-Sister workshop in New York. It was a tearful, joyous ending to a day of soul-searching for pairs of women bonded by blood and sisterhood. The most surprising development for me was the moment when two sisters, while role-playing under Gallahue's watchful eye, enacted the sense of guilt and entrapment the older sister feels about being the "responsible one." "Let me be myself," she pleaded with her younger sister, who seemed amazed that her older sister even harbored such feelings of rebellion. "I don't want to carry all the responsibility you've given me." Several women cried at that scene, and they weren't all elder sisters.

By midlife, many of us are more apt to forgive our sisters for what they could not possibly have given us as children. Remember the testimony in these chapters: the sister who laments how she couldn't laugh with her younger siblings while taking care of them; the sister who carries the guilt that she didn't "give all" to her baby sisters when she was twelve and her mother was depressed; the sister who regrets that she didn't help her sister through her teenage depression; and the sister who feels uncomfortably guilty for having received more love and attention from the parents.

Long after I had completed all my interviews, I met a woman in her early fifties who was mourning the recent death of her sister, who was four years older and had suffered from ovarian cancer. Filled with guilt for not reciprocating her sister's lifelong "brilliant love," this woman vehemently claimed that the imbalanced dedication had begun when she was just a baby and her big sister played the "fortune-telling game" at a family picnic. "My sister held a buttercup under my chin, saw the yellow, and told my parents, and all my aunts and uncles, that she would take care of me the rest of her life." The prediction came true, says this woman, whose life fell into tragedy with addiction and poor health. Now that her sister is gone, she is determined to stay in recovery and preserve her health, something her sister had yearned for her for so long.

So many sisters—no matter if they are the oldest, the middle, or the youngest—carry the burden of being the all-perfect mother and woman, sensitive and giving to all within the family; just as so many sisters, no matter what their position, carry the burden of being the receiver of that love.

There is Tillie Olsen's wisdom, gleaned at the ironing board where she mapped out much of her later written inspiration on women's issues: "Women are traditionally trained to place others' needs first . . . their satisfaction to be in making it possible for others to use their abilities."[3] We know all too well that our blessing in being women who care carries its trouble spots in a society that doesn't treat us equally or fairly. But we need to recognize that the hierarchy between sisters also doesn't escape such trouble spots. Sisters are their own worst judges. One of our tasks in lessening the distance between our sisters, then, is to forgive and let go of our guilt for what we didn't do, or what they didn't do in the roles of the sister caretaker or the little sister.

Monica McGoldrick, director of the Family Institute of New Jersey, urges therapists to "challenge traditional assumptions" about caretaking and maintaining relationships—the mainstay privilege and task of daughters.[4] When a woman comes to therapy with the concern that her sister didn't give her enough as a child or now, says McGoldrick, the task is to help her "question the negative focus she may have on another sister for letting her down, rather than appreciating the unreasonable expectations she or the family may have for the sister, which match the overly demanding expectations she has for herself to be sensitive to everyone else.

"We must validate the sisters' experience of the burden of family responsibilities and encourage them to use each other for support rather than viewing each other as competitors."[5]

It is my belief that validating the experience of traditional roles means validating the experiences on both sides. There is no need to judge which sister hurts more—the "big" sister trying to be perfect and the substitute mother, or the "little" sister who can't get enough love or gain her sister's approval. It is crucial, however, to acknowledge that the patterns of being responsible or involved with one another can be cause for lifelong grievances.

Women with sisters often spoke to me about watching other women and their sisters to find clues as to what "sisters" is all about. They typically felt they were mishandling their relationship and wanted to know how other women managed the complexities of sisterhood. I hope with this discussion women will have a more grounded understanding of why that complexity exists. Here is a relationship that from early childhood affects our lives as girls and as women, and yet we know so little about it. Privately, we believe we are biological partners in love, and yet we feel this ambivalent love.

We sisters, as women, expect too much from one another. We expect the perfection of ourselves and/or of the mother we never had, so we are disappointed and critical. With stubborn energy we obsess over the past as well as our present relationship. Why didn't my sister include me with her friends? Why didn't my sister leave me alone? Why is my sister so bossy? Why doesn't my sister speak her mind?

Is there any critic more ruthless than a sister? But then again, is there any relationship more lasting and complex, and more *capable of resolve* than sister-to-sister? Our parents die, our children leave, we can separate from our husbands and lovers, but a sister remains part of us long after we place the snapshots back in the drawer, or wave good-bye from the car window.

The saying goes that sisters are bonded by their "shared

273

history." I don't agree with such a maxim because it implies that the history is agreed upon, or experienced equally or similarly. Sisters are bonded *by their gender,* which is trained from early childhood to be sensitive to others; but just as they are keenly aware of each other, sisters are keenly, covertly involved in criticism and their competition, caused and fueled by their *different perspectives* of their family history. To meet a resolve, they develop and hone their non-judgmental and sensitive perspectives. If they can, they talk about and understand each other's different position in their parents' eyes and within the framework of the family. If talking is too threatening, a sister may elect to do her own interior examination. No matter what the course of action, with this knowledge and understanding of their history and roles, in time such sisters may come to accept their separate identities and be rewarded with the embrace of sisterhood experienced by untold numbers of women.

Notes

Preface
1. Christine Downing, *Psyche's Sisters,* pp. 9–10.
2. Grace Weinstein, "Crisis of Elder Care," *Ms.,* October 1989 (from *The Elderly: Opposing Viewpoints*), p. 47.
3. Robert Coles, *The Call of Stories,* p. 7.
4. Ibid., p. 19.

Chapter One
1. Carol Gilligan, *In a Different Voice,* p. 20.

Chapter Two
1. Walter Toman, *Family Constellation,* pp. 7–22.
2. Alice Miller, *The Drama of the Gifted Child,* p. 27.
3. Toman, p. 34; Stephen Bank and Michael Kahn, *The Sibling Bond,* pp. 4, 12.
4. Toman, pp. 24–25.
5. Timmen Cermak, *A Time to Heal,* p. 72.

Chapter Three
1. George Eliot, *Middlemarch,* pp. 20–21.
2. Jane Austen, *Pride and Prejudice,* p. 9.

3. Barbara Raskin, *Current Affairs,* p. 22.
4. Ibid., p. 25.
5. Ibid.

Chapter Four
1. Natalie Low, "The Sisterly Relationship," p. 13.
2. Ibid., p. 11.
3. Lillian Rubin, *Just Friends,* p. 83.
4. Nancy Friday, *My Mother/My Self: The Daughter's Search for Identity,* p. 267.
5. Luise Eichenbaum and Susie Orbach. *Between Women,* p. 122.
6. Rubin, *Just Friends,* p. 83.
7. Eichenbaum and Orbach, p. 92.
8. Sigmund Freud, *Collected Papers,* p. 269; Freud, *An Outline of Psychoanalysis,* p. 51.
9. Juliet Mitchell, *The Selected Melanie Klein,* p. 78.
10. Eichenbaum and Orbach, pp. 100–101.
11. Anne Frank, *The Diary of Anne Frank,* p. 295.
12. Jane Smiley, *A Thousand Acres.*
13. Simone de Beauvoir, *The Second Sex,* p. 279.
14. Toman, p. 20.
15. Amy Tan, *The Joy Luck Club,* pp. 37–38.

Chapter Five
1. Terri Apter, *Altered Loves,* p. 144.
2. Freud, *An Outline of Psychoanalysis,* p. 50.
3. Nancy Chodorow, *The Reproduction of Mothering,* p. 127.
4. Ibid., p. 127.
5. Jane Howard, *A Different Woman,* p. 19.
6. Elizabeth Fishel, *Sisters,* p. 13 (taken from Robert White, *Enterprise of Living* [New York: Holt, Rinehart, 1976], p. 106).
7. Apter, p. 181.

8. Selma Fraiberg, *The Magic Years*, pp. 228–229.
9. Bank and Kahn, p. 24.
10. De Beauvoir, *The Second Sex*, p. 521.
11. Miller, p. 28.
12. Marianne Walters, *The Invisible Web*, p. 40.
13. Emily Hancock, *The Girl Within*, pp. 182–183.
14. Erik H. Erickson, *Identity: Youth and Crisis*, p. 33.
15. Jill Barber and Rita E. Watson. *Sisterhood Betrayed*, p. 146.

Chapter Six
1. Lillian Rubin, *Intimate Strangers*, p. 130.
2. Ibid., p. 151.
3. Austen, *Pride and Prejudice*, by Donald J. Gray, p. vii.
4. Deborah Tannen, *You Just Don't Understand*, p. 77.

Chapter Seven
1. Bank and Kahn, p. 24.
2. Michael Nichols, *The Power of the Family*, p. 47.
3. Jane Dunn, *A Very Close Conspiracy*, p. 32.
4. Ibid., p. 126 (from Vanessa Bell's *Recollection from Virginia's Childhood*).
5. Ibid., p. 130.
6. Michael Kahn and Karen Gail Lewis, eds., *Siblings in Therapy*, p. 4.
7. Nichols, pp. 47–48.

Chapter Eight
1. Monica McGoldrick, Carol Anderson, and Froma Walsh, eds., *Women in Families*, p. 262.
2. Ibid., p. 263.
3. Thomas Bouchard, et al., "Sources of Human Psychological Differences," p. 223.

Chapter Nine

1. Toni McNaron, *The Sister Bond*, p. 64.
2. Toman, p. 40.
3. Catherine Sanders, *Grief*, p. 82.
4. Joseph H. Smith and William Kerrigan, eds., *Images in Our Souls* (chapter by Bruce H. Sklarew, "Ingmar Bergman's *Cries and Whispers:* The Consequences of Pre-oedipal Developmental Disturbances," pp. 172–173).
5. McNaron, p. 25.
6. Ibid., pp. 25–26.

Chapter Ten

1. Birgitta Ralston, caption of photo at photo exhibit, Radcliffe College, Schlesinger Library, Cambridge, Massachusetts, December 1990.

Chapter Eleven

1. Erik H. Erickson, *Identity and the Life Cycle*, p. 127.

Chapter Twelve

1. Leo Tolstoy, *Anna Karenina*, pt. I, chap. 1.
2. Harriet Lerner, *Dance of Intimacy*, p. 126.
3. Tillie Olsen, *Silences*, pt. 1, p. 35.
4. McGoldrick. p. 264.
5. Ibid.

Bibliography

Apter, Terri. *Altered Loves: Mothers and Daughters During Adolescence.* New York: St. Martin's Press, 1990.

Austen, Jane. *Pride and Prejudice,* Donald J. Gray, ed. New York: Norton, 1966.

Bank, Stephen, and Michael Kahn. *The Sibling Bond.* New York: Basic Books, 1983.

Barber, Jill, and Rita E. Watson. *Sisterhood Betrayed: Women in the Workplace and the All About Eve Complex.* New York: St. Martin's Press, 1990.

Beauvoir, Simone de. *Memoirs of a Dutiful Daughter.* New York: Harper Colophon Books, 1974.

_____. *The Second Sex.* New York: Vintage Books, 1989.

Bouchard, Thomas, and David Lykken, Matthew McGue, Nancy Segal, and Auke Tellegen. "Sources of Human Psychological Differences: The Minnesota Study of Twins Reared Apart." *Articles,* October 12, 1990.

Cermak, Timmen. *A Time to Heal: The Road to Recovery for Adult Children of Alcoholics.* New York: Avon, 1989.

Chodorow, Nancy. *The Reproduction of Mothering: Psychoanalysis and the Sociology of Gender.* Berkeley: University of California Press, 1978.

Coles, Robert. *The Call of Stories.* Boston: Houghton Mifflin, 1989.

Downing, Christine. *Psyche's Sisters: Re-Imagining the Meaning of Sisterhood.* New York: Continuum, 1990.

Dunn, Jane. *A Very Close Conspiracy: Vanessa Bell and Virginia Woolf.* Boston: Little, Brown, 1991.

Eichenbaum, Luise, and Susie Orbach. *Between Women: Love, Envy, and Competition in Women's Friendships.* New York: Viking, 1989.

Eliot, George. *Middlemarch.* New York: New American Library, 1964.

Erickson, Erik H. *Identity: Youth and Crisis.* New York: Norton, 1968.

———. *Identity and the Life Cycle.* New York: Norton, 1980.

Fishel, Elizabeth. *Sisters: Love and Rivalry Inside the Family and Beyond.* New York: Morrow, 1979.

Fraiberg, Selma H. *The Magic Years.* New York: Scribner, 1959.

Frank, Anne. *The Diary of Anne Frank: The Critical Edition.* Doubleday, 1989.

Fraser, Rebecca. *The Brontës: Charlotte Brontë and Her Family.* New York: Fawcett Columbine, 1988.

Freud, Sigmund. *Collected Papers of Sigmund Freud,* ed. Ernest Jones. Vol. 2, no. 8. New York, Basic Books, 1959.

———. *An Outline of Psychoanalysis.* New York: Norton, 1969.

———. "Some Reflections on Schoolboy Psychology" (originally published in 1914). *Sigmund Freud: The Standard Edition, Vol. 13.* London: The Hogarth Press, 1969.

Friday, Nancy. *My Mother/My Self: The Daughter's Search for Identity.* New York: Delacorte Press, 1977.

Gilligan, Carol. *In a Different Voice: Psychological Theory and Women's Development.* Cambridge, Mass.: Harvard University Press, 1982.

Hancock, Emily. *The Girl Within*. New York: Fawcett Columbine, 1990.

Horney, Karen. *Feminine Psychology*. New York: Norton, 1967.

———. *New Ways in Psychoanalysis*. New York: Norton, 1939.

Howard, Jane. *A Different Woman*. New York: Dutton, 1973.

Kahn, Michael D., and Karen Gail Lewis, eds. *Siblings in Therapy: Life Span and Clinical Issues*. New York: Norton, 1988.

Lerner, Harriet. *The Dance of Anger: A Woman's Guide to Changing the Patterns of Intimate Relationships*. New York: HarperCollins, 1985.

———. *The Dance of Intimacy: A Woman's Guide to Courageous Acts of Change in Key Relationships*. New York: Harper-Collins, 1989.

Low, Natalie S. "The Sisterly Relationship." Based on a paper presented at a meeting of the American Family Therapy Association, Montreal, June 1988. *Radcliffe Quarterly* (March 1990).

McGoldrick, Monica, Carol Anderson, and Froma Walsh, eds. *Women in Families: A Framework for Family Therapy*. New York: Norton, 1991.

McNaron, Toni A. H., ed. *The Sister Bond: A Feminist View of a Timeless Connection*. New York: Pergamon, 1985.

Miller, Alice. *The Drama of the Gifted Child: The Search for the True Self*. New York: Basic Books, 1990.

Mitchell, Juliet, ed. *The Selected Melanie Klein*. New York: Free Press, 1986.

Nichols, Michael. *The Power of the Family*. New York: Fireside/Simon & Schuster, 1988.

Olsen, Tillie. *Silences*. New York: Dell, 1989.

Raskin, Barbara. *Current Affairs*. New York: Random House, 1990.

Rose, Phyllis. *Woman of Letters: A Life of Virginia Woolf.* New York: Oxford University Press, 1978.

Rubin, Lillian. *Intimate Strangers: Men and Women Together.* New York: HarperCollins, 1983.

_____. *Just Friends: The Role of Friendship in Our Lives.* New York: HarperCollins, 1985.

Sanders, Catherine. *Grief: The Mourning After.* Wiley, 1989.

Smiley, Jane. *A Thousand Acres.* New York: Knopf, 1991.

Smith, Joseph H., and William Kerrigan, eds. *Images in Our Souls: Cavell, Psychoanalysis and Cinema.* Baltimore: Johns Hopkins University Press, 1987.

Tan, Amy. *The Joy Luck Club.* New York: Putnam, 1989.

Tannen, Deborah. *You Just Don't Understand: Women and Men in Conversation.* New York: Ballantine, 1991.

Tolstoy, Leo. *Anna Karenina.*

Toman, Walter. *Family Constellation: Its Effects on Personality and Social Behavior.* New York: Springer, 1976.

Walters, Marianne, Betty Carter, Peggy Papp, and Olga Silverstein. *The Invisible Web: Gender Patterns in Family Relationships.* New York: Guilford Press, 1988.

Weinstein, Grace W. "Crisis of Elder Care." In *The Elderly: Opposing Viewpoints,* ed., Karen Swisher. San Diego: Greenhaven Press, 1990.

Acknowledgments

Two years ago when Peggy Hackman, my "Style Plus" editor at *The Washington Post,* asked me to write an article on sisters, she said very pointedly, "I have a good feeling about this one."

Good indeed. Thank you, Peggy.

Once the article was written and plans for the book were subsequently made, I was supported by countless numbers of friends—women and men—who offered names of sisters throughout the country and abroad. Because the anonymity of these sisters is so important, I cannot cite my friends by name, though I am indebted to each and every one, not only for their assistance but for their enthusiasm and belief in this project.

In addition, I am grateful to Al Sanoff for his professional support and wisdom. To Sarah Ban Breathnach for her faith in me and for sharing her writer's survival techniques. And to Priscilla J. Friesen (Georgetown Family Center) and Dr. Fonya Lord Helm for their reading and analysis of my manuscript.

I am grateful to my agent, Chris Tomasino, who has

watched over me beautifully, and whose talents include a sensitive awareness of the reader's needs and questions. And to my editor at Delacorte, Cynthia White, who so gracefully and unoffensively showed me how to balance these sister stories with my own family history.

BARBARA MATHIAS